Praise for

ABANDONED IN HELL

"Why read a book about a battle in a war everyone is trying to forget? Because you will learn an important secret. Are there other ways to learn it? Yes, but you do not want them. *Abandoned in Hell* is an epic tale of junior officers and NCOs salvaging a clusterf**k with minimum losses and maximum damage to the enemy. Nasty war. Great book."

—Jim Morris, author of *War Story* and *Above and Beyond*

"Surrounded, vastly outnumbered, pounded day and night by incoming fire, and all but abandoned, tiny Firebase Kate should have fallen within twenty-four hours. That it did not is a testament to Captain Albracht and the fighting tenacity of those around him. This is an exceptional account, told in much detail."

—Major John L. Plaster, US Army Special Forces (Ret.) and author of *SOG* and *Secret Commandos*

"Marvin Wolf and William Albracht have produced in *Abandoned in Hell* a riveting, dead-true account in the tradition of *Black Hawk Down* and *We Were Soldiers Once . . . and Young*—that is, an in-detail narrative of events that could be studied by historians or by cadets in academies of war, but that also reads like a breathless, hair-raising novel."

—Steven Pressfield, national bestselling author of *The Lion's Gate*

"Albracht's gallantry defending Kate, and his actions in the days that followed, reached mythical proportions. *Abandoned in Hell* is essential reading about the brave men who lived and died fighting an unpopular war."

—David Hume Kennerly, winner of the 1972 Pulitzer Prize for Feature Photography

"Wolf and Albracht have interwoven the history, the tumult of battle, and the spectrum of personalities that turn up on a forlorn red dirt hill on the Cambodian border in the crunch year of 1968. It's a story that grabs you by the throat and won't let go."

—Tim Page, photojournalist and author of *Another Vietnam*

continued . . .

"This gripping, gritty, and cinematic blow-by-blow account of outnumbered Americans locked in a desperate battle with the North Vietnamese Army is destined to become a classic of its genre. If you read only one book about Vietnam this year, this must be the one."

—Major General Paul Vallely, US Army (Ret.), two-tour Vietnam veteran, Fox News senior military analyst, and author of *Endgame: The Blueprint for Victory in the War on Terror*

"This extraordinary narrative about leadership, loyalty, and trust grabbed me from page one. It should be required reading for anyone who wants to know what really happened in Vietnam."

—Rocky Bleier, decorated Vietnam veteran and four-time Super Bowl champion

"A riveting look at a little-known but compelling Vietnam War story."

—*Publishers Weekly*

"Albracht and Wolf present a vivid, often gripping account of the attack by four thousand members of the People's Army of Vietnam. . . . This fast-paced narrative encapsulates Vietnam War themes, significantly the bravery of grunts and company grade officers and their loyalty to one another. . . . Readers of such excellent battlefield works as Harold Moore and Joseph Galloway's *We Were Soldiers Once . . . and Young* will delve into this one."

—*Library Journal*

Also by Marvin J. Wolf

For Whom the Shofar Blows

Family Blood

Where White Men Fear to Tread

Beating the Odds

Fallen Angels

Rotten Apples

Perfect Crimes

Buddha's Child

CAPT. WILLIAM ALBRACHT (RET.)
AND CAPT. MARVIN J. WOLF (RET.)

ABANDONED IN HELL

THE FIGHT FOR VIETNAM'S FIREBASE KATE

NAL CALIBER
Published by New American Library,
an imprint of Penguin Random House LLC
375 Hudson Street, New York, New York 10014

This book is a publication of New American Library. Previously published in an NAL Caliber hardcover edition.

First NAL Caliber Trade Paperback Printing, February 2016

NAL CALIBER TRADE PAPERBACK ISBN 978-0-451-46809-3

THE LIBRARY OF CONGRESS HAS CATALOGED THE HARDCOVER EDITION OF THIS TITLE AS FOLLOWS:

Albracht, William.
Abandoned in hell: the fight for Vietnam's Firebase Kate / Captain William Albracht (Ret.) and Captain Marvin J. Wolf (Ret.).
pages cm
ISBN 978-0-451-46808-6 (hardback)
1. Albracht, William. 2. Firebase Kate (Vietnam) 3. Vietnam War, 1961–1975—Personal narratives, American. 4. Escapes—Vietnam—Central Highlands—History—20th century. 5. United States. Army. Special Forces—Officers—Biography. 6. Soldiers—United States—Biography. 7. Heroes—United States—Biography. 8. Command of troops—Case studies. 9. Courage—Case studies. I. Wolf, Marvin J. II. Title.
DS559.5.A43 2015
959.704'342—dc23 2014028501

Printed in the United States of America
10 9 8 7 6 5 4 3

Designed by Spring Hoteling

PUBLISHER'S NOTE
While the author has made every effort to provide accurate telephone numbers and Internet addresses at the time of publication, neither the publisher nor the author assumes any responsibility for errors, or for changes that occur after publication. Further, publisher does not have any control over and does not assume any responsibility for author or third-party Web sites or their content.

Penguin
Random
House

This book is dedicated to the 150 Rhade Montagnard soldiers from Civilian Irregular Defense Group companies based at Special Forces Camps Trang Phuoc and An Lac who fought the North Vietnamese Army's murderous attacks on Firebase Kate. I have good reason to believe that every striker who survived the hellish five-day siege is now almost certainly dead, either from natural causes, from the hazards of a long, brutal war, or, sadly, from the campaign of savage repression waged by the Communist regime that followed the fall of Saigon. None of the 27 Americans who served on Firebase Kate would have survived the enemy's onslaught if these short, wiry, dark-skinned, and unshakably loyal fighting men had not stood their ground, bled and died and fought as bravely and as well as any soldiers on the planet.

I'd like to have two armies: one for display with lovely guns, tanks, little soldiers, staffs, distinguished and doddering Generals, and dear little regimental officers who would be deeply concerned over their General's bowel movements or their Colonel's piles, an army that would be shown for a modest fee on every fairground in the country. The other would be the real one, composed entirely of young enthusiasts in camouflage uniforms, who would not be put on display, but from whom impossible efforts would be demanded and to whom all sorts of tricks would be taught. That's the army in which I should like to fight.

—Jean Lartéguy (nom de plume of Jean Pierre Lucien Osty), 1920–2011

CONTENTS

Foreword xiii

Glossary of Military Terms xvii

Maps xxi

Introduction 1

PART ONE 7

Chapter One 9

Chapter Two 23

Chapter Three 45

Chapter Four 65

PART TWO 83

Chapter Five 85

Chapter Six 95

Chapter Seven 107
Chapter Eight 123
Chapter Nine 129
Chapter Ten 141
Chapter Eleven 153
Chapter Twelve 161
Chapter Thirteen 173
Chapter Fourteen 185
Chapter Fifteen 199
Chapter Sixteen 209

PART THREE 217
Chapter Seventeen 219
Chapter Eighteen 229
Chapter Nineteen 243

The Aftermath 253
Views from Higher Up 259
Finis 263
Epilogue 267
Appendix: The Spooky Chronicles 297
Acknowledgments 345
Index 349

FOREWORD

By Joseph L. Galloway

In war, each day brings thousands of decisions—some good, some bad, some deadly for those who must carry out the orders that flow from such decisions. This book is about a deadly decision taken in the fall of 1969 to create a small artillery firebase in the Central Highlands of South Vietnam and dangle that post as bait for thousands of North Vietnamese Army regulars just two miles away behind the Cambodian border.

At this point in the Vietnam War, President Richard Nixon desperately wanted a big battle that would force the South Vietnamese Army to prove that it *could* fight and that it *would* fight. He wanted a success to show that his strategy of handing over the war to the South Vietnamese—Vietnamization—was working. Nixon's intent trickled down to the Pentagon, and from there to the US headquarters in Saigon, and thence to subordinate headquarters.

Thus was born Firebase Kate, one of three such bases created around Bu Prang Special Forces Camp deep in the Central Highlands. No part of this grand strategy was communicated to the handful of Americans and a larger handful of Montagnard tribal mercenaries who would occupy a makeshift hilltop fortress urgently constructed with shovels and sweat and sandbags out of the hard red clay of a grassy knob overlooked by higher surrounding mountains. Not for nothing did the arriving Americans immediately think of Dien Bien Phu and a similar French mistake in 1954. Nor did anyone bother to tell these men or their commander, Special Forces Captain Bill Albracht, that the dense triple-canopy jungle that ran back into nearby Cambodia was absolutely crawling with thousands of enemy troops who would soon be coming for them.

Huge US helicopters lifted in two 155 mm artillery pieces and one 105 mm howitzer, along with 27 American artillerymen to serve the big guns. Other helicopters lifted in 156 Montagnard soldiers of the so-called Civilian Irregular Defense Group—a collection of lightly armed tribal militias—to provide security for Firebase Kate. The closest road was five miles away. All their supplies, including drinking water, would have to be delivered by helicopter.

Among the North Vietnamese troops sheltering across the Cambodian border, waiting for the signal to attack, was the 66th NVA Regiment, well-known as the outfit that started the American war by attacking the 1st Cavalry Division battalions in the Ia Drang Valley in November 1965. Bled white with hundreds dead and wounded there, it came back to lead the Battle of Hill 875/Dak To against American airborne troops in 1967. The 66th fought again in the siege of Khe Sanh in 1968. Now, in the fall of 1969, it had been reinforced and refitted, and was ready to get back in action killing Americans.

That Firebase Kate survived an all-out North Vietnamese attack for five days and nights is little short of a miracle, given that the enemy opened up with heavy artillery from its Cambodian sanctuary and brought in 37 mm anti-aircraft weapons and plenty of .51-caliber heavy machine guns to make helicopter support a true nightmare. Mortars and B-40 rockets rained fire on the base. One by one, the firebase's own artillery pieces were knocked out.

Between the endless artillery and mortar barrages came human waves with hundreds of attackers. The Montagnard troops, reinforced here and there by a handful of the bravest artillerymen, fired off tens of thousands of rifle and machine-gun rounds every single day.

What kept the troops at Kate alive were brave helicopter crews bringing in ammo and water, Air Force fast movers delivering napalm and bombs from F-4 Phantoms and F-100 Super Sabres during daylight hours, and Air Force C-47 Spooky gunships that came out after dark to pour 6,000 rounds of minigun fire a minute onto the surrounding hills and the swarms of attacking enemy troops.

Ground attacks were almost continuous during daylight, while mortars and rockets landed around the clock. No one on Kate slept more than one hour in twenty-four. No one had time to eat beyond snatching a mouthful of C rations during the fighting. Water was in short supply until it was gone entirely. Leaving a foxhole to relieve yourself invited death or dismemberment.

In the midst of this hellish battle for survival, Captain Albracht would be stunned when his urgent radio request for a huge ammunition resupply to beat off the unceasing attacks was arbitrarily cut in half by a rear-echelon weenie whose reaction was: *There's no way those guys need this much ammo.*

Near the end of the fight, with 15 of the 27 artillery troops wounded and one dead, and a third of the 156 Montagnard defenders dead or wounded, Albracht was hoping and praying for a relief force to rescue Kate. He didn't care if that force was American or South Vietnamese: the American 4th Division or the ARVN 23rd Division. Senior US commanders were hoping that the ARVN would move, but all they heard were reasons why it would not. It was only a few Americans and a company of Montagnards, who were hated by the Vietnamese anyway. The Americans weren't coming either, hoping to avoid another pointless battle with heavy American casualties in a war that the leadership back home wanted to end soon.

That left only US Special Forces, Albracht's last best hope, and they ordered two companies of Mike Force Nung troops under an Australian commander to air-assault into the area and attempt to break through the North Vietnamese cordon around the firebase. The Mike Force troops ran into a buzz saw and were forced to pull back and hunker down. If the men on Firebase Kate were going to survive, they would have to save themselves by escaping under the noses of the enemy encircling them and then finding and linking up with the Mike Force troops several miles away.

The survivors, including the wounded, destroyed the already disabled big guns and the radios and generators and weapons and escaped under cover of darkness. The column of exhausted, shell-shocked men stumbled through dense jungle and bomb craters and broken trees on a long night's march until they found the Mike Force troops who would lead them to safety.

On his way back to headquarters, Captain Albracht looked up the officer who had cut the shipment of ammunition in half, then chased him around his office with violence on his mind until he was restrained by two sergeants while the offending officer ran out the door and down the street.

Albracht and his coauthor, former Army captain Marvin Wolf, have told the story of Firebase Kate splendidly and in great detail. They found and interviewed half the surviving Americans and have woven their individual stories into the larger tapestry. There are tales here that will chill the blood, accounts of incredible sacrifice and bravery in a battle that more closely resembles those in Europe in World War II, or those during the first months after the Chinese intervened in the Korean unpleasantness, than those in Vietnam.

GLOSSARY

of Military Terms

12.7: PAVN (see below) 12.7 mm (.51-caliber) machine gun often used in an anti-aircraft role.

105: A howitzer firing 85-pound explosive shells that are 105 mm (4 inches) in diameter.

155: A howitzer weighing six tons and firing 100-pound explosive shells that are 155 mm (6 inches) in diameter.

AK-47: Chinese, Russian, Viet Cong, and PAVN infantry rifle. Fires semi or full auto.

Arc Light: A B-52 strike.

ARVN: Army of the Republic of [South] Vietnam.

B-40: A rocket-propelled grenade, also called an RPG.

Chief of Smoke: The senior noncom in charge of an artillery battery's guns.

CIDG: The Civilian Irregular Defense Group, a sort of militia, used for defense of Montagnard and other rural villages. They were led by US Special Forces troops.

Cobra: Fast, extremely agile, and heavily armed helicopter used as a gunship.

commissioned officer: Appointed by the president and confirmed by the Senate to serve in pay grades from second lieutenant through general.

CONEX: A large steel shipping container with doors.

deuce-and-a-half: A 2.5-ton (cargo capacity) truck. *Also:* Six-by (6x6 for six wheels with driving power).

dink: Pejorative term for a Vietnamese individual of any description, but especially the enemy.

FAC: Forward air controller—Army or Air Force officer in a small plane who directs the activities of attack aircraft in support of ground troops.

fast mover: A USAF or USN jet aircraft that carries bombs, rockets, and cannon.

Firebase Kate: Small hilltop with three US howitzers and crews, a fire direction center, two Special Forces dudes, and 156 CIDG strikers (after reinforcement).

gook: Derogatory slang for an Asian, especially one with a weapon.

Green Weenie: The Army Commendation Medal.

hooch: A dwelling. It might be a hole in the ground or a cinder-block building. On Kate it was usually a hole in the ground, covered with sandbags.

Huey: One of several different models of the UH-1, a jet-turbine-powered helicopter used in a variety of configurations as cargo/troop carrier, gunship, command and control center, and platform for collecting intelligence or spraying various chemicals.

Lima Charlie: Military phonetic alphabet for "loud and clear." Also "Five by five."

LOACH: Small, agile, unarmed helicopter used for reconnaissance, observation, and carrying small loads.

M16: Basic US Army rifle. Uses a 20-round magazine and fires semi or full automatic.

M79: A shotgunlike weapon that fires a 40 mm grenade at ranges up to 450 meters.

MACV: Military Assistance Command, Vietnam. The umbrella organization for all US military in Vietnam.

Mike Force: An elite force of volunteer strikers (see below) held as a general reserve and used in the most serious situations. Led by US Special Forces and Australian Special Air Service noncoms and officers.

military time: Midnight is 2400. Noon is 1200. A minute after midnight is 0001.

MOS: Military occupational specialty.

noncom: A noncommissioned officer, e.g., a corporal or a sergeant of any pay grade, appointed by authority of the Secretary of the Army. *Also:* NCO.

NVA: North Vietnamese Army (see PAVN below).

OCS: Officer Candidate School. A demanding, six-month path to becoming a commissioned officer.

Old Man: A commanding officer, whatever the chronological age or gender.

PAVN: People's Army of [North] Vietnam. The regular army of the Hanoi regime.

PIO: Public information officer. Army public relations and media liaison.

Prick 25: AN/PRC 25 backpack radio, 20 pounds with battery; operates on FM frequencies.

punji pit: A hole filled with sharpened bamboo slivers, often coated with excrement.

push: A radio frequency.

regenerate: To refuel and rearm an aircraft to prepare it to resume a previous mission or begin a new one.

RPG: Rocket-propelled grenade—fires B-40 rocket with explosive warhead up to 200 meters effective range.

RTO: Radio-telephone operator.

TAOR: Tactical area of responsibility—the geographic area over which any particular unit was expected to operate in and exercise military control over.

TOC: Tactical operations center—a bunker or tent where combat operations were planned and monitored.

Shadow: An AC-119G gunship similarly equipped as a Spooky (see below).

slick: Huey (see above) configured to carry troops and cargo.

SPAD: USAF A-1, a single-engine attack plane that carried 4 tons of ordnance and enough fuel to loiter for hours over the battlefield.

Special Forces: Elite US unit trained in unconventional warfare.

Spectre: AC-130H, the USAF's newest and most fearsome gunship, armed with 20, 40, and 105 mm cannon and a host of defensive devices.

Spooky: AC-47 (DC-3) aircraft converted to gunship with three electrically driven Gatling guns firing 6,000 bullets each per minute.

striker: A Yard (see below) who serves in the CIDG.

VNAF: The South Vietnamese Air Force.

warrant officer: A rank above sergeant major and below second lieutenant. Rates a salute by lower ranks, receives pay similar to junior officers, but is limited to technical specialties. Most Army warrant officers are helicopter pilots, and most Army pilots are warrant officers.

Yard: Slang for Montagnard, a member of one of thirty indigenous tribes that inhabit the Central Highlands. Small, dark-skinned, and no friend of the lowland Vietnamese, who regarded them as dangerous savages.

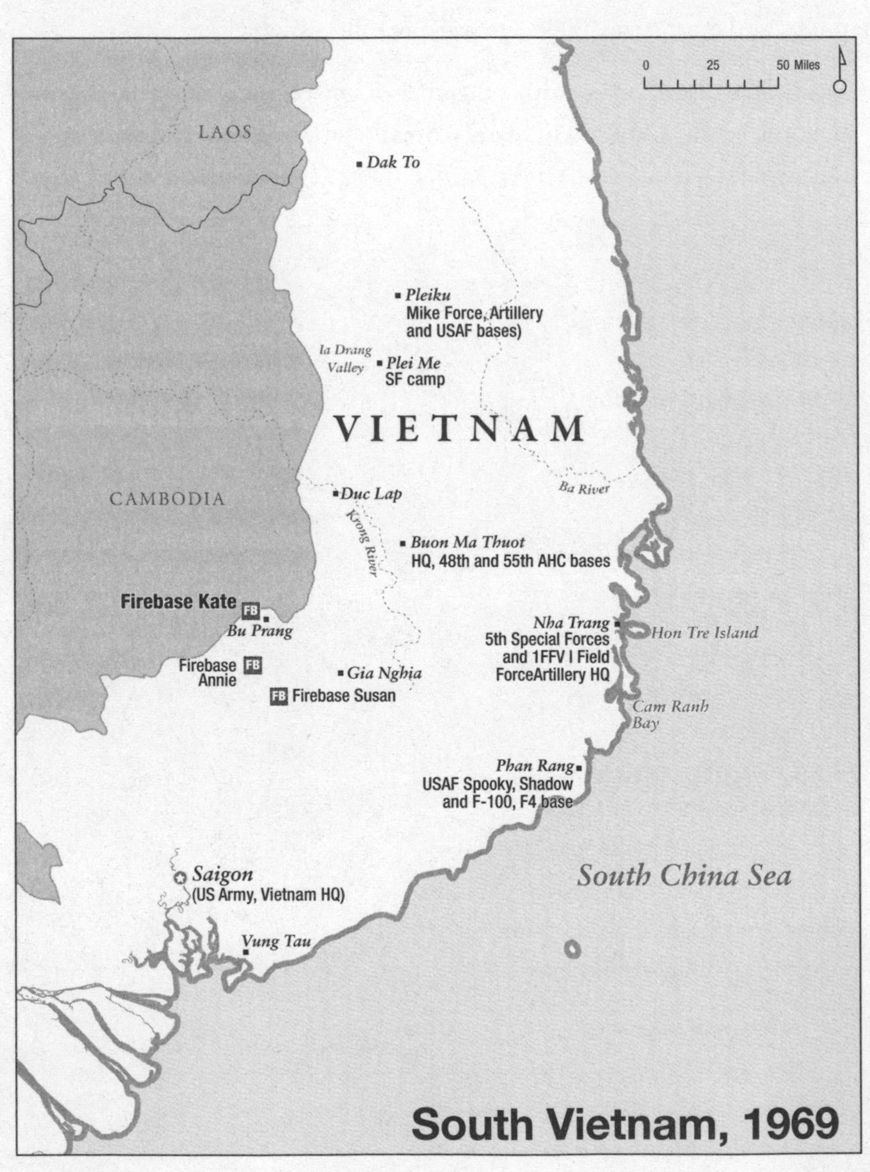
0 25 50 Miles
LAOS
Dak To
Pleiku
Mike Force, Artillery
and USAF bases)
Ia Drang
Valley
Plei Me
SF camp
VIETNAM
CAMBODIA
Duc Lap
Ba River
Krong River
Buon Ma Thuot
HQ, 48th and 55th AHC bases
Firebase Kate
FB
Bu Prang
Nha Trang
5th Special Forces
and 1FFV I Field
ForceArtillery HQ
Hon Tre Island
Firebase
Annie
FB
Gia Nghia
FB Firebase Susan
Cam Ranh
Bay
Phan Rang
USAF Spooky, Shadow
and F-100, F4 base
Saigon
(US Army, Vietnam HQ)
South China Sea
Vung Tau
South Vietnam, 1969

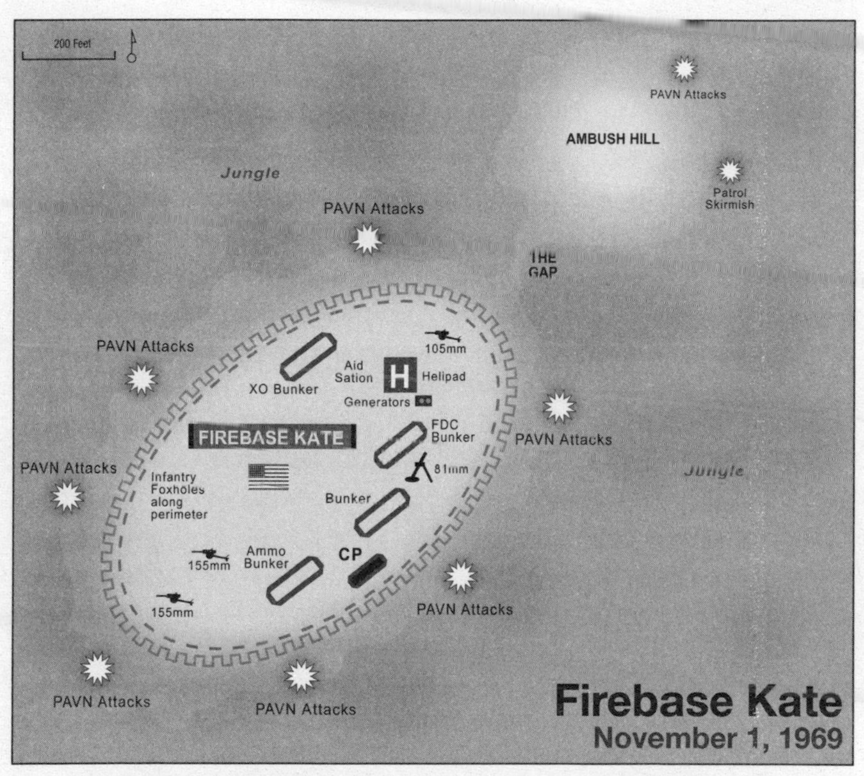
200 Feet
PAVN Attacks
AMBUSH HILL
Jungle
Patrol
Skirmish
PAVN Attacks
THE
GAP
PAVN Attacks
105mm
Aid
Sation
Helipad
XO Bunker
Generators
FDC
Bunker
PAVN Attacks
FIREBASE KATE
PAVN Attacks
81mm
Jungle
Infantry
Foxholes
along
perimeter
Bunker
Ammo
Bunker
CP
155mm
155mm
PAVN Attacks
PAVN Attacks
PAVN Attacks
Firebase Kate
November 1, 1969

ABANDONED IN HELL

Not for fame or reward, not for place or for rank, not lured by ambition, or goaded by necessity, but in simple obedience to duty as they understood it, these men suffered all, sacrificed all, dared all.

—Randolph Harrison McKim, inscription on the Confederate War Memorial, Arlington National Cemetery

INTRODUCTION

This is the tale of an almost forgotten fight for a small, worthless hilltop in Vietnam's Central Highlands. It is about some of the finest soldiers who ever served their country. It is a chronicle of shared hardship and danger, of the very young men with whom I served and their constant, casual courage. It is an attempt to describe functioning as a soldier while gripped by deathly fear, the soul-shattering effects of betrayal, and the lifetime bonds that form between fighting men. It is also about the life-changing loss of innocence that follows the death of a close comrade. In a lesser way, it is about a tiny part of a large, strategically vital campaign.

The five-day siege of Firebase Kate took place in 1969, at a turning point in what now seems like an ancient and misbegotten conflict. Four years earlier, American ground forces went to war against a well-armed and highly motivated North Vietnamese invasion force. America sent its best troops into battle, sent them to grapple with the enemy, to punish and to kill, certainly, but also to take our foe's measure and to learn if and how a road to victory was possible.

The year 1969 marked the abandonment of that road. Kate was an ephemeral, cautionary signpost in history's rearview mirror on what would become a detour to a costly and ignominious failure.

As late as the previous year, the route to American victory had appeared to be well paved and wide-open. Defeated in the field at every turn, the Viet Cong were seemingly reduced to small, mostly homegrown guerrilla bands. They were a nuisance, but no longer much of a threat. The 1965 invasion by the People's Army of Vietnam (PAVN), as the North Vietnamese Army called itself, had been turned around by a half million American and Allied troops. Pursued by our highly mobile infantry, attacked high and low by our deadly warplanes, pounded by our armed helicopters and long-range artillery, the PAVN fought hard and fought well but repeatedly was forced to retreat to its sanctuaries in supposedly neutral Cambodia and Laos. Hanoi's official records show that at least twenty-four PAVN or Viet Cong were killed for every American whose name would be engraved on our wall of tears on the Washington Mall.

Meanwhile, day after day, US bombers flattened Hanoi and its environs, to say nothing of large parts of South Vietnam, with thousands of tons of explosives—more bombs than were dropped by all sides during World War II. Through America's largely compliant media, top Pentagon and White House officials assured the nation that even with support from the Soviet Union and Red China, a country as small and resource-poor as North Vietnam could not prosecute war on this scale much longer.

Then came Tet, a national and regional celebration of the Chinese lunar new year. Until 1968, in the course of this war, Tet was a brief midwinter pause for an informal countrywide truce. Tet 1968 was instead a surprise surge of simultaneous, well-coordinated, and deadly Viet Cong attacks on every major city in South Vietnam. Tet was a shock to America's nervous system, a blow to the national solar plexus.

From a purely military perspective, however, the Tet Offensive was a Viet Cong disaster. The nationwide civilian uprising against American forces that the VC had expected to trigger died stillborn. Fighting in some cities persisted for months; when it was over, most of the best VC troops, and virtually all its experienced leaders, were dead.

In addition, and not least, the usually lethargic Army of the Republic of [South] Vietnam, the ARVN, which bore the brunt of Tet's urban fighting, acquitted itself with surprising distinction: "Initially outnumbered and under fierce attack, the ARVN closed ranks and fought," wrote General Nguyen Cao Ky, then vice president, and a former commander of the South Vietnam Air Force (VNAF). "From the top down, senior officers led by example, sharing the risks of battle . . . We kicked the VC out of our cities, we kicked their ass. The little Vietnamese soldier will fight hard under good leadership."[1]

Tet was nevertheless a huge propaganda victory for the Hanoi regime. It told the American public that the Pentagon's rosy predictions of imminent victory were at best wishful thinking but possibly a campaign of deliberate deception. Millions of Americans held a personal stake in the war—those who had served in Vietnam and those at or near draft age who could expect to be called up, as well as their families and loved ones. After Tet, a large and noisy proportion of these citizens demanded an end to the war.

The public relations disaster of the Tet Offensive forced President Lyndon Johnson to abandon his quest for a second full term. It helped to enable former vice president Richard M. Nixon to win the White House on a fuzzy platform that included a "secret plan" to end the war.

Soon after his inauguration in January 1969, Nixon revealed this plan: Under "Vietnamization," the ARVN, whose petite soldiers struggled with large, heavy, obsolete American weapons left over from World War II, was to be equipped with the same weaponry as US units. ARVN was then to gradually take over the ground war. America would fund a rapid expansion of the VNAF, and provide air, artillery, and logistical support to the ARVN. As they engaged the enemy, America would disengage.

By late 1969, most of the million-man ARVN was equipped with lightweight, modern infantry weapons, supported by American and VNAF airpower and an enormous collection of US artillery, and sustained by a generous and efficient US logistics system.

---

1 Full disclosure: Coauthor Wolf cowrote General Ky's wartime memoir, *Buddha's Child* (New York: St. Martin's Press, 2002), from which the above is drawn.

An impatient White House now demanded that ARVN demonstrate the commander in chief's wisdom: South Vietnamese units must start to take the lead in ground combat. They must fight and win battles. Americans were expected to do everything in their power to help make that happen.

If that was Washington's view of things, it was not necessarily what the Saigon leadership, singular and plural, might have wished for. And it was not necessarily realistic: For one thing, the easy familiarity that American officers and senior noncoms had with complex, combined-arms operations, with coordinating the movement of men and machines—tanks, artillery, aircraft—through four dimensions of time and space while dealing with complex logistics, as well as making full use of the capabilities of helicopters, represented skills that few ARVN officers had acquired, particularly at the company and battalion levels, where they were most needed. Moreover, virtually every man in every US combat unit could read and write and was hands-on familiar with machinery; the typical ARVN soldier was a peasant with fewer than five years of schooling and little experience with machinery, much less the complex apparatus of modern warfare. After 1969, it was not unusual to hear of ARVN artillery shelling its own troops, or of a VNAF strike on friendlies or civilians. Exhibit One: Associated Press photographer Nick Ut's horrifying photograph of nine-year-old Phan Thi Kim Phuc running naked from a VNAF napalm strike on her village. And that was in 1972.

ARVN also lacked an effective logistical system, and much of the war material provided by the US was siphoned off through a web of graft. ARVN troops in the field were often expected to forage for their own food, a huge distraction and an unwanted burden that did not endear them to the local populace.

While these obstacles could be overcome with time and patience, both were in as short supply in the White House as in the Pentagon.

Not incidentally, ARVN's generals and colonels realized that the departure of US forces would dam the Niagara of American cash—billions every month—flowing into South Vietnam's war economy, much of which trickled into their own pockets. They therefore sought to find ways to postpone the day when that river ran dry.

Just as unwelcome in Saigon was the fact that taking over the ground war inevitably meant many more ARVN casualties, which from the beginning of the war had been anathema to its commanders. This was, and still is, hard for Americans to accept: By the end of 1969, upwards of 220 GIs were zipped into body bags every week. Americans served one-year tours, however, while ARVN's troops remained in uniform until they were killed, horribly maimed, or too old to fight. And America's population was a dozen times the size of South Vietnam's 16 million people.

Moreover, despite the influx of new weapons and hardware, despite advisers, training programs, and the demonstrated capacity of properly led Vietnamese soldiers to fight well, many ARVN units were even less than what they seemed.

According to General Nguyen Cao Ky, as many as 10 percent, and in infantry units, even more, of the ARVN's rank and file were "ghost soldiers," young men whose well-to-do families bribed a senior commander to report them present for duty while they were in fact happily elsewhere. Legions of these young draft dodgers, dubbed Saigon Cowboys, roamed the capital mounted on new Japanese motorbikes, noisily peddling black-market goods, illicit drugs, and prostitutes, mostly to Americans. Other draft dodgers worked in family businesses. Thousands lived or studied abroad.

Ghost soldiers' salaries disappeared into their commander's pocket; he also sold their rations, uniforms, and sometimes even their weapons. Regimental and battalion commanders knew that any period of protracted combat would reveal the hollowness of their formations. They therefore avoided it.

Americans advising senior ARVN commanders were not blind to their shortcomings. They were well versed in the commanders' personal idiosyncrasies, of their eagerness for battle or their aversion to it, and of their units' combat capabilities. These advisers, however, were also keenly aware of their commander in chief's desire that Vietnamization show results: ARVN battlefield victories. Most of all, these regimental and division advisers, US Army officers in the crucial middle years of their careers, knew that if reports that they sent up their chain of command described the commander whom they advised, the officer they had been sent to educate while enhancing his unit's combat effectiveness, as cowardly, or corrupt, or thickheaded, or as someone who displayed little regard for troop welfare, or was reckless and mistaken in his choice of tactics—if they painted a picture of ARVN cowardice or ineptness, they were likely to be replaced by an adviser who wrote more optimistic reports, to the detriment of their own career.

So the White House demanded ARVN victories, ARVN generals promised that battlefield success was around the corner, and US advisers pretended to believe them.

As for me, until the previous year, when I was stationed in nearby Thailand, I would have been pressed to find Vietnam on a world map. All that I knew of this war was that America was fighting Communists, and it was my duty to help my country. At age 21, I believed that I was seven feet tall, bulletproof, invisible when needed, and that Vietnam was to be the greatest adventure I could ever hope for.

I had had three years' service but not a minute in combat. My troops were very young—many still in their teens. Like me, most had enlisted or been drafted straight out of high school. A few had several months of combat under their belts, but even they could not have been prepared for what awaited us in late October 1969.

And so we went more or less happily onto the isolated hilltop called Kate, ignorant of the misaligned forces that controlled our fate, never expecting a bloody five-day monsoon of steel and fire, and entirely unaware that the ARVN generals responsible for our lives loathed and feared the mountain tribesmen on whom we relied to defend us and our isolated hilltop from the fierce and relentless PAVN infantry.

This is how it went, to the best of our recollections.

PART ONE

Cannon to right of them,
Cannon to left of them,
Cannon in front of them
Volley'd and thunder'd;
Storm'd at with shot and shell,
Boldly they rode and well,
Into the jaws of Death,
Into the mouth of Hell
Rode the 600.

—Alfred, Lord Tennyson

ONE

Bu Prang, Republic of Vietnam, October 1969

I did not want to go to Fire Support Base Kate. It was about six kilometers southeast of Bu Prang Special Forces Camp, close to the Cambodia border. There was nothing going on there, not a damn thing, and I'd barely gotten my feet on the ground in my first combat assignment as executive officer (XO) of Special Forces Team A-236.

A few days earlier, intelligence officers had warned that Special Forces camps along the border at Bu Prang and Duc Lap could expect an attack soon. I told Lieutenant Colonel Frank Simmons, commander of B-23, my boss's boss, that my talents would be wasted on Kate. I had much to do to prepare Camp Bu Prang for the expected attack. I didn't want to go out to Kate and sit on my ass.

Simmons said that he understood my feelings. And that I was going to Kate.

Maybe it was because an "A" Team authorized only one captain and one first lieutenant—but at the moment, ours had one lieutenant and three captains, and I was the greenest of the trio. I presented myself at six feet and

200 whipcord-lean pounds of rough, tough, romping, stomping, face-chewing, bullet-spewing, airborne Green Beret hell—but I'd just turned 21. And I had just pinned on captain's bars. I'd never commanded troops in the field, never heard a shot fired in anger. Surely I was the youngest Special Forces captain in South Vietnam—very likely the youngest captain of any description among the half million American soldiers, sailors, marines, and airmen stationed there.

So maybe, in Simmons's mind, sending me to sit on my ass on a remote hill for a few weeks was just the thing to start breaking me in. Or something.

A typical Vietnam-era Green Beret "A" Team of two officers and ten non-coms, A-236 was based in the tiny market town of Bu Prang, close to a contested salient along the porous, ill-defined Cambodian border, and about forty air miles southwest of Buon Ma Thuot, capital city of Dak Lak Province and the strategic linchpin of South Vietnam's enormous but thinly populated Central Highlands region. To save ourselves the anguish of learning Vietnamese and its tones—to most American ears, they are all but indistinguishable from one another—we called Buon Ma Thuot by its initials, BMT.

The highlands are a series of vast, contiguous plateaus bordering the lower part of Laos and northeastern Cambodia. For more than a thousand years, these jungle-covered hills have supported at least thirty distinct tribal societies spread among six different ethnic groups speaking dialects and languages drawn primarily from the Malayo-Polynesian, Tai, and Mon-Khmer language families. Collectively, these minority societies call themselves the Degar.

Until the eighth century, the Degar tribes thrived in the lowlands and valleys along Vietnam's warm, fertile coast. Over the next thousand years, however, they were steadily pushed into the damp, malarial mountains and valleys of Laos, Cambodia, and Vietnam, first by the Cham and Khmer peoples, most of whose descendants now populate Cambodia, and then by the Kinh, the lowland Vietnamese whose ancestors migrated southward from China and multiplied into Vietnam's majority ethnic group.

The first Europeans to encounter the diminutive, dark-skinned mountain tribesmen were seventeenth-century Jesuits. These French missionaries noted that while the more numerous Kinh had lighter skins, an advanced culture, and a sophisticated language closely related to the neighboring Chinese, the mountain people were seminomadic, Bronze Age primitives subsisting on hunting, gathering, and slash-and-burn agriculture. Possessed of no written language, they worshipped local spirit pantheons and spoke in a babble of tongues. French missionaries dubbed them "Montagnards," mountain people, and set out to convert both them and the Kinh to Christianity.

The Jesuits modified the Roman alphabet and added diacritics to accommodate the Kinh tonal language (six tones in the north, five in the south), as well as certain vowels and consonants, then translated the Bible into this *quốc ngữ* alphabet. They won many converts among the Kinh, especially in the hunger-haunted, hardscrabble northern regions, but few among the shy peoples of the misty highlands. This was mostly because, every six or seven years, each Montagnard clan abandoned its tiny farmstead, burned its thatched huts, and moved a few miles to another clearing, where they hacked new fields from the thin jungle soil and started over. Missionaries found it hard to maintain contact.

If they clung tenaciously to their old gods and animist spirits, if they resisted change, most Montagnards nevertheless regarded the French as friends, or at least not as enemies. Then and now, however, the Kinh, whether North Vietnamese or South Vietnamese, regarded the mountain people as *moi*, literally savages—inferior, even subhuman creatures—and proceeded to murder and subjugate them, meanwhile shamelessly exploiting their lands and resources. To put it plainly: The Kinh view the various Montagnard tribes much as nineteenth-century Americans reckoned the indigenous peoples of the Great Plains—the Lakota, the Pawnee, the Arapaho, the Comanche, the Kiowa, etc. To most Kinh, the only good *moi* is a dead *moi*.

North America's indigenous peoples were considerably better fed than the Montagnards. They were taller, more muscular, longer lived, better suited physically and temperamentally to war, and far quicker to adapt European ways—notably, the horse—in defense of their homes. Neither the

Native American nor the Montagnard had much success resisting the more technologically advanced cultures that invaded them.

Starting in the seventeenth century, France colonized Indochina. After World War II, she granted political autonomy to Montagnards in the Central Highlands' five provinces. The tribes were in no way prepared to capitalize on this: They had been oppressed for so long that they had few educated people, and fewer still that were capable of governing or administering. Despite their supposed sovereignty, nothing changed for them.

In 1952, Vietnam's French puppet emperor, Báo Đại, abolished Montagnard autonomy but allowed them to retain their lands. Two years later the Viet Minh communists drove the French out; the 1954 Geneva Accords placed all Montagnard tribes under the authority of the new South Vietnam government. When Ngo Dinh Diem was elected president in 1955, he immediately labeled the Montagnard, Cham, Khmer, and Chinese peoples "ethnic minorities." Under the pretense of bringing them into Kinh culture, oppression became systematic and open. Nearly a million lowland Vietnamese were resettled in the highlands on Montagnard lands.

While the highland tribes feared and distrusted the southern Kinh, the northerners presented a greater and more immediate threat to the Degar. Invading their forested slopes, they enslaved able-bodied men as porters, conscripted younger ones into their military, stole food, and, when it suited them, liquidated entire communities.

Seeking safety, by the sixties many Montagnards had abandoned their seminomadic lifestyle to live in government-sponsored villages with rudimentary sanitation and bare-bones social services and schools.

Team A-236 worked with the Montagnard clans in and around Bu Prang, trained their men to defend the community, and recruited able-bodied adults into the Civilian Irregular Defense Group, a kind of mercenary militia equipped as light infantry and deployed in a wide variety of mostly defensive roles.

CIDG was originally a CIA program. Created in 1961, four years before US combat units were deployed, the CIDG was intended to counter expanding Viet Cong influence and control in the Central Highlands, both to defend settlements against attack and to deny Viet Cong the ability to conscript Montagnards as slave labor.

"A" Teams from the Army's newly minted Special Forces moved into selected Montagnard hamlets and villages and set up "area development centers." Each small unit drew upon the specialized training of its NCOs in weapons, intelligence, engineering, communications, and medicine. They concentrated on local defense and initiated such civic action projects as digging wells, teaching sanitation essentials to families who had never known soap, and building schools and rudimentary hospitals. Green Berets trained villagers and provided weapons, equipment, and supplies for defense. They handpicked the best militiamen for further training, recruiting them into quick-reaction forces poised to respond to nearby Viet Cong attacks. The program was almost instantly successful. As each village was pacified, it served as a training camp for neighboring settlements.

By 1963, the CIA believed that greater success against the Viet Cong could be realized by moving both CIDG units and Special Forces teams to military control, where they could carry the fight to the enemy instead of waiting to be attacked.

Operation Switchback transferred the CIDG program to MACV. To manage it, the US Army's Fifth Special Forces Group moved to Vietnam from Fort Bragg, North Carolina. CIDG units were employed in support of conventional military operations, especially patrolling border regions. It quickly became apparent that with patience, training, and leadership these diminutive soldiers could become a loyal, reliable, well-disciplined, and highly effective fighting force.

Nevertheless, South Vietnam's systematic oppression of minorities, and especially Montagnards, continued. In 1964, the Montagnard autonomy movement turned militant. On September 20, 1964, the Degar Highlands Liberation Front revolted, killing many government officials. Several sympathetic Special Forces soldiers volunteered to become "hostages" in order to serve as negotiators. Saigon made concessions and released movement leaders from prison. At the insistence of the US Embassy, the Saigon government, then run by a former Diem supporter, General Duong Van

Minh, restored Montagnard institutions and took steps to win back their loyalty.

Still suspicious of Saigon, organizations advocating for autonomy for the Cham and Kampuchean minorities joined with the Montagnards to create an umbrella organization called the United Front for the Liberation of Oppressed Races (in French, Front Unifié de Lutte des Races Opprimées). FULRO was chaired by Y Bham Enuol, a charismatic and often-imprisoned Montagnard.

Leaders of the three organizations agreed that their first priority must be to win the war against the Communists. While accepting the need for Montagnard CIDG units, South Vietnam's leaders nevertheless viewed FULRO with hatred and suspicion. FULRO went underground, meeting in secret, biding its time.

THE CIDG program grew rapidly and was largely effective, but it could not stop the infiltration of PAVN regiments from Laos and Cambodia. By mid-1965, these units were poised for a quick strike at the Central Highlands aimed at cutting the country in half at its narrow waist, where South Vietnam was only fifty miles wide. If the North Vietnamese attacked in force, there was little hope that the undisciplined, poorly trained, and ill-equipped ARVN, with its notoriously corrupt and venal leadership, could stop them.

To counter this threat, in July 1965 the newly appointed South Vietnamese prime minister, Nguyen Cao Ky, until a few weeks earlier the flamboyant yet relatively obscure VNAF commander, asked President Lyndon Johnson for an immediate infusion of American combat troops.

This was the start of an enormous buildup that would reach, at its peak, more than half a million US soldiers, sailors, aviators, and marines in South Vietnam and its waters. At the same time, billions of US dollars poured into the country to train and advise the ARVN. To support ARVN, US, and other Allied military units, Fifth Special Forces created the Mobile Strike Force. Dubbed the Mike Force, its units were based in each of Vietnam's four military areas and composed of elite, battalion-size CIDG formations led by US Green Beret and Australian Special Air Service advisers.

Mike Force was a "force multiplier," designed to supplement and enhance conventional military forces.

Mike Force troops were mercenaries, including Chinese Nung tribesmen, feared fighters whose ancestors had been pirates in the Gulf of Tonkin, and members of the Degar tribes, Cambodians, Laotians, and other persecuted minorities: the Bahnar, Nung, Jarai, and Khmer Krom. Collectively, it was a countrywide quick-reaction force "for securing, reinforcing, and recapturing CIDG 'A' Camps." Mike Force also conducted long-range recon patrols that reaped valuable intelligence, went on search and-rescue missions for US and Allied prisoners of war, and carried out raids on PAVN and VC units.

Mike Force also played a critical role in the rescue of downed American airmen. These highly mobile units moved through even the most challenging terrain, and were often stationed close to the so-called Demilitarized Zone between the two Vietnams. Mike Force established and secured drop zones for paratroop landings and landing zones for helicopter assaults. Equipped with the most advanced radios of the era, Mike Force advisers called in artillery and air strikes on high-value targets.

In short, for an eager Special Forces officer anxious for action and yearning to carry the fight to the enemy, Mike Force was the place to be. By 1969, the largest Mike Force unit was based at Pleiku under Headquarters, Fifth Special Forces Group. It had about as many infantrymen as a US Army brigade or regiment, but lacked the combat support elements of these organizations: Mike Force was all teeth, no tail.

Thanks to my older brother, Bob, a Green Beret sergeant, this was what I had envisioned as my combat assignment when I repeatedly volunteered for Vietnam. And that was why, after completing the Army's tough Special Warfare course at Fort Bragg, North Carolina, then spending a comparatively laid-back year in Thailand training the Royal Thai Army, I had volunteered yet again for Vietnam.

Thus my assignment as XO of A-236 was something of a disappointment.

Nevertheless, in the weeks since coming to Bu Prang, I had worked hard at supervising construction of in-depth defenses of the camp and surrounding area to withstand attack by a large, well-equipped, and determined enemy force.

FOR both political and military reasons, South Vietnam's forty-four provinces were grouped into four geographic districts, called Corps, and numbered north to south. II Corps, commanded by an ARVN general, was headquartered in Pleiku City and covered thirteen provinces, from Kontum in the northwest and Binh Dinh in the northeast to Quang Duc, Lam Dong, and Binh Thuan Provinces in the south—the largest Corps in geographic area.

US, ARVN, and Allied military units within II Corps, including two Republic of Korea infantry divisions, were under the operational control of I Field Force Vietnam, a US Army headquarters then commanded by Lieutenant General Charles A. Corcoran. (Corcoran wore another hat: He was the MACV assistant chief of staff for operations.) In size, military components, and organization, it was much like a larger US Army corps—several infantry divisions with supporting units—but designated a "field force" to avoid confusion with South Vietnam's nationwide military-political corps system. Unlike a corps headquarters, however, IFFV had more than a purely tactical function. Its responsibilities also included logistics, running pacification efforts in rural areas, and providing advisers to the ARVN and other South Vietnamese government organizations.

In late September 1969, the G2 (intelligence) staff at IFFV headquarters in Nha Trang—before the war a sleepy resort town with gorgeous white-sand beaches and more than its share of equally lovely women—began to assemble the jigsaw puzzle that is tactical and strategic military intelligence.

G2's puzzle pieces were diverse. In that era before spy satellites were flexible and reliable, ELINT (electronic intelligence, e.g., monitoring enemy radio and radar emissions) was developed from data captured by the NSA, and by Army Security Agency monitoring units; aerial reconnaissance data came from Air Force sources, including high-flying U-2 spy planes, EC-47s—converted WW II–era cargo aircraft jammed with state-of-the-art electronics—and Army OV-1 Mohawks, Grumman's small twin-engine turbo prop surveillance platform, equipped with side-looking radar or infrared cameras. Mohawks flew in the dark, often at treetop level, popping infrared flashbulbs and snapping large-format images that captured the heat from campfires, engine exhaust, or groups of men. Other Mohawks flew between hills, their radar looking for anomalies in ground cover or movement where none should be.

But the terrain along both sides of the Cambodian and Laotian borders was made for concealment. Thick jungle covered steep hillsides and watercourses. Ground fog and heavy rain often obscured visibility. A U-2 at 60,000 feet is all but blind over these jungles. The EC-47's sensitive electronics could detect the radio-frequency energy produced by a spark plug from miles distant—but not with rain absorbing that energy before it reached the aircraft. And while the OV-1 was designed to fly at very low altitudes, few pilots could fly daily nap-of-the earth missions through monsoon rains and live to tell about it.

US Army aviation units also deployed the tiny but safer O-1 Bird Dog, a single-engine Cessna designed for spotting artillery, and helicopters for tactical patrolling.

July through September, however, is monsoon season in the Central Highlands—not the sort of weather that lends itself to aerial reconnaissance. In that era, the military's most sophisticated snooping gear was of little value while heavy rains drenched the highlands nonstop for upwards of a week at a time. Wind-driven torrents wash out roads and bridges, trigger landslides, drive rivers over their banks, turn the ground into an impassable quagmire, and cover the mountains with low, thick clouds.

Nevertheless, tough, motivated, and well-trained infantry can function even in such conditions. Thus, even before American combat troops arrived, the North Vietnamese had used this season to move men and equipment down the long network of trails and roads they'd established in Laos and Cambodia—the so-called Ho Chi Minh Trail. Every October since 1965, when the skies cleared, they launched a new offensive.

As the rains faded in mid-October 1969, I Field Force aviation launched aerial surveillance, including a small helicopter fleet equipped with ungainly sensor arrays designed to detect ammonia in air flowing through a scoop beneath the fuselage.

Ammonia is a mammalian waste product, found in sweat, feces, and urine.

These sensors were unreliable—a high reading might indicate a troop concentration—but might as well be elephant dung, tiger, bear, a monkey troop, a previously unknown Montagnard village, or nothing at all. Sniffer sorties over thick, trackless jungle with an uncooperative population were usually only a bit better than nothing at all.

Based in BMT, the 155th Assault Helicopter Company began flying sniffer missions along the border and found data suggesting either several previously unsuspected monkey troops and elephant herds, or a tremendous upsurge in enemy activity in the areas around Bu Prang and Duc Lap.

By late October, intelligence had further indications of large troop movements along the Cambodian border north of Bu Prang. Mike Force units patrolling the border confirmed reports from "special agents"—local people paid to keep their eyes open and share what they saw with CIA or Military Intelligence agents—of a buildup of regimental-size units in Cambodian sanctuaries just across the border. On about October 22, the PAVN 66th and 28th Infantry Regiments, supported by elements of the 40th Artillery Regiment and the K-394 Artillery Battalion, whose 37 mm antiaircraft guns were a new addition to the PAVN arsenal in South Vietnam, crossed the border and melted into the jungles north of Bu Prang and south of Duc Lap.

The PAVN 66th was a familiar foe that had earned our respect. In August 1965, the 66th had slipped out of its base in coastal Thanh Hoa, about a hundred miles south of Hanoi. With some 1,600 men in its headquarters and component infantry battalions, the 7th, 8th, and 9th, the regiment made a grueling, three-month, 500-mile march across the width of North Vietnam, then turned south through Laos and Cambodia to a fateful encounter with elements of the First US Air Cavalry Division at LZs X-Ray and Albany in the valley of the Drang River.

This bloody clash, the Battle of Ia Drang, was the first large encounter between the regular armies of North Vietnam and the United States. Both sides paid dearly in blood: 241 Americans killed or missing, and 258 wounded, while the 66th lost upwards of three-fourths of its men, about half dead and half wounded.

The regiment withdrew into Cambodia to rest and replenish its ranks with replacements from the stream of PAVN troops flowing down the Ho Chi Minh Trail.

Almost a year later, back at full strength, the 66th joined the PAVN 32nd, 24th, and 174th regiments in a months long campaign on the massive hills south and southeast of Dak To. Opposed by elements of the US 173rd Airborne, 1st Cavalry and 4th Infantry divisions, and by the ARVN's elite First Airborne Division, the 66th engaged in some of the hardest-fought and deadliest battles of the war. Battered and bloodied, it again retreated to its Cambodian sanctuary.

The 66th returned to combat in January 1968 with a night attack on Khe Sanh village in northern Quang Tri Province, a settlement defended by a South Vietnamese Regional Force company—lightly armed infantry—and a US Marine rifle company. The Allied forces held their position until first light, when they called in air strikes and artillery from the big Marine combat base nearby. Relentless, the 66th continued the attack through the day and into the next night. The Marines and the RF withdrew after daylight on January 22. This pyrrhic victory cost the 66th Regiment 154 killed and 496 wounded; again it retreated into Cambodia to replenish its ranks and train for battle. By October 1969, the 66th was again combat ready and headed for Bu Prang.

BU Prang and Duc Lap were each defended by an "A" Team and CIDG forces; the team at Duc Lap was A-239. To IFFV intelligence officers at Nha Trang, and to the Green Berets of these "A" Teams, however, it was plain that their camps and garrisons were merely nuisances, obstacles to be removed en route to the main objective, the garrison city and provincial capital, Buon Ma Thuot.

Home of the well-regarded 23rd ARVN Division and internationally famous for a hunting lodge built by Theodore Roosevelt, BMT had two airports and straddled a strategic crossroads. A good road led east to a still better one, the coast highway that runs southward to Saigon and northward to Hue, Vietnam's ancient imperial capital, just below the fortified 17th Parallel dividing North and South Vietnam.

The other highway past BMT ran south to Saigon and north through Kontum to Da Nang. Taking BMT would allow the PAVN to funnel large forces with tanks and heavy artillery into the heart of South Vietnam. If they could seize that prize, it might panic the 23rd Division and BMT's civilian population. That would hasten the disintegration of ARVN defenses and its certain and rapid capitulation.[2]

But in October 1969, before the NVA could attack BMT, they had to get through us: the Green Berets and our CIDG forces at Bu Prang and Duc Lap.

---

2 In March 1975, more than a year after US combat troops withdrew from Vietnam, the North Vietnamese took BMT. Surrounded by PAVN regiments backed by heavy artillery and Soviet-built tanks, the 23rd Division offered stiff resistance for a few days, then broke. In panic, retreating troops stripped off their uniforms, threw away their boots, and fled into the countryside. Two months later, 100,000 PAVN troops seized Saigon to complete their conquest and end the war.

"We advanced down a gradual descent . . . with the batteries vomiting forth upon us shells and shot, round and grape, with one battery on our right flank and another on the left, and all the intermediate ground covered with the Russian riflemen; so that when we came to within . . . fifty yards from the mouths of the artillery . . . we were, in fact, surrounded and encircled by a blaze of fire. . . .

"I think that every man who was engaged in that disastrous affair at Balaklava, and who was fortunate enough to come out of it alive, must feel that it was only by a merciful decree of Almighty Providence that he escaped from the greatest apparent certainty of death which could possibly be conceived."

—Major General, the Earl of Cardigan

TWO

Infantry proudly styles itself Queen of Battle. Like the queen on a chessboard, but with more firepower, infantry goes anywhere: frozen mountains, steaming equatorial swamps, forests, jungles, deserts, plains, tundras, savannahs—to almost any terrain and under virtually any condition on earth. From the middle of the nineteenth century on, however, the Queen of Battle has relied upon support from the King: artillery.

Between the ninth and eleventh centuries, the Chinese invented gunpowder, which led them to rockets and then artillery. Starting in the twelfth century with bamboo barrels, then graduating to bronze, iron, and steel, steadily achieving greater accuracy at longer ranges, artillery became infantry's best friend and most feared foe. By the American War Between the States, advances in metallurgy, chemistry, and manufacturing made possible the development of large-caliber guns with rifled barrels. Hurling time-fused shells that burst into deadly shrapnel, field artillery accompanied infantry on the front lines and was employed with deadly effect.

But not until the Franco-Prussian War of 1870 did artillery achieve its modern form and assume its present role in warfare. German engineers built enormous guns that could lob explosive death up to 75 miles. Though lacking in accuracy, these guns introduced the concept of indirect fire.

On the other side of the lines, the French developed the first modern field gun. First deployed in 1870 and steadily improved for decades, the French 75, towed by horses or by a motorized vehicle, went into service with a range of about five miles (8 kilometers); over time that increased to almost eight miles (12.9 kilometers). The gun's rifled barrel imparted a spin to projectiles that enhanced their accuracy. A hydro-pneumatic mechanism absorbed the recoil of firing over a two-second cycle; this kept the gun trails and wheels locked and unmoving during the firing sequence and enabled subsequent shots without reaiming. Unlocking the loading door at the rear of the gun ejected the spent brass cartridge. A fresh cartridge containing bags of gunpowder and affixed to a projectile was thrust into the breech, the door locked and the gun ready to fire again in as little as two seconds—faster than bolt-action rifles of that era.

Along with breakthroughs in battlefield communications, the French 75, and other guns based on its design, changed the way artillery was used. No longer did the big guns deploy alongside infantry. Towed behind trucks or mounted on an armored, self-propelled chassis, artillery took up positions miles to the rear and fired over the heads of friendly troops. Forward observers on the ground or aloft in balloons fed target information to the guns over telephone lines or, later, by wireless.

Cannon with a variety of barrels were developed. Long barrels hurled huge shells over enormous ranges. Equipped with shorter barrels and consequently possessing a lower center of gravity, howitzers could raise their tubes to almost vertical, allowing them to be sited on a reverse slope to fire on high trajectories that soared over a ridge or summit to find targets in defiladed valleys. For centuries employed as heavy siege weapons, mortars became small and light enough to be carried into battle by infantry.

In the US Army, artillery assumed new roles. Artillery battalions were integrated into infantry divisions to provide direct support to ground troops. Because the demands of a fully engaged division exceed the capabilities of these battalions, additional artillery units, often with heavier guns capable of firing at greater ranges, were placed under the control of higher headquarters, such as the corps and field army. These guns were to provide "general support," and responded to fire missions from any unit within their range and geographical area of responsibility.

Now removed miles from the front lines, unable to see their targets and firing projectiles weighing hundreds of pounds, cannoneers relied upon the discipline of ballistics. By World War II, it was no longer enough to know merely the range and direction to a target. After selecting the most effective trajectory, fire direction specialists could also calculate the time of the projectile's flight; the effects of barometric pressure and air temperature at firing elevations; the speed, altitude, and direction of winds aloft; the difference between magnetic north and north as indicated on firing maps ("magnetic declination"); and, at longer ranges, even the rotation of Earth.

Accomplished with speed and precision, such calculations allowed artillery to fire over great distances with impressive accuracy. Such computations, however, demanded individuals with the aptitude and training for complex mathematics. While gun crews remained the domain of brawny men capable of manhandling heavy projectiles and guns, artillery officers were selected for their mathematical acumen no less than for their leadership qualities.

Which was why in 1968, when tall, thin, calmly intense John Kerr graduated from the University of Iowa at age 22 with a degree in mathematics and a shavetail ROTC commission, he chose to become an artillery officer. "For my senior year, our professor of military science was a field artillery officer," Kerr recalls. "I liked him, and I liked math, and when he explained that ballistics is based on differential equations and calculus, I wanted to serve in the artillery, instead of some other branch."

Kerr spent his first year in uniform learning about field guns and troops at hot, dusty Fort Hood, Texas. After a promotion to first lieutenant, he received orders for Vietnam, where he was assigned to Charlie Battery, 1st Battalion, 92nd Artillery.

Charlie Battery 1/92 was the designated II Corps "swing battery" and boasted the region's only airmobile 155 mm howitzers. From the worm's-eye perspective of tall, rangy Kenn Hopkins, 21, a Charlie Battery ammunition handler and surfer out of Chula Vista, California, things appeared somewhat different. "Charlie Battery was an experiment," he says. "They'd send us out during the monsoon to see if we could last without helicopter support. They sent us to a place like Kate, stuck us next to an NVA training camp a couple clicks away from what we were told was Cambodia."

Hopkins had a certain perspective on this: Although he was young and very junior in rank, he'd been in-country since March of that year, and had served on several firebases that were involved in almost constant fighting. "At Ben Het, we were getting anywhere from 200 to 300 rounds a day of incoming—mortars, rockets, and artillery," he recalls. "And lots of small-arms fire."

At one firebase, he says, many Montagnard infantrymen were accompanied by their older children. "Ben was 12, Mo was 14, and the rest of the kids were 13. We got hit one night, and we gave our M60 [light machine gun] to Mo," he recounts. "A flare went off and I saw Mo down there with the M60! I called to him. He turned around with a big shit-eating grin on his face, and then he turned back and *brrrrrrrrrap!* He was firing that gun John Wayne–style, this 14-year-old kid, doing this stuff. Just phenomenal."

Hopkins arrived on Firebase Kate on September 13, 1969, just about the time that I was assigned to Bu Prang. His platoon's two 155 mm howitzers—six tons each!—were sling-loaded, one at a time, beneath a behemoth CH-54 Sikorsky Flying Crane. The troops were delivered in big-bellied CH-47 Chinooks. The rest of their field gear, along with such construction materials as pierced steel planking, railroad ties, plywood, and fasteners, was packed into big cargo nets and slung beneath a Chinook to be delivered to this steep, football-shaped hilltop, elevation 910 meters, less than two miles from Cambodia. With the guns came a Charlie Battery fire direction team.

In charge of Kate's guns was First Lieutenant Mike Smith, 25, Charlie Battery's executive officer. (Unlike the infantry, where the XO is largely an administrative job, an artillery XO takes charge of the guns.) Handsome, very short, and wiry, Smith grew up on a ranch outside Muleshoe, Texas, about twenty miles southeast of Clovis, New Mexico, and fifty miles northwest of Lubbock, Texas.

In 1964, he was working as a Lubbock hospital orderly and getting tired of Texas. He planned to strap on his hog and head for California. "I was pretty much a ne'er-do-well motorcyclist, Harley-Davidson type," he recalls.

At the hospital he met Elizabeth Clark, 21, a nursing student and the daughter of a Southern Pacific Railroad employee. She was from Sanderson, Texas, on the northern edge of the Rio Grande Valley. "A week before she graduated, she asked me to a dance at the nursing school," Smith recalls. "I never went to California."

A few months later, Smith's mother signed a consent form allowing the State of Texas to let 20-year-old Mike marry Elizabeth. Two years later, they decided to escape the heat and monotonous flatness of West Texas and move to the cool, green, rumpled landscape near Fort Collins, Colorado. Elizabeth found a hospital job as a registered nurse; Mike took veterinary classes and worked as an emergency room orderly. Life was good. "We lived in a little cabin, paid $60 a month rent, had a pickup and a dog, had each other, a fireplace, and we were living in the Colorado mountains—a heck of a time!"

Then came 1967. American soldiers were dying in Vietnam by the thousands, and Mike's friends began receiving draft notices. "I got wind that the draft was getting worse," he says. "I called the Muleshoe draft board to see where I stood, and they said, 'You're about number four on the list, and we need five people.' "

Mike had a friend in Oklahoma, an Army lieutenant, who opined that if Mike wound up going to Vietnam, he'd "want to be an officer because you'll get more money and life is a little better than it is as an enlisted man."

So Mike found the Fort Collins Army recruiter. "He said, 'Oh, yeah, if you sign up, I guarantee you'll go to OCS. If you don't sign up—well, they hate draftees and you'll never get to OCS.' "

Smith took basic training at Fort Bliss, Texas, then went to Fort Sill, Oklahoma, for training in artillery, and then OCS. "But while I was in [artillery school], they changed the rules," he says. "You had to have two years of college to go to OCS, and I had only a smattering."

It looked like he was headed for a firing battery. But Smith had learned to type in high school, a highly valued skill in the Army. He became a battery clerk. "I wound up with a helluva job, inside, no heavy lifting. The first sergeant was death on errors, didn't allow any at all, but he made a damn good clerk out of me. So I did that for several months," he continues. "Then, I guess, a bunch of guys got killed in 'Nam, and they needed more officers, and they took that college restriction out, and six months later I bounced out of OCS as a second looey. I spent some time training cannon cockers, which was enjoyable; by and large I enjoyed my military experience. And then I was sent to Vietnam."

SHARING space on Kate with Charlie 1/92's men and guns was a 105 mm howitzer section from Charlie Battery, 5th Battalion, 27th Arty—half a dozen men ramrodded by a burly sergeant in his mid-twenties named Houghtaling.

Protecting Kate's artillerymen from ground attack was a CIDG company of about 100 Montagnards from Special Forces Team A-233 at Trang Phuoc (also, for obscure reasons, known as Ban Don). CIDG units were nominally under the command and control of ARVN Special Forces; an ARVN officer therefore commanded Bu Prang's CIDG forces, and the yellow-and-red-striped flag of the Republic of Vietnam flew over the camp, as it did over every Special Forces camp in Vietnam.

In practice, however, ARVN Special Forces officers rarely accompanied CIDG troops into potentially hazardous places or situations. I could never decide whether the ARVN officers were more afraid of their Montagnards, or of the North Vietnamese. Either way, I never saw an ARVN officer on Kate or with a CIDG patrol out of Bu Prang. To be fair, however, I must say that when I later served in a Mike Force unit, a few ARVN Special Forces officers operated with us in the field.

Lacking ARVN boots on the ground, on Kate and other firebases protected by CIDG units, the US Army Special Forces, although officially mere advisers, exercised control of Montagnard CIDG troops through the power of our Army-implanted charisma: They obeyed our orders, but only because they chose to do so.

In mid-September, as the artillerymen began building Kate, they were defended by a hundred-man CIDG company led by Captain Lucian "Luke" Barham, commander of Team A-234 at An Lac, and Staff Sergeant Santiago Arbizo, a demolitions specialist from A-233 at Ban Don.

Forrest Scott, 22, a Georgia native with a Gumpian accent to match, graduated from an Atlanta trade school with a certificate as a sheet metal mechanic in 1967 and was drafted the following year. He joined Charlie Battery as a fledgling gun bunny in January 1969, when the entire battery was at beleaguered Firebase Swinger, fifteen clicks west of Ben Het. "We were there for about 97 days and took incoming rounds continuously for 87 or 88 days," he recalls.

And that was the easy part. "When we got there, the North Vietnamese were on the hill and we shot and killed them, drove them off before our infantry got there. And then we set up and got the guns going, built the fire pit, the ammo pits, and dug our underground two-man hooches," he says matter-of-factly, in the manner that only combat veterans and homicide detectives use to tell a story. "[The firebase] was near Mile-High Hill, so they called our hill *Half*-Mile Hill. It was real steep on all sides except one, and that was kind of a semigrade that they used to shield the choppers to keep the enemy from knocking them out of the air when they came in. But that was Charlie Company, and all of those guys were accustomed to that."

Scott and the rest of Mike Smith's cannoneers were already digging and filling sandbags on Kate when their infantry defenders arrived. Alighting from helicopters, the Montagnards discovered termite mounds concealed in the high grass. As the Americans watched in amazement, they began kicking in the mounds and grabbing up as many insects as they could cram into their mouths, swallowing their surprise feast with great gusto down to the last crawler.

When Barham regained control of his troops, he spread them around the hilltop just far enough below the summit that a man could stand erect behind his firing position without being silhouetted against the sky, the so-called military crest. He stationed fewer men on the three steep, almost vertical sides, which rose several meters above the jungle's highest treetops.

He reasoned that attack would be more likely on the gentler slopes. With their entrenching tools, the Montagnards began to hack firing positions from the hard red clay.

"They started digging a perimeter right at the edge of the hill," Scott recalls. "They started out at about two feet deep and they'd throw the dirt on the outside and put their pup tents inside, uphill, so that they could just slide out of their tents and down into the hole, which was then about three feet deep and three feet wide."

Mike Smith stepped off the chopper onto Kate and was instantly smitten by the beauty of the landscape before him. "When I first saw it, I thought, *Damn, this is great!* We could see everything. Kate was on a little hill out in the middle of lots of valleys; when I look back on it now, [I realize] Vietnam was a beautiful country," he recalls. "It was a bald hill with lots of tree cover around it, grassy, but not incredibly tall grass, and with really red, hard-to-dig-in dirt. Filling sandbags was filling dirt bags. From the air it looked like a guitar. The firebase was on the big part of the guitar, then there was a neck, and then a smaller knoll where the fret—the fingerboard—was. In profile it was a big hill, then a little narrow area, and then another hill that we started calling Ambush Hill because it looked like a natural place to set up if you wanted to shoot out the bigger hill."

Four or five hundred meters to Kate's southeast was a high, steep ridge, thickly forested and ending in a long, sharp summit that gave it the look of a knife blade. It was higher than Kate and much bigger, slanting away to the southeast at some twenty or thirty degrees from the parallel. Kenn Hopkins didn't much like that ridge: "It was within range of my M79 grenade launcher. The enemy could have the high ground," he wrote.

"Kate was barren of trees; basically it was a place that you could look at and think, *Boy, I could defend this forever,*" says Smith. "We were dropped in by chopper, with a fair amount of ammo, and we set to filling sandbags to protect the ammo, then building rudimentary bunkers to protect the troops. Nobody got to sleep until everyone had overhead cover. That's the way it was, everywhere in 'Nam."

All that took a couple of days. Even with axes and big shovels, it was hard going. "There was lots of grumbling because people were tired and worn-out from filling sandbags," Smith continues. "But as soon as we were all under reasonable cover, we were fine. At that time there was no indication that there was any real problem."

No problem, except hungry bugs. For their first three days on Kate the artillerymen and their Montagnard security force were under constant assault from tiny, gold-colored insects. "It was about a quarter-inch long and sucked your blood . . . They came up from the south side of the hill in late morning, landed on anything with blood, and began biting. After the first day, when the swarm came up, everyone ran for cover," Hopkins recalls. The gold bugs were soon superseded by six-legged black critters as big as a man's fist. "They didn't swarm in by the hundreds like the gold bugs, they didn't bite or suck blood, but they were so big that they became a distraction," Hopkins adds.

While Smith's men were sandbagging gun emplacements, digging bunkers for ammo storage, a command post, and a fire direction center, Charlie Battery's Second Platoon, with two 155 mm howitzers, was building Firebase Susan. Three 105 mm howitzer crews from Second Battalion, 17th Artillery, were meanwhile building Annie. All three bases were named for the daughters and wife of IFFV Artillery's deputy commander, Colonel Anderson.

Kate's three howitzers were of designs that had gone into service almost thirty years earlier. They were built to be towed behind trucks, and were equipped with 180-degree aiming mechanisms designed for wars like WW II and the Korean War. Wars with front lines, where howitzers were emplaced in the rear to fire toward the front. In those wars, guns were usually emplaced with enough overhead cover to protect their crews from a direct hit by enemy artillery.

Vietnam's battlefields, however, lacked front lines. Guns could be tasked to fire at targets through all 360 degrees, and at any angle up to almost vertical. Accordingly, Kate's howitzers had no overhead cover; they were protected only by chest-high sandbag parapets that would allow gunners to level their muzzles for direct fire against close targets.

Before dark on the second day of Kate's creation, two enormous boxes of heavy corrugated steel, called CONEX containers, were airlifted in beneath Chinooks. Set into a shallow pit, then surrounded and topped with sandbags, one served as Kate's command post, medical aid station, and officer sleeping quarters. The other became the fire direction center, or FDC.

As soon as the FDC was set up, the fire direction officer and his assistant, Specialist Four Bob Johnson, 24, a native New Yorker and recent Cornell graduate, began working with the gun crews and observers on firebases Susan and Annie, fourteen and ten kilometers distant, respectively, to register their guns. This involved picking out a prominent landmark and firing a smoke round at it, then adjusting range and deflection until the target was hit three times. Then, using map and compass, they went on to plot, calculate, and confirm range and deflection data for likely targets around their sister bases and Bu Prang Camp.

Kate, Susan, and Annie, along with a trio of bases around Camp Duc Lap, were the brainchildren of IFFV Artillery planners. They were established to provide artillery support to these camps for the expected PAVN offensive.

SHORT, wiry, and unusually savvy for a man his age, First Lieutenant Reginald Brockwell, 23, was from Paris, Tennessee, a hundred miles west of Nashville. A Vanderbilt graduate with an ROTC commission, he was trained as a chemical engineer and worked in that field before being called to active duty in October 1968. He was a quick study of his new trade in the artillery business, and a few months in combat with the 5/22 Artillery earned him a reputation as an effective forward observer, an outstanding fire control officer, and an all-around up-and-comer.

In September 1969, shortly after I arrived in Vietnam, Brockwell was tasked to help assemble artillery firing charts as a component of IFFV Artillery's plans for the defense of Bu Prang and Duc Lap.

At the time, IFFV Artillery controlled more than twenty US Army artillery battalions firing about 300 tubes, including 175 mm guns; eight-inch, 155 mm and 105 mm howitzers; 4.2-inch and 81 mm mortars; and M-42 "Dusters"—track-mounted, twin 40 mm Bofors-type cannons—anti-aircraft guns employed as direct-fire anti-personnel weapons.

This arsenal was expected to cover IFFV Artillery's tactical area of responsibility (TAOR), which encompassed 79,140 square kilometers, amounting to 47 percent of South Vietnam's landmass.

US Army personnel policies then in effect reflected military, medical, and political considerations. In WW II, draftees and enlistees alike had served for the duration of the war. Those in war zones were awarded "points" that shortened their exposure to hazard in direct proportion to the degree of danger they experienced. Thus, an air crewman might be pulled from further flight duty after 25 or 50 missions. An infantryman served fewer months in a frontline unit than a finance clerk in that same unit. In contrast, everyone in Vietnam served a year, unless killed or evacuated for wounds before the year was up. This policy was designed to lower the incidence of what we now call PTSD, and to reduce casualties among draftees. Career soldiers, however, could expect multiple tours, with Stateside or European duty in between.

By 1969, noncoms who had served in World War II and Korea were retiring in droves to avoid another tour in Vietnam. IFFV Artillery thus suffered from a severe shortage of midlevel NCOs in firing batteries and artillery operations billets. To fill this gap, promising men in lower ranks were promoted. The command also had several recent graduates of the Fort Sill NCO Academy. These were junior enlisted men with good technical skills but little or no experience. Even so, the shortage of experienced NCOs for such vital positions as battery first sergeants and gun section chiefs "at times degraded the combat effectiveness of the units," according to its commanding general's after-action report.

IFFV Artillery was also short of field artillery officers. A third of its captains and almost half its majors had been trained for air defense artillery, which was chiefly surface-to-air missiles with some anti-aircraft guns for low-level defense of tactical units. Most of these officers were assigned to headquarters jobs.

To compound these personnel problems, by 1969 many of the command's guns were wearing out from overuse.

Despite such strictures, IFFV Artillery was obliged to create and staff a forward post in BMT to coordinate all artillery fire for the defense of Duc Lap and Bu Prang, and to cannibalize its firing battalions to assemble a provisional group—what an infantry or armor commander might call a "task force"—to handle all general support artillery missions in the southern II Corps area. Instead of deploying intact batteries, 105 mm and 155 mm howitzers, with crews and bare-bones fire direction sections, were borrowed or swapped from among the group's firing batteries. These guns and FDC teams were emplaced on fire support bases around Bu Prang and Duc Lap.

The firebase concept was invented in Vietnam, although it would be resurrected decades later for the US war in Afghanistan. Like the isolated forts of the Indian Wars, a firebase was a fortified redoubt, deep in contested territory, or "Indian Country," often erected on a height and usually supplied by air. A large, permanent base might host an entire artillery battalion, as many as eighteen howitzers. Most firebases, however, deployed a battery of six or fewer. Built by Army engineers, permanent bases included underground ammunition storage, troop billets, a fire direction center, a mess facility, showers, and latrines. Infantry—US, ARVN, or CIDG—dug in on the base perimeter to protect the base from ground attack.

"IFFV's Provisional Artillery Group included all artillery units in southern II Corps under its command; it would establish fire support bases around Bu Prang and Duc Lap," Brockwell explains. Colonel Francis Bowers, commander of the Provisional Artillery Group, told him that firebases hacked out of the jungle for this campaign were *not* intended to serve as permanent locations. They would get little, if any, engineer support in their construction and would offer none of the creature comforts or amenities found on permanent bases.

Kate's guns were placed under the 5/22's operational control. Commanded by Lieutenant Colonel Elton Delaune, Jr., the 5/22 was headquartered in Phan Rang. It coordinated the fire from its own batteries, and that of others on firebases. Most of these firebases had guns or fire control sections from one or another battalion. The men on those firebases, however, also reported to their original battery or battalion commanders. Infantry protecting each base against ground attack reported to its own commanders, be they ARVN, US Army, or CIDG. Green Beret advisers to the CIDG units reported to still another chain of command, that of the Fifth Special Forces Group. Orders, reports, munitions and supply requests, intelligence advisories, and other messages moved by radio, back and forth between levels of each chain of command. Between the multiple parallel command chains, however, there was little communication.

To any reasonable military observer, the low end of the operational chain of command on Kate—the part that actually fired at the enemy—and on other firebases established to support Bu Prang, Duc Lap, and each other was a convoluted mess, resembling nothing quite so much as one of those puzzling yet clearly erotic friezes found on ancient Indian temples—or, as most infantrymen would say, in our profane but eloquent way, a clusterfuck. But I would not learn this fact until much later.

NOT long after his briefing on the IFFV Artillery firing plans, Brockwell was put on a short list to interview for a new job: aide-de-camp for Colonel Charles Hall, the new commander of IFFV Artillery, who was slated for promotion to brigadier general.

Depending on who you ask, serving as a general's aide is either the best job a junior officer could aspire to or the worst, most thankless duty ever invented. On the plus side, it was an opportunity for a young officer to observe firsthand how large Army organizations are run, how generals actually carry out their duties, and to some extent what goes through senior commanders' minds when making decisions. A successful tour as a general's aide would lead to accelerated promotion and elevated odds of eventually wearing a general's star. Since the end of World War II, there has hardly been a general in the US Army who did *not* serve as an aide at least once in his or her career.

On the downside, it was a 24/7 job that quickly lost the aide every Army buddy he'd ever had. He was at the general's beck and call, expected to serve as his eyes and ears, playing no favorites, reporting what he observed directly to the general, carrying private messages not meant for the record up and down the chain of command. An aide was presumed to speak for the general he represented, which created potentially awkward situations when he addressed officers far more senior than himself. The young aide might be his general's sounding board, or his errand boy, but either way, none of his brother officers would ever treat him with the same sense of comradeship that they had once shared.

Brockwell never learned who nominated him for the job—he suspected it was General Winant Sidle, the outgoing commander, a gentleman of the old school whose own career was headed for a type of greatness—and Brockwell wasn't even sure that he wanted to be a general's aide. He arrived for his interview directly from the field, caked in dust and reeking from days without a shower, and learned that Colonel Hall was expected to return from the field at any time. Brockwell spent a cordial half hour with Hall's deputy, Colonel Anderson, making small talk about duck hunting and family.

Then he was shown a map overlay of the Bu Prang and Duc Lap artillery defensive scheme. Bu Prang was defended by firebases Kate, Susan, and Annie in a triangle formation south and east of A-236. In similar fashion, Helen, Martha, and Dorrie supported Duc Lap and were between it and the border.

"I thought I knew about the . . . splitting of batteries for internal fire support to each firebase," recalls Brockwell, "but when I saw how close to the Cambodian border [the firebases] were, I asked if [my understanding] was correct."

Colonel Anderson solicited Brockwell's impression of the plan. The younger and less experienced Brockwell replied that he understood how, in theory, firebases sited in a triangular formation would allow each to support the others while also supporting a central strong point like Bu Prang, "but since we could not fire into Cambodia and we would have only twenty-five to thirty US artillerymen on each base, it seemed to me that the number of [suspected] NVA in the vicinity could easily effect a siege on all three bases at once and that [none of the firebases] would be firing for anyone but themselves."

Long after the fact, reconsidering his briefing by Colonel Anderson, Brockwell realized that the size of the attacking NVA force had never been a factor in IFFV Artillery planning; the planners had assumed that Bu

Prang was the sole objective. It had never entered their minds that with enough troops at their disposal, taking Kate would have seemed important enough to justify the effort required. In addition, Brockwell surmised, none of the planners had considered that an NVA base would be established just across the border in Cambodia in support of their attack.

With the clarity of hindsight, this presents an eerie parallel to the French mind-set at Dien Bien Phu in 1954. Supposing that the Viet Minh enemy had no artillery and in any case no way to emplace big guns beyond the reach of French air support, the French put their base in a broad valley, established a chain of outposts with mutually supporting fields of fire, and waited for the enemy to attack, certain that their superior firepower would systematically chew them up.

Instead, working at night, General Võ Nguyên Giáp's troops and thousands of conscripted laborers dragged heavy artillery onto the rugged heights overlooking the French positions. They dug caves and deep emplacements, and proceeded to pulverize the French with well-placed fire. Giáp accepted enormous casualties to overrun one French outpost after another with repeated ground attacks and bitter hand-to-hand fighting. In the end, the French surrendered the bulk of their troops and accepted defeat.

Nevertheless, at his unscheduled and serendipitous briefing in 1969, Brockwell was assured that with on-call air strikes, the support of nearby ARVN units, the Special Forces, and CIDG troops, "this would not be a problem." His subsequent interview with Colonel Hall seemed to go well, and he left Nha Trang "feeling confident about everything except finding myself on Kate, Susan, or Annie."

"UNTIL the very end of my time as Charlie Battery commander, the only time I had the whole battery together in one place at the same time was at the very end of my tour, just before I left," recalls Klaus Adam, then a captain. "We were always split up. Most of the time I had four guns with me and the other platoon was out doing something else. We were always deployed as General Support Reinforcing [backing up artillery units that were in direct support of a particular infantry or armor unit].

"I can't even tell you how many men I had in the battery, because all the paperwork, the morning reports, were done in the rear," says Adam. "I was almost always on a firebase with the guns. But I seem to recall that we were usually at about 95 percent strength."

Adam was born in Saarbrücken, Germany, in 1942. The following year his father was killed, and Adam went to live with an aunt in southern Bavaria, which was then beyond the reach of Allied bombers. When the war ended, he was reunited with his mother, and they moved to Wiesbaden, where she found work as a translator for the Occupation forces. "She met an alcoholic American Air Force sergeant, and in order to help her family and help him, she accepted his marriage proposal," Adam explains.

The family came to the US in 1951; young Klaus suffered from the effects of his stepfather's alcoholism, and his parents divorced when he was in his early teens. "As a result of a lack of parental control, I ended up on the streets, did a little gang running—petty theft," Adam says. "I graduated to major theft. I got caught." He was 17. A small-town judge offered him a choice of reform school until he was 21 or three years of military service. "When you get an honorable discharge, I'll purge your records," the judge promised.

Adam enlisted in the summer of 1960. After infantry training and jump school, he was assigned to the 101st Airborne Division at Fort Campbell, Kentucky. During his in-processing, a personnel clerk learned that Adam had taken a high school typing class. Army typists are always in short supply; he was assigned to the division Military Intelligence Detachment. "The top kick was an old airborne infantryman who would not have made it in today's Army," Adam says. Short and fat, he looked like a bowling ball on toothpicks. "He was the finest man I ever met," Adam insists. "He decided to make a human being out of me and sent me to get a high school GED; because my scores were so high, he sent me back to the Education Center to get a one-year college GED. Then he sent me to the Adjutant General school at Fort Benjamin Harrison, Indiana."

There Adam met Úrsula Viera-Vazquez, daughter of a master sergeant, and fell in love. The attraction was mutual. "Clerk school was six weeks. I called my first sergeant to ask if I could stay a little longer—so he made me a personnel management specialist and gave me another six weeks of classes."

Afterward, accompanied by his fiancée, Adam returned to the 101st Airborne. After their marriage, Úrsula began to worry about the part of Adam's job that involved jumping out of airplanes in flight. To placate her fears, in 1962 he reenlisted in return for an assignment to an air defense unit outside Austin, Texas.

As a battalion personnel specialist, Adam learned that his upward mobility was limited by his occupational specialty. The specialty with the highest possible rank in his air defense unit was fire control maintenance technician, so Adam requested training in that. The course was almost a year long and came with a one-grade promotion upon graduation; instead of returning to Austin, however, Sergeant Adam remained at Fort Bliss as an instructor. Less than a year later, he was again promoted. In that era, it was not unusual for a soldier to complete a twenty-year career and retire at the pay grade of E-6, but Adam was not satisfied with his status. "I thought, *Here I am, five years into my career and I'm only an E-6! And I only have three more steps to the maximum enlisted pay grade, E-9.*" The notion of rising to become a sergeant major, an exalted personage who sits at the commander's right hand, and doing so while still in his thirties, did not satisfy him.

So Adam applied for flight school; graduation would mean promotion to warrant officer. Adam completed ground school at Fort Wolters, Texas, as an honor graduate, but failed to master the multiple intricacies of flying helicopters; after five months he washed out. As it turned out, that was a good thing: "There were 122 guys in my class; after Vietnam we had only two survivors—me and the other washout."

Adam was assigned to a missile site near Lincoln, Nebraska. He didn't mind the duty, but Úrsula, pregnant with their second child, hated everything about the state. So Adam applied for Artillery OCS. After graduation, he went to yet another school to learn artillery communications. Then he spent a year in Korea. Through a combination of luck and his father-in-law's connections, Adam was tapped to serve as a general's aide in the Korean Military Advisory Group. After six months in that job, he took charge of an advisory detachment.

Leaving Korea, Adam picked up his family and went to West Germany, where he took command of a surface-to-surface missile battery. In November 1968 he was promoted to captain; a month later he came down on orders for Vietnam.

IN time of peace, US Army officer promotions were determined by the size of the armed forces, which has always been regulated by Congress. Peacetime armies are small, and upward mobility in the officer corps is slow. In the decade following the Korean War, second lieutenants served eighteen months before they could be considered for promotion. First lieutenants needed four years in grade before becoming eligible for promotion to captain. The vast majority of OCS and ROTC graduates, Reserve officers, left active duty after two years. Only those with sterling efficiency reports were retained on active duty, and even in training commands, most companies, batteries, and troops were led by captains with upwards of six years' service. Selection for a command was based on seniority and perceived capabilities, as described in efficiency reports. Once in command, an officer could expect at least a year in that position.

All that changed with Vietnam. Between 1965 and 1970, Army troop strength grew by more than 50 percent. Officer promotions accelerated—one year from second to first lieutenant, and one year more from first lieutenant to captain. There have always been more staff officers than commanders; as the Army ballooned, staff officer billets grew faster than command slots. Common wisdom among senior officers held that successful command time was a prerequisite for advancement to the highest ranks—an officer who had never commanded a company, battery, or troop would be an unlikely choice to command a battalion. An officer without battalion command would probably never command an artillery group, infantry brigade, or cavalry regiment, and officers without command experience at the brigade level would never be considered to command a division, and thus would never become generals. To ensure that as many officers as possible had the opportunity to demonstrate their command chops, and thus ensure all an equal shot at promotion to the highest ranks, a Pentagon policy limited command time at the battalion level and below to six months, with few exceptions.

This was, of course, careerism at its most insidious. It takes months on the job before almost any officer reaches his full potential as a battery or company commander, and during that very demanding learning curve, new commanders will make mistakes. Mistakes in combat cost lives. By giving almost every captain a shot at command, and limiting this assignment to six months, Pentagon planners ensured that few American soldiers would fight our difficult war under an experienced and capable commander. This is not to say that there were no good unit commanders, or that even the best and most experienced officers don't make mistakes. But when the average unit commander has three months' job experience, his troops suffer for it, and some will die.

Captain Klaus Adam had eight years on active duty when he arrived in Vietnam. He had attended nine Army schools, and graduated with distinction from eight. He had commanded a Sergeant Missile battery in peacetime Germany. But he had no experience whatsoever with field artillery, so his first combat assignment was as assistant operations officer of the 52nd Artillery Group, a headquarters for several field artillery battalions under IFFV Artillery. "I was basically the night duty officer," he explains. Six months after arriving in Vietnam, in August 1969, he took command of Charlie Battery, 1/92 Artillery.

In late September he flew into Kate for a look-see. "I met the CIDG force commander [Special Forces Captain Lucian Barham]," recalls Adam. "I surveyed the defensive positions and made sure that my guys were adequately defended, because artillerymen can't fire their guns and take care of themselves at the same time. You either shoot or you duck; you can't do both. At the time, I still had the stupid idea that they were out there to support the Mike Force and the South Vietnamese forces that were supposedly out there; artillery is never told the plan of action for the ground forces. There was no need to brief us, because all the ground forces need do is call for fire. It didn't matter *why* they called it in; we just sent the fire where and when they wanted it. So, my assumption was that there were combat teams out there doing sweeps, and patrols, and going after the bad guys, and we were there to support them."

In fact, there were almost no US or ARVN forces in the area at all. Adam was later told by an IFFV Artillery colonel that his men had been positioned as bait, designed to lure the North Vietnamese across the border, where they could be destroyed.

Nobody on Kate was ever told about that.

After looking around for some twenty minutes and finding nothing to complain about, Adam got back in his chopper and flew away.

When you heard your country calling, Illinois, Illinois,
Where the shot and shell were falling, Illinois, Illinois,
When the Southern host withdrew,
Pitting Gray against the Blue, There were none more brave than
you, Illinois, Illinois,
There were none more brave than you, Illinois.

—Illinois State Song

THREE

Rock Island, Illinois

The first train to link Chicago with the Mississippi River arrived at the sleepy river town of Rock Island, Illinois, in February 1854 on the tracks of the just-completed Chicago & Rock Island Railroad. Building across the river's largest isle to save construction costs, the rail company thrust two bridges over to what is now Davenport, Iowa, opening Chicago's slaughterhouses, grain mills, and rail network to the farmers of the Great Plains. Rock Island boomed. In 1880 the US Army opened the Rock Island Arsenal, today the nation's largest federal armaments manufacturer, and the Quad Cities—Rock Island and neighbors Moline, Illinois, and Davenport and Bettendorf, Iowa—became a manufacturing center. (Even after East Moline was incorporated in 1903, these five tough river towns with closely connected economies remained known as the Quad Cities.) Dominated by the United Auto Workers, they were a union bastion whose blue-collar members swore allegiance to FDR and the New Deal and could be counted on to vote Democratic in every election.

I was born in Rock Island in August 1948, the third of five children of second-generation German American farmers. I am certain that my father, Leander, a welder at John Deere, the giant manufacturer of tractors and farm implements, loved me and all his children. But he rarely showed this affection; taciturn and emotionally closed, a compact, muscular, and short-fused man, he punched like a prizefighter and relied mostly on his fists to communicate his displeasure with me. As I entered puberty, my beloved mother, Germaine, a sensitive and intelligent woman, was diagnosed with depression and hypertension. Like many depressed women of that era, she was severely overmedicated. She was soon bedridden, and rarely left her room for days on end. Mom died of a stroke in 1965. My relations with Dad, which had never been good, chilled to an icy truce.

I am the middle child: Sister Nancy and brother Bob were the oldest, while Don and Mary Beth followed me in birth order. We had always looked out for one another; after our mother died, we became even closer. When Bob finished high school, he escaped the limited horizons of small-town life and enlisted in the Air Force.

Our family wasn't poor in the classic sense. We had enough to eat, a safe roof over our heads, decent clothes to wear, and we all went to Catholic schools. But there was no money for anything else, period. When it was time for me to start high school, we didn't have enough for tuition at the diocese school, Alleman High, where all my elementary school friends were enrolled. I found an after-school job in a grocery store to help pay my tuition.

Alleman was coed; most of our teachers were nuns or priests. Student discipline was strict, and most teachers enforced school policies and their own classroom rules with corporal punishment. I soon learned not to complain to my father about being spanked or slapped or having an ear twisted: That always triggered a second beating, from him.

At this time in my life, academics didn't much interest me; studying was not my thing at all. Instead, I devoted my high school years to enjoying myself. Soon the nuns had labeled me: I was the boy who would never live up to my potential. Held to such low expectations, I did my best not to disappoint anyone: I was happy to earn a C and believed that my parents should also have been happy. I was a classic underachiever—but I *was* voted "Most Fun to Be With" by my senior classmates.

I was big and strong but, in the grand scheme of things, only an average athlete. I was desperate to make the varsity football squad, to become a prince of the campus. In my junior year, however, my job conflicted with football practice. I deferred varsity dreams until my senior year; by then, I had enough work seniority to demand a schedule that allowed for after-school practice. With much help from my coaches—and I mean they gave me every possible break and spent hours and hours with me—I made up for my lack of native ability and playing experience with sheer desire. I never started a game, but I played often enough and well enough to earn the respect of my coaches and teammates—and a prized varsity letter.

This became tremendously important to me for reasons I had no way to predict: Being part of a team, as I saw and experienced, was a powerful force multiplier. Earning that letter was the turning point in my young life, my first glimmer of the power of my own possibilities.

But only a glimmer. As I approached graduation, the future I envisioned for myself was much like the one most of my classmates imagined: I would get obligatory military service out of the way, return to the Quad Cities, and find an apprenticeship in the building trades.

Yet I was anxious to put the humdrum ordinariness and rigidity of small-town life aside, if only for a few years. I wanted adventure. I wanted to break out of the Quad Cities cycle of going nowhere in record time.

With my best friend, Joe Murphy, I spent a few weeks considering service options. I could enlist for three years in the Army, or four in the Marines, Air Force, or Navy. I could volunteer for the draft, or wait to be drafted, which meant only two years.

Joe and I decided that the Marines offered the biggest challenge and the most possibilities for adventure.

I idolized my brother Bob—and he wouldn't hear of me joining the Marines. After completing a four-year Air Force hitch, instead of returning to Rock Island, he re-upped! Reenlisted in the *Army*, spent eight weeks in advanced infantry training, then went to jump school and volunteered for Special Forces.

Bob was a paratrooper! In the entire eighteen years of my life, I had never even *met* a paratrooper! So when Bob said, "Forget about the Marines," I listened. In the Gospel According to Brother Bob, Special Forces was where the action was. He laid it out for us: Enlist in the Army, volunteer for airborne infantry, then ask for Vietnam.

This was the summer of 1966. Nearly half a million American men had already been drafted for Vietnam service; by the end of that year, some 385,000 US troops would be serving in Vietnam or its waters. Twice that many were in various stages of training for deployment to the war zone. Across America, millions of young men about my age were going to extraordinary lengths to get into perennially understrength National Guard and Reserve units that almost overnight had filled up and grown waiting lists. Men with family, business, or political connections, or with relatives serving in Guard units, proved far more successful in their quest for an honorable, or at least legal, way to avoid the draft and the hazards of combat.

Those lacking such connections—tens of millions of them—began applying for student draft deferments, enrolling in divinity schools or other graduate programs where they would find shelter from the monsoon of draft notices falling on America's youth. Thousands more had fled the country or faced prison by declaring themselves conscientious objectors. Navy and Air Force recruiters were swamped by a flood of highly qualified applicants that allowed them to pick and choose, while their opposite numbers in the Army and Marines struggled to meet monthly quotas.

Many, perhaps most, of those who approached Army recruiters were seeking to do better for themselves than simply waiting to be drafted. Often accompanied by a parent or older brother, potential enlistees came prepared with pointed questions and lists of Army schools. They demanded a written guarantee of training as a dental technician, electronics repairman, military policeman, radar operator, aircraft mechanic, chaplain's assistant, finance clerk—schooling in any military occupational specialty that might offer safety from the danger and privation of a wartime combat unit.

But Joe and I lived in Rock Island. Our parents, our uncles, our older brothers, had all served in the military. As bored as I was with life along the Mississippi, I knew that I lived in the greatest country on earth. I was proud to be American. That we were at war in Vietnam meant that I *needed* to join up, get trained to fight and get to the war zone before it was over. I was almost desperate to do my part for America.

Right after graduation, Joe and I found Rock Island's Army recruiting office and asked about signing up for airborne infantry. The sergeant questioned us for a long time, until he was convinced of our sincerity. Then he smiled.

"This is your lucky day," he drawled. "I've got exactly *two* quota slots left for airborne infantry. If you're *truly* interested in a life of adventure, in joining a military *elite*, so prized that most who volunteer are turned away or wash out of training, you'll have to sign up right away. Today. Right now."

Before some friend or relative could talk us into changing our minds.

On October 2, 1966, Joe and I took the train to Chicago, where we reported to the Armed Forces Induction Center. After a physical and a battery of tests, we were sworn in to the United States Army. A little before midnight, just like the lyrics of the Monkees hit song, we "caught the last train to Clarksville," Tennessee, gateway to Fort Campbell, Kentucky.

Joe and I were assigned to the same basic training company. A day or so later, we took another battery of exams, including the OCS test. OCS might have stood for Oklahoma Cooking School, for all I knew—I had never heard the term "Officer Candidate School." I had no idea that such a place existed, any more than I had the merest inkling that there was something called the Reserve Officer Training Corps for college students. I thought that every Army officer came from West Point.

Becoming an officer was not part of my escape-boring-Rock-Island-adventure dream. Officers, I supposed, must have a lot more responsibility than the men in the ranks. They had to be pretty smart, I guessed, because officers would have to know a lot of stuff. They would have to set an example for everyone else. That felt a lot like getting an "A" in every class and being on the student council. It felt like it was going to be an awful lot of work. A lot of responsibility. Not much fun.

It didn't feel like *me* at all.

Joe, who'd earned better high school grades than I did, wanted that kind of responsibility. His score on the officer candidate exam missed the cutoff by one point.

I *passed* by one point.

GROUND war is particularly hard on junior infantry officers and noncoms. They're the sharpened tip of the spear; in combat, platoon and squad leaders are killed or wounded far more often than almost any other infantrymen, and the better they are at leading their men against fire, the more likely it is that they will become a casualty. By the autumn of 1966, when I enlisted and, coincidentally, when my coauthor was commissioned as an infantry second lieutenant at An Khe, Vietnam, the Army was so desperate for infantry platoon leaders that the Secretary of the Army, the authority who, with congressional approval, appointed individuals to the officer ranks—until then, virtually without exception, they were physicians, dentists, nurses, clergy, attorneys, and other professionals—delegated this power of direct commissioning to the commanding general of US Army, Vietnam, for the purpose of awarding direct appointments to outstanding sergeants and warrant officers. The Army also opened six new Officer Candidate Schools geared to turning out armor, engineer, ordnance, transportation, signal, and quartermaster officers, respectively.

When my OCS test results were published, I was summoned to my company commander's office, along with everyone else who had passed. It's rare for a basic training company commander to have direct contact with trainees: He has a first sergeant and a cadre of drill instructors for that. When my coauthor went through Army basic training at Fort Ord, California, in 1959, when he was himself a Fort Jackson, South Carolina, drill instructor in 1961, and when he spent a month reporting on a basic training company at Fort Benning, Georgia, for a national magazine in 1979, he never saw a company commander address a group of trainees smaller than a platoon, and then only to scold them.

But it isn't every day that a young captain gets a chance to talk to future officers, an opportunity to impart his wisdom and insight and perhaps influence both their immediate futures and their entire lives. Even as my CO outlined what was ahead for us, he made it clear that some of us would *not* get into OCS, and that fewer still would graduate. But once we did, he explained, once we were appointed Reserve officers, our lives would be far different from those of the enlisted men we left behind.

When he finished talking, the captain asked if we had any questions. I raised my hand and he nodded at me—permission to speak.

I took a deep breath and said, "What if I don't *want* to go to OCS?"

"Private, let me explain how the Army works," he replied. "I have a levy to fill, and with everyone in this room, I'll just make my OCS quota. You *will* be going to OCS. Any more questions?"

There were none.

Now that I'd made the OCS cut, I noticed that my drill instructors paid a bit more attention to me. At the time, I didn't understand just how much more. I didn't know that achieving a satisfactory grade on a multiple-choice test wasn't enough to show that an individual has the ability to learn critical leadership skills. My DIs were obliged to take note of my progress, my successes, and my failures. They looked for evidence of personal initiative as well as obedience to discipline, and they made subjective evaluations of my leadership ability, my capacity to learn and adapt to changing situations, my physical conditioning, and my progress in learning the soldierly skills. If I failed to meet their expectations, I would never have been allowed to start OCS.

Looking back, I realize it's a good thing I didn't know any of that.

While Fort Campbell is the home of the 101st Airborne Division, for some reason most of my company's drill instructors were tankers—what the Army calls the armor branch. These men seemed to assume that those of us headed for OCS would go to nearby Fort Knox, the Armor Center and School.

I did *not* want Armor. No steel coffin for me! Bob had made it clear that the action was in the infantry. But by then, I'd been in uniform long enough to know better than to argue with a drill instructor. Or to voice an unsolicited opinion.

Following the eight-week basic course, where I learned the rudiments of soldiering—how to march, how to wear the uniform, how to care for and shoot a rifle, how to throw a hand grenade, make proper use of a gas mask, live in the field while practicing good hygiene, use a map and a compass and, most of all, get into good physical shape, I was shipped to Fort Knox for a two-week leadership preparation school. Then I started the eight-week Advanced Individual Training Course in Armor.

In February 1967, as I approached the midpoint in my Armor training, those of us bound for OCS were called together to hear that the Fort Knox program was at maximum capacity. We would attend *Infantry* Officer Candidate School at Fort Benning, Georgia.

I was the only one who cheered this news.

I arrived at Fort Benning in March 1967. Now that I'd been in the Army for a few months and had begun to grasp the width and depth of the chasm that separates the enlisted ranks, including even the oldest, most experienced noncoms, from the rarefied peaks inhabited by commissioned officers—now that I realized that pinning on the gold bar of a second lieutenant brought not only freedoms and privileges unimaginable to a lowly private but also enormous, life-or-death responsibilities—the notion of becoming an officer at the tender age of 19 was more difficult to comprehend than ever. Each successive day made me more apprehensive: I'd grown up being told by my parents and teachers that I would never amount to anything. That I wasn't smart enough or enterprising enough or reliable enough to be entrusted with serious responsibility. If I managed, somehow, to get through OCS and become an infantry platoon leader, I would be responsible for the lives of about forty men, most of them my elders. I knew that I wasn't capable of that. I was almost certain that I lacked what becoming a leader of men in combat would require of me.

My first day as an officer candidate in 84th Company did nothing to bolster my self-confidence. Standing in ranks in the company street, we heard my company commander issue a challenge: "Look to your left. Look to your right. Get a good look at those men, remember their faces, because chances are they *won't* be here on graduation day."

Much later in my life I would learn that this is much the same challenge laid down by generations of professors to each new class of law and medical students—to say nothing of the three service academy plebe classes.

At that moment, however, I was certain that my CO was talking directly to *me*.

Over the decades since that day at Fort Benning, I have learned that the US Army has long operated under the doctrine that *leaders are made, not born*. While not every soldier has the capability to learn and apply leadership skills, the Army has devoted enormous resources to finding the best and most efficient ways to train leaders at every echelon, from squad and fire team leaders to the very senior officers who serve in the Army's highest commands. Over the last century, the Pentagon has often contracted with academia, both public and private educational institutions, to construct and supervise hundreds of long-running experiments involving tens of thousands of soldiers, all aimed at finding the keys to motivating men to lead others, and then quickly and efficiently training them in the requisite skill sets. Thus it has acquired a vast reservoir of experience in identifying and nurturing those with leadership potential.

So even if *I* didn't think that I had what it would take to learn military leadership skills, even if *I* felt that I lacked the gumption, fortitude, confidence, and ineffable je ne sais quoi required to inspire respect, to direct men's actions under the most urgent, trying, and hazardous conditions, the Army was pretty sure that I did, because even before Fort Benning, it had made an investment in me, had evaluated me many times.

The Army selection mechanism can make mistakes about a particular individual's leadership potential and personal integrity, especially in wartime. Consider, for example, the officers responsible for the 1968 My Lai massacre. But usually the Army knows exactly what it's doing when it selects a man for officer training.

The Army began to envision Officer Candidate Schools in 1938; to meet the threat of rising militarism in Japan and Germany, the Pentagon planned to draft millions of recruits. They would need officers to lead them, and the US Military Academy and university ROTC programs around the country would not be able to meet the demand. In 1941, the Army Signal Corps launched the first OCS program, and the Infantry followed suit almost immediately. By eliminating the field training segment of its 13-week curriculum, Infantry OCS beat Signal Corps OCS and graduated the first batch of OCS-trained second lieutenants. Eighty percent of them died in World War II.

In my time, OCS was a grueling 23-week course structured to operate with a high attrition rate, to weed out the weak and unmotivated before they were in a position to endanger the lives of their men. Our curriculum had two categories:

General subjects were mostly taught in the classroom and included leadership; communications; airborne-, airmobile-, artillery-, joint-command, and Air Force operations; combined staff subjects; equipment; serviceability; and unit readiness.

Critical subjects were taught in the field or on the range, and mastering all of them was considered vital to becoming an officer. They included map and aerial photo reading, the care and employment of small arms, anti-tank missiles, mine warfare, recoilless rifles, mortars, and combined tactics for platoon and company.

To help digest this Niagara of information, we were obliged to spend two hours a day in study hall. To graduate, we had to achieve a grade of 70 percent or better in each and every subject. This translates to a C average.

But that was only *one* dimension of OCS, and for most candidates, the easiest. Added to the classroom work were field training, unremitting harassment, and physical stress. We candidates were hardened by daily physical training and constant running—we moved at double time between classes, to the mess hall and back; we ran everywhere. Infantry tactics discussed in classrooms were put into practice in the field, starting at the squad level, at all times under the intense supervision of young, fit, and tough-minded tactical officers (TACs), all of them recent OCS graduates, all looking for any reason or no reason to put pressure on individuals no less than on a squad or platoon. We got very little sleep, we were forced to eat hurriedly and without conversation, and until the last few weeks of the course we had almost no time off. The slightest slip, the most passing, momentary failure—a speck of rust in a rifle barrel, an almost microscopic thread on a uniform pocket, a bed blanket lacking the required degree of tautness—was punished instantly with push-ups or extra duty or loss of some privilege.

OCS was not a place for men who needed peace and quiet. Many college graduates, especially those who grew up in calm homes surrounded by protective parents, found the stress and the constant in-your-face hazing insufferable.

I grew up in no such home.

My OCS experience began with meeting two of the finest men who have ever walked the earth, Lex Crane and Ed Baltzly—my roommates. An Irish kid from Staten Island, New York, Lex challenged me intellectually, forced me to defend my beliefs and many of my decisions. He is a truly great man, a true friend who taught me more about life than anyone else on the planet. Ed was another native New Yorker who had moved to New Rochelle. Big and tough, he's an absolute wild man who attacked the Army, OCS, and everything else he encountered with an abundance of enthusiasm.

With Lex's and Ed's support, I took to OCS like a duck to water. As a little kid, I liked baseball and football—but I *loved* playing Army. I loved exploring the woods above the Mississippi's eastern bank in Black Hawk State Park, playing Army with my buddies. We'd set up L-shaped ambushes on the trails and come out with blazing cap pistols. Those were the happiest times of my childhood. But while I always knew that someday I'd be a soldier, I never dreamed that I'd be a leader. While I was growing and learning the OCS brand of self-confidence, I began to notice that some of my classmates, men a little older than me, men mostly much smarter than me, men with a few years of college, even men with college degrees, gave up. They quit the program, gladly returning to the ranks of the common soldier.

As their desire waned, mine intensified. I became bolder and more confident. I began to understand leadership. At the Benning School for Boys, I learned the most important leadership lesson of all, the lesson that I have carried with me always and applied to any situation of command or management: the three M's—the Mission, the Men, and, only then, Me. The mission must be accomplished at all costs. Once it is, take care of the men who enabled you to accomplish it. *Me*—a distant third on the list. Once the mission was done and my men's needs provided for, any reward or accolade that came my way could and should be accepted.

It sounds simple, and it is; outside the military, it's not put into practice enough. Most of the corporate or political leaders and managers that I've met put themselves first, then the mission—and their men are left to fend for themselves.

When it came to OCS academics, I was astonished to learn that I actually wasn't stupid: I graduated with a B+ grade average. The class work was challenging, but now, suddenly, I was motivated. I accepted my mediocre grades but worked hard to do better. Then came field exercises, and the realization that *this* was my moment. When we started the Ranger phase, long-range patrols under sometimes very severe conditions, I knew that I would make it.

For example, at first we operated in very hot weather, and we had no water. Then it was cold and rainy. Several candidates quit during this phase. But once our squad adapted to the weather, once we learned that if we couldn't be comfortably dry, then all wet is better than partly wet, the weather was simply an inconvenience that could be ignored. We just went with it—accepted that this was how it was just then—and let's go! Find the enemy, complete the mission, and let the good times roll. In the end, we had a great training exercise, while the other squads, operating under the same conditions, made themselves miserable.

As for the rest of OCS—maintaining a personal and unit spit-and-polish environment, constant marching and drill formations, parades—it wasn't fun, but it was tolerable. As a survivor of parochial schools and corporal punishment by unbending priests and nuns, as the frequent object of my father's fury, the constant hazing and harassment never really fazed me. The trick, I learned, was to understand that it was pretty much all a game. So I played the game. My dad could yell and scream better and louder than any TAC officer; they might get in my face, but I was sure that, unlike Dad, they wouldn't hit me. Let's make that I was *pretty* sure, but not completely.

Later, of course, I learned that TAC officers have *never* been allowed to strike an officer candidate or any other soldier. It's a very rare event when one of those bright, intense young officers fails to remember this. Their supreme gift is planting that doubt in the candidate's mind.

As the days turned into weeks and weeks into months, the schooling, the pressurized environment, the young officers pushing and prodding me and my classmates, awoke something in me. One day I realized that, despite my best intentions, despite the years that I had sabotaged myself by clinging to the comfort of underachievement, I had become a *leader.* Was I born one, or created? It doesn't matter. Weeks before the Army made it official, I knew that I could command and that I could lead. When the shock of that realization wore off, I felt very good about myself. It had been a long time coming.

Twenty-two days past my nineteenth birthday, on the last day of August 1967, I was commissioned a second lieutenant in the US Army Reserve, the first in my family to become an officer.

A couple of weeks before graduation, our class was allowed to request individual duty assignments. Some put in for Germany, where the Army kept an enormous garrison, nearly a quarter of a million men, in support of NATO treaty obligations and its policy of containing the Soviet Union. Some asked for South Korea, where some 50,000 American soldiers and airmen remained as a counterweight to the threats of the bellicose North Korean regime. Still others were eager to go to Vietnam. Recalling brother Bob's advice, I asked for assignment to Special Forces at Fort Bragg, North Carolina.

Immediately after graduation, I moved half a mile across Fort Benning's vast cantonment and reported for Basic Parachutist School, a three-week course that included a week of ground school—training in the apparatus of military parachuting, learning how to exit an aircraft door, and to land safely while encumbered with a spare parachute, a rifle, and field gear. During Ground Week, we ran everywhere, toughening our legs for the shock of landings, and made several jumps from a 34-foot tower in a parachute harness. The fall is arrested after about ten feet by a steel cable; then we slid down the cable a hundred meters or so to an embankment, where we were caught by a couple of classmates. For week number two, Tower Week, we were dropped from a 250-foot tower under fully inflated parachutes to practice landing falls. During Jump Week, we made five parachute jumps from various types of aircraft, including a night drop. After the last, the graduation leap, I was awarded the silver wings of a parachutist.

More than a year earlier, as a raw recruit, I had applied for Special Forces, only to learn that enlisted personnel under age twenty did not qualify. There is no restriction on officers, probably because it was and is exceedingly rare to find an officer under that age.

Like me.

After jump school, I reported to Third Special Forces Group at Fort Bragg, North Carolina. Both Lex and Ed, my OCS roommates, were also assigned. We shared a rented house in Spring Lake, just off the post, which we lovingly referred to as the ABC (Albracht, Baltzly, Crane) House.

The Army Special Warfare Center is an elite academy. In the earliest days of America's Vietnam adventure, when US involvement was limited to an advisory role, it minted hundreds of new Green Berets, the vast majority of them career officers and noncoms. Their previous postings reflected a peacetime Army, where promotions were slow and officers and sergeants gained valuable experience in a wide variety of staff and troop-duty assignments within their combat arm or specialty branch. With the introduction of US combat forces to Vietnam in mid-1965, Special Forces expanded exponentially and the school added faculty and facilities. Even so, by the time I headed for Bragg in September 1967, the waiting list for the Special Forces Officers' Course was almost a year long.

I got lucky. For reasons unknown, perhaps a death, a serious injury, an extended illness, a family emergency—I never learned why—a slot had opened in the next starting class of the three-month course. If I could start the following Monday, the slot was mine.

How could I say no to that?

Lex and Ed had enjoyed a few days' leave before reporting to the Special Warfare School. They spent months in Special Forces units getting on-the-job training—but never cracked the school waiting list before they were assigned overseas.

OCS was a demanding and ultimately satisfying undergraduate program that taught me how to use the contents of the small-unit leader's toolbox: the weapons and tactics of an infantry leader. The Special Forces Officers' Course taught me how to think *outside* that toolbox. It was like skipping past the master's curriculum and jumping directly into a doctoral program. It was physically demanding, of course, but I was fresh from OCS and jump school and in the best shape of my entire life.

The skull work, however, included short, intensive, college-level courses. For some reason, I did very well in those that presented theoretical concepts, while technical subjects emerged as a formidable challenge. My classmates were mostly college graduates who had long ago mastered subjects that I only dimly understood. For example, I was hardly ready for the application of algebra and geometry to such ordinary Special Forces tasks as setting up an aircraft resupply mission: The resupply aircraft is flying north at X knots, the wind is blowing at Y knots from the southeast, the supply bundles will be kicked out at altitude R, each weighs Z, and they fall at rate of speed Q. So how big should I make my drop zone?

And I had barely graduated from Alleman! Because I did poorly in tech classes, when we went to the field, instructors gave me the hardest practical exercises—and I shined at them. The extra points I earned helped my overall grade average, and that, probably, was the only reason I got through this exceedingly tough school.

I was the only student just out of OCS. Most of my classmates had served a year or more in various infantry units, and very few, if any, lacked at least some exposure to post-secondary education. But time in a college classroom doesn't always prepare an officer for the challenges of high-risk, high-stress, unconventional warfare. I recall a particular lieutenant who was brilliant in class but could not operate in the field. He was reassigned to the 82nd Airborne a few days before he would have graduated.

By then I had realized that Special Forces was where I wanted to be as long as I was in uniform. There was nothing about it that I didn't like. I'd found a home—a real home with brothers for whom I would die.

As graduation day approached, I was again given the opportunity to state my preference for a duty assignment. As every good Green Beret officer would, I put in for Vietnam. Bob was there with Fifth Special Forces, but I didn't think it mattered.

I know now that it may have. Since the death of the five Sullivan brothers of Waterloo, Iowa, when the light cruiser USS *Juneau* was sunk during World War II, every branch of the US armed forces has shown extreme reluctance in assigning siblings to the same wartime combat unit, although there is no regulation on this subject for officers. More likely, if Bob's presence in Fifth Special Forces was noted against my desire to join him, it was because he was a noncom and I was a commissioned officer. If we were in the same unit, and he disagreed with one of my decisions, what would happen? Some savvy officer in Special Forces Personnel might have wanted to avoid even the possibility that an awkward situation might arise.

Or maybe that didn't enter into the decision at all. The Special Forces mission was then mostly about imparting expertise in a variety of military specialties to Third World allies, which is to say, training their regular and irregular forces in counter-insurgency warfare. I was still a teenager. I had no experience leading troops. I had never taught a class. Up to then, my entire Army career, just over a year, had been spent going from one Army school to the next.

Ed, Lex, and I remained at Fort Bragg until summer, when Ed went to Vietnam and Lex and I were assigned to the 46th Special Forces Company in Thailand. I became the S-4, or logistics officer, of a "B" Team. The team mission focused on training the Royal Thai Army in counterinsurgency techniques. It was a relatively undemanding assignment that afforded me the opportunity to serve in the field, where I could perform useful work while observing and learning the myriad small but vital ways that Special Forces officers and enlisted men work together.

After six months in that job—around the time, actually, that I had figured out what I was supposed to be doing—I became the executive officer of an "A" Team at Thailand's extreme southern tip. Except for a resident CIA officer, there were no other Americans for many miles around.

I had enlisted for three years. When I accepted a commission as a Reserve officer, however, this became moot: I was obligated to two years' active duty from that date. Unless I volunteered to stay on indefinitely, with a minimum of one more year, I'd return to civilian life in late August 1969 without ever having heard a shot fired in anger.

But the Army that needed thousands of new junior officers as it expanded into a wartime force also sought to protect its investment in these new lieutenants. It did so in several ways, most obviously by speeding promotions. If I accepted a promotion to captain, I would owe Uncle Samuel only one more year of service.

About a month before I was due for discharge, I told our personnel officer that I'd stick around for that extra year—but only if I could serve it in a Special Forces unit in Vietnam. He gave me a funny look. I remembered that look: It was just like the one the Rock Island recruiter had flashed when Joe and I asked about enlisting for airborne infantry.

The personnel officer smiled. "This, my friend, is your lucky day!"

My dream had become real! I was headed for combat with the Special Forces.

OR maybe not.

Most of the Army's thousands of new first lieutenants had completed their two-year service obligation and left active duty. Before boarding a plane to Vietnam, I learned that there was an acute shortage of infantry captains—and Special Forces captains arriving without specific orders to Fifth Special Forces were usually diverted to shorthanded infantry battalions to serve as company commanders.

That was not why I'd volunteered for an extra year in uniform.

I had no orders for Fifth Special Forces—but I was determined to get some.

I arrived in Vietnam on August 25, 1969. Before going through inprocessing in Long Binh, I sought out the commanding officer of the 90th Replacement Battalion and pleaded my case. He very kindly heard me out, and then obligingly made sure I was on orders to the Fifth Special Forces.

I hitched an airplane ride to Nha Trang and reported to Headquarters, Fifth Special Forces. There I had a sit-down with a light colonel, who matter-of-factly told me that I was slated for a headquarters job. I would command a desk and do hand-to-hand combat with the paperwork of war.

That was even worse than leading a rifle company in an infantry division! There, I would at least have a good chance of seeing action. I wasn't about to take a staff job if I could help it, so I asked for an assignment to the Mike Force. He looked at my records, and then shook his head. No combat experience. The Mike Force was out of the question.

"What about an 'A' Team?" I asked, and he nodded yes. I asked for one in II Corps, where Bob had served, and again he agreed.

But first I had to go back to school: the MACV RECONDO Combat Orientations Course (COC), staffed and run by veteran Special Forces types. This was mandatory for all members of Special Forces serving their first Vietnam tour. On the last day of August, a boat took me to Hon Tre Island in Nha Trang Bay. For the next ten days I polished my combat mojo with an intense refresher course in patrolling, jungle operations, communications, and working with forward air controllers (FACs) and artillery forward observers (FOs) to call in supporting fire and air strikes. Not a bad way to get acclimated to Vietnam while picking up very useful, hands-on experience.

What I learned on Hon Tre would soon save my life.

On September 11, I reported to Company B, Fifth Special Forces, in Pleiku, a dusty, backward, and distinctly unlovely provincial capital. Three days later, I was flown down to BMT, where I was assigned to A-236 in Bu Prang, reputedly the crown jewel of Central Highlands "A" Team camps. I signed in to Bu Prang on September 19 and assumed the duties of executive officer. A-236 was commanded by Captain William Palmer, a National Guard officer on active duty. He was a graduate of the Military College of South Carolina—the Citadel—which has operated a well-regarded West Point–style ROTC program going back to 1842. Palmer was due to rotate home in December, which left me with the inside track to succeed him. He was a nice enough fellow who seemed to fancy himself a Southern gentleman, not much for mingling with the unwashed masses, the sergeants who comprised most of his team. As a recent escapee from those unwashed ranks—and, more important, a small-town Midwestern working-class guy—I found the company of these vastly more experienced men in many ways more convivial and interesting than that of Captain Palmer.

Some of the sergeants at Bu Prang had served with my brother Bob. I proudly learned that his combat exploits had made him an almost legendary figure in the Green Berets' fighting fraternity. I hoped a little of that would rub off on me.

The other officer at Bu Prang was Lieutenant George Tierney, a good guy. He was wired—a skinny kid seemingly brimming with nervous energy; someone nicknamed him Arc Light. He was busy electrifying various things. Palmer was busy being Olympian, and I was just plain busy, working long hours to get the camp and surrounding areas prepared to withstand a prolonged attack. Almost before I started, however, I was ordered to go to Kate.

Now this is the Law of the Jungle
as old and as true as the sky;
And the Wolf that shall keep it may prosper,
but the Wolf that shall break it must die.
As the creeper that girdles the tree-trunk,
the Law runneth forward and back
For the strength of the Pack is the Wolf,
and the strength of the Wolf is the Pack.

—Rudyard Kipling, *The Law of the Jungle*

FOUR

Firebase Kate, September 1969

First Lieutenant John Kerr flew into Kate on September 20, 1969, replacing the previous FDC officer, who had been reassigned; they met only in passing as Kerr hopped off a Huey and the other lieutenant got on it and flew away. "I never got his name," muses Kerr. "I think he became the assistant ammunition officer, or something like that."

Among all the others that I could find who had served on Kate, none can recall this lieutenant's name. I mention this to make the point that while Firebase Kate was not quite as big as a football field, and while there were never as many as thirty Americans on it at the same time, such was the compartmentalization of duties that, after the passage of more than forty years, few of Kate's survivors can recall the names of more than the handful of men with whom they worked the most closely.

Kerr settled into Kate's FDC, communicating with Susan and Annie and 5/22 headquarters with one of two AN/GRC-46 radios. Normally mounted in vehicles and connected to a whip antenna on a spring mount, these FM radios have a useful range, on a vehicle, of three to five miles. On

Kate, however, the antenna was emplaced on a thirty-foot pole; at some 3,000 feet elevation, it had line-of-sight communication with units at far greater distances.

That pole also told anyone who could see it exactly where the FDC was.

FDC radios were powered by a collection of truck batteries charged by a three-kilowatt diesel generator. Two smaller generators provided light and power for the FDC and for its new FADAC computer.

"FADAC [Field Artillery Digital Automatic Computer] was a big ungainly thing," recalls Bob Johnson. "We were not supposed to use it to actually issue [firing] instructions, but only to double-check; I think the idea was to get field confirmation that the information coming out of FADAC was reasonably consistent with the manual process.

"FADAC required elaborate information, including temperatures and wind directions at different altitudes," Johnson adds. Until this device came into use, however, weather data had not been provided to Kate's FDC. "We began to get that information, but how accurate and timely it was—that was a different matter. In my experience, temperature information did not seem important; generally, temperatures in the Central Highlands were in a fairly narrow band. Wind information was important, but usually the wind was not very strong; most of the time these factors were not a consideration."

Tall, skinny, and very well-spoken, Johnson was an unusual man to find in a Vietnam FDC. A Cornell graduate with a degree in economics, he had been an actuarial trainee for the Equitable Life Assurance Society (now called AXA Equitable Life Insurance Company), an enormous company headquartered in New York City. At 24, surrounded by men in their teens or barely beyond them, he was among the oldest GIs on Kate.

"After my junior year at Cornell, I worked in a summer intern program for Equitable, and they offered me full-time work in the actuarial program following graduation," Johnson explains. At that time, anyone draft-eligible and employed in an actuarial-training program like Equitable's was eligible for a Public Health Service commission. "I expected to receive my commission during the summer following my graduation," Johnson adds. For that reason, he elected not to apply for graduate school and a student deferment.

After he graduated, however, but before his application was processed, Congress decreed that Public Health Service commissions would require a *graduate* degree. Now classified 1-A, Johnson immediately enlisted for Artillery OCS. While in advanced artillery training, however, he discovered that he could opt out of officer training and still serve only a two-year enlistment, "with the understanding that I'd be sent to Vietnam."

Johnson had—correctly—assumed that everyone who completed OCS would also go to Vietnam. "It was a question of whether I wanted to serve almost three years, which would be the total period if I accepted a commission and went to Vietnam, or a shorter period," he explains. He opted out of officer training. After arriving in Vietnam in October 1968, Johnson was assigned to Charlie Battery, and he worked in the FDC on several firebases.

Kate was established in mid-September; Johnson should have completed his combat tour at the end of that month—except that he voluntarily extended it until December 25. If he returned to the US on or after that date, he would then be less than five months from the end of his enlistment. Army policy, he had learned, was to grant early discharge to those returning from overseas duty with fewer than 150 days remaining in uniform. Johnson had gamed the system to reduce his twenty-four-month obligation to nineteen. But first he had to survive Vietnam.

KERR'S FDC crew worked with Smith's gunners to register their guns on possible trouble spots—obvious avenues of approach to their hill, as well as trail and stream junctions and nearby hilltops. They did the same for targets near Susan and Annie, adjusting their own fire with reports from observers on the distant bases. Kerr then adjusted Susan's 155 mm howitzers on preplanned targets around Kate. The idea was to have guns on all three firebases ready to fire in support of an attack on any other base.

For the guns on Susan, however, this was risky; Kate was almost at the maximum range for a 155 mm howitzer, about 14,000 meters. Howitzers are not precision weapons, so there is always a small degree of uncertainty about exactly where any particular shell will land; as long as the impact point is within the warhead's bursting radius, it's considered on-target. However, as range-to-target distance increases, error probability increases with it: the greater the range, the greater the probability of error. Moreover, ballistics and hardware characteristics dictate that the greater degree of error will be in range, rather than deflection. Having one of Susan's guns fire at a target on or near a line between the two firebases increased the chance of a shell landing shorter or longer than planned. This is to say, landing on Kate.

Once their guns were registered, Kate's gunners were rarely asked to fire them. "There were no US or ARVN troops in the area," recalls Kerr. "We weren't in direct support of an infantry division on the ground. Once or twice we shot for LRRPs, long-range recon patrols, and the LRRP guys were impressed with what we could do. But that was only once or twice. I'd been in Vietnam only a month when I got to Kate, and it was only my second firebase, so I didn't really know *why* we were there, except that we were supposed to shoot for whoever asked us to shoot."

"We went days without firing our guns," Smith confirms. "There was a lot of boredom. Day to day to day, we wondered what the hell we were doing there."

For a morale-building break in the tedium, Smith once had his guns target the ruins of a stone building. "We could see this old stone building that sort of looked like a church; according to the map, that was in Cambodia," he says. "We shot at it just to see if we could hit it, just dinking around. We probably weren't supposed to [fire into Cambodia], but it gave us something to do."

Including the three gun crews and the FDC staff, there were never more than twenty-seven artillerymen on Kate. From time to time, men came or left for R&R, to go on sick call, or for some other official reason.

The CIDG strikers were issued their own food, while the GIs dined twice daily on C rations; once a week, a Huey brought in hot food. Some artillerymen scavenged steel ammunition boxes and turned them into makeshift stoves and cooking pots. "We'd take an ammo box, put some water and rice in it, maybe scrounge some spices or peppers from the CIDG guys," recalls Bob Johnson.

Artillery units stocked C-4 plastic explosive in case they had to fell trees to clear space for their guns. They'd pull the lid off a steel ammo box and lay it at right angles under their cooking box, pinch off a squib of C-4, and light it in the lower box, add the contents of whatever C ration meals were available—chopped ham and eggs, turkey loaf, tuna and noodles, ham and lima beans—then mix them into the spiced rice and cook up GI slumgullion stews on their little C-4 stoves.

One afternoon, the pilots of a passing helicopter radioed Kate and offered to swap a freshly killed deer for a case of C rations. "Their door gunner saw something moving near the edge of a clearing and opened up on what turned out to be a deer," Smith recalls. "They landed and threw it on the chopper. I don't know why they wanted C's. They were living in much greater comfort than we were; they ate in a mess hall every night, but they offered us the swap, so we took it."

Gerald "Tex" Rogers, a gun section chief, knew just what to do with the deer. An avid hunter, he dressed the carcass, butchered it, and distributed the meat to be cooked in ammo-box stoves. For one meal, at least, Kate's artillerymen had fresh meat.

THE Montagnard infantry was a CIDG company from Special Forces Camp A-233 at Trang Phuoc under Captain Lucian "Luke" Barham, five feet nine inches and a lean, sinewy 130 pounds. Born in Riverdale, Maryland, Barham was 23, the oldest of nine children in an Air Force family. He had lived all over the world. After taking classes at a community college in Sacramento, California, he enlisted in the Army in 1965 and graduated OCS in November 1966. After jump school, he spent a year in language school learning Cambodian, then attended the Special Warfare School at Fort Bragg. Following a year in Okinawa, he arrived at the Special Forces camp at Duc Lap. By his account, almost every day he or Staff Sergeant Arbizo led a dozen or so "Yards," as GIs called them, to patrol the jungle around Kate's isolated hilltop, looking for anything that might indicate the presence of enemy troops. He recalls finding no sign of the enemy at all. "On one of the patrols we ran into an [abandoned] French plantation close to the Cambodian border," Barham says. "It was made of concrete, and the jungle had overtaken it. I couldn't believe it."

On a fine late-September day, Mike Smith joined one of these patrols, which descended Kate's steep eastern slope through thick jungle. At the bottom of a deep ravine large enough to conceal a regiment, the patrol picked their way through dense vegetation. They crossed a stream perhaps eight inches deep, with trees growing out of it.

Past the stream, the patrol climbed the steep, forested flank toward that long, high, narrow ridge that ran away from Kate to the southeast. They paused in a clearing well below the ridge. Smith was perhaps 250 meters from Kate, well within small-arms range, and just below the line of CIDG foxholes encircling the base. He could see CIDG troops clearly, as well as gun parapets, the sandbagged FDC, and the command post bunker. Early in his tour, Smith had purchased a good camera and habitually carried it almost everywhere. Now he took out this Minolta SLR and took a photo on color slide film.

As on their other patrols, Barham's CIDG found no sign of the PAVN. Yet we now know, from POWs, from US Army after-action reports, and from postwar PAVN unit histories, that from late September on, several thousand PAVN troops were on the Vietnam side of the border within a few kilometers, or less, of Kate. Helicopters landed on the firebase from time to time; someone in a PAVN recon unit observing these flights could easily have pulled out a compass and shot an azimuth along the aircraft's course. The big guns were fired from time to time, and the bald hilltop offered no concealment. Every few days, the human waste from Kate's garrison was burned with diesel fuel, sending a column of black smoke skyward for a few hours. Anyone within a mile or two could hardly have been unaware of the presence of American troops on Kate.

The North Vietnamese, however, are masters of camouflage, tireless diggers who obsessively fashioned elaborate underground facilities and long bunkers connected by tunnels. It is easy to believe that Barham and his CIDG troops patrolled widely and diligently, yet simply failed to find a wily and elusive foe.

Yet many others on Kate say that after a couple of weeks or so, CIDG recon expeditions from Kate became much less frequent and more often resembled hunting excursions than recon patrols. Occasionally, a few GIs from one or another gun crew accompanied the Yards on these hunts.

Skilled trackers and stalkers, the Yards rarely failed to return without something for their stew pots: a wild pig, a small, furtive *muntjac* deer, a monkey of one species or another, a hare or a big snake or a lizard, a badger or a brush-tailed porcupine—it was all welcomed as fresh meat by the CIDG troops.

"I have a picture of the CIDG bringing in a big-ass pig," confirms Mike Smith. "They shot deer, and once I watched them cook a monkey, which looked like a little human. They poked it around in the pot to get the hair off, and then ate the whole thing."

"I'm not taking anything away from the [Green] Berets who were there prior to Captain Albracht. They were good guys—but we partied," says Kenn Hopkins. "We didn't do anything else *but* party. We didn't send out any patrols until Albracht came. We went hunting for deer, pigs, monkeys, and all that good stuff. I was very apprehensive at the staging area, but once we got there, after a couple of days it became relaxed vacation time. We'd fill empty powder canisters with water, put them on top of the hooch during the day, and we'd have hot water to take our little whore's bath, then sit up there and watch the sun go down. It was ideal, a beautiful place. After the previous stuff we'd gone through, this place was a vacation wonderland."

To further dispel boredom, a volleyball net and a ball were obtained, and a makeshift court set up between the gun pits for occasional matches, fast and furious games that relieved the tedium and encouraged aerobic fitness. At night, Kate practiced light and noise discipline, but often as many as eighteen officers and men crowded into the FDC for a poker game in the only space with electric lights.

As the monsoon season tapered off, days on Kate became hotter and dusty. Water, always at a premium, became scarce. When the contents of their huge, cylindrical neoprene "blivet" ran low, some troops collected rainwater. Some afternoons, rain clouds marched across their valley; anticipating its arrival, everyone not otherwise occupied stripped off their clothes to stand in the rain, soap up, and hope that the brief shower would continue long enough for them to rinse off.

Field sanitation, always an issue on isolated bases, was rudimentary. Men urinated anywhere outside the barbed wire surrounding their positions. More moving issues were handled at an open-air latrine that was no more than two halves of 55-gallon diesel drums with a wooden bench laid across them and holes cut above each drum. Kate's garrison included a medical corpsman—like others of his trade, he went by "Doc," and no one I spoke with about this book could now recall his name. Each week, Doc removed the wooden bench, poured diesel oil over the waste in the steel drum halves, and set it afire. When the waste was consumed and the containers had cooled, the latrine was reassembled.

Personal hygiene was an effort. When they had enough water, some cannoneers filled an empty powder canister, put one or two garments in with soap, and used their hands and an arm as a plunger to circulate the water. From time to time, resupply choppers brought in batches of recycled fatigues; dirty uniforms and underwear were sent to the rear.

SPECIALIST Four Warren Geromin, 20 years old, had a head of thick, moplike dark red hair. Pale as an Irish coal miner and skinny as a starving ferret, he carried a mere 130 pounds on his five-foot-ten frame. He grew up a Connecticut Yankee, in a blue-collar Middletown family, and was drafted after graduating from high school. After basic training at Fort Dix, New Jersey, Geromin went to Fort Belvoir, Virginia, where the Corps of Engineers trained him to operate and maintain generators.

When he reported to Charlie Battery, however, the man he was scheduled to replace had two months remaining on his tour, so they stuck Geromin on a gun. "I filled sandbags and moved shells. Sometime I'd help break down powder charges; when we got a fire mission, after the shell went in, I would come up and throw in the powder," he says, still proud to have served as a fighting man, however briefly.

Geromin maintained three FDC generators, one to recharge the radio batteries, another for lighting, and a third to deliver DC power to the FADAC.

On a few occasions, he and a few other artillerymen, accompanied by a squad of CIDG troops, would descend Kate's eastern flank into the jungle, following a game trail to a small clearing cut by that swift, shallow creek. "It was thick and really dark in there," Geromin recalls. "You couldn't see more than a few feet ahead."

Of the officers who served on Kate and shared their recollections for this book, none recall being aware that their men left the firebase and went into the jungle below. On the other hand, personal experience teaches me that officers often don't know everything that their men are up to. That's why they have sergeants.

Kenn Hopkins joined a couple of these expeditions as well. While CIDG strikers took turns on guard, the GIs bathed or washed clothes in the cold creek. Some men went a little way upstream and filled their canteens. "When I was in high school, a guy who'd been with the 101st Airborne in Vietnam told me that a stream running fast through rocks for a few hundred feet is basically good enough to drink," Hopkins recalled.

Hopkins's job on the howitzer was preparing powder charges and attaching fuses to 155 mm projectiles in a gun section under Tex "Don't Call Me Gerald" Rogers. Tex was a 21-year-old draftee; his promotion to sergeant came just three days after the platoon and their guns landed on Kate. Tall and brawny, ruggedly handsome, with a taste for alcohol and a devil-may-care grin, Rogers grew up in Crane, Texas, population 3,000, about thirty miles south of Odessa, amid the endless oil fields of the Permian Basin. He left school after the tenth grade to work in his dad's construction outfit. Weekends, he went hunting or wrestled steers at local rodeos, collecting a little cash, a saddle, and a roomful of belt buckles. As big and burly as Tex was, however, his body was slowly being ravaged by diabetes, a condition that would not be diagnosed for several years.

ON October 15, 1969, 18-year-old Specialist Four Nelson Koon flew into Kate to join Tex Rogers's section as assistant gunner. Tall and muscular, a handsome, serious-minded Ohioan, he was eager to serve his country. Like Captain Klaus Adam, he had been trained in several military specialties—but not on howitzers.

A year earlier, when Koon was in his senior year of high school in rural Mifflin, Ohio, a tiny town a few miles east of Mansfield, he decided to enlist. But he was only 17, and needed parental permission. His father, a World War II combat veteran, refused to sign unless the Army guaranteed that Nelson would be trained for a military occupational specialty that would keep him out of combat in Vietnam.

To please his father, "I enlisted for Honest John rockets," Koon recalls.

Already obsolete, the Honest John was an unguided, solid-fuel missile launched from a five-ton truck. It accelerated to Mach 2 by the time it was airborne and could reach targets up to 15 miles distant. While the three-stage missile lacked accuracy, it delivered a huge payload of conventional explosives—or one of three types of nuclear warheads, the largest of which packed 50 percent more punch than the bomb dropped on Hiroshima during World War II.

Despite his enlistment contract, when Koon graduated from basic training at Fort Gordon, Georgia, in September 1968, he received orders for infantry training. "Dad came to my graduation. In World War II, he had served in the same outfit with my training brigade commander," Koon explains. "Dad complained to him about my assignment, and that colonel put me in his staff car and took me to the personnel office. He told them that the recruiter had screwed up or something. Then he told me that because it would take a while for my orders to get changed, he suggested that I go to infantry school anyway because it wouldn't hurt to have the training."

When Koon got to Fort Jackson, South Carolina, however, his new unit commander told him that orders for Honest John school at Fort Sill had arrived.

"I told him, 'I don't want anything to do with Honest John rockets. I want to stay infantry.'" Koon was allowed to remain at Fort Jackson and complete infantry training.

Upon graduation, he received orders for Vietnam, with leave en route to a California port of debarkation. While he was at home in Ohio, however, someone from the Department of the Army called and told him that he was *not* going to Vietnam. He *would* report to Fort Sill, Oklahoma, for Honest John school.

Koon protested—and then reported to Fort Sill.

Five days after he started Honest John school, Koon's class, and all future Honest John training, was canceled as part of a program to phase out the weapons system.

So Koon went to fire direction control school. "I was gung ho and I just wanted to get to Vietnam somehow, so I kind of screwed around in classes. They sent me to the commander, and he chewed me out a little. He said, 'If you keep this up, I'm going to send you back to the infantry.'

"I said, 'Great! That's what I want!'"

Whereupon young Nelson Koon discovered that this is not how the Army works.

"My CO said, 'You're too anxious. Get back into class and stay with it.' I would have graduated from FDC, but then almost everybody in my class was sent to Vietnam."

The exceptions were Koon and two classmates, who went to FADAC school, just down the road at Fort Sill. After completing the three-week course, almost everyone in Koon's class got orders for Vietnam.

Not Koon. With two classmates, he went to Germany.

"They put me in an Honest John unit, in the FDC. Then one of my buddies reenlisted for duty in Vietnam. Until then, I had no idea that I could do that. I went down and reenlisted. I wanted infantry or artillery, and the recruiter said, 'The only two places I can give you are Vietnam or Italy.'

"I took Vietnam, and he said, 'You've got to be a 13-Bravo.'"

Military Occupational Specialty 13B was a crewman on a towed howitzer, a weapon that Koon had seen only at a distance. But the MOS was Koon's ticket to Vietnam, and he took it. En route from Germany to Vietnam, Koon had thirty days of leave. "My father told me that I was crazy for wanting to go to Vietnam, but I told him I had to find out for myself what war was like," Koon recalls.

He landed on Kate on October 15 and was introduced to his first howitzer. For everything and anything worth doing—and for a few things that are not—there is a right way and, usually, a multitude of wrong ways. As everyone who ever wore Army green knows, there is also the Army Way. The Army Way for getting a howitzer to do its thing goes like this:

Using the sight and aiming stakes, the gunner sets the azimuth and elevation. One man sets the fuse on each projectile. Another man opens powder canisters and selects the proper number of bags for each shot, based on range to target. Two men place the 96-pound projectile on a basketlike loader and carry it to the gun, positioning the projectile behind the open breech. A third man positions the projectile in the lip of the breech. A fourth, using an eight-foot steel pole with a rubber tip, rams the shell into the howitzer barrel. The powder man drops the bags of powder behind the projectile. A firing cap is inserted in the door, the door is locked, and the assistant gunner yanks a lanyard to fire the gun.

That's how things are done at the artillery school at Fort Sill.

In the field, in combat, in Vietnam, gun crews were rarely at full strength. Somebody was always on R&R, or detailed to fill sandbags or burn shit, load or unload something, dig a hole or fill one in. Somebody was always on sick call or in the hospital, or on emergency leave, or back at base camp for some reason. For example, Sergeant Tidmore, a Charlie Battery gunner, who had had all his teeth pulled in August, returned to base camp in late October to be fitted with new dentures. And Sergeant First Class Jimmy Gooch, the much-beloved battery Chief of Smoke, a tall, lean, grizzled Korean War veteran, left on R&R two days before I flew into Kate.

So the eleven-man crew that Fort Sill taught was more often six or seven men in Vietnam. This is how they rolled in Charlie Battery: One strong man picked up the 96-pound projectile, carried it to the howitzer's breech, and shoved it as far up the barrel as he could. Then another man used the eight-foot pole to shove the projectile all the way into the barrel, followed, as before, by powder bags and a firing cap.

Most people, including artillerymen, are right-handed: Before the rammer can do his thing, he has to wait a second or two for the loader to get out of his way. But if the loader is right-handed and the rammer is left-handed, the rammer can immediately follow a shove with a push, saving precious seconds.

Koon is left-handed. He soon learned to use the ramming pole; when he became assistant gunner, he sometimes then pulled the lanyard to fire the gun.

Section chief Tex Rogers didn't need a ramming pole. "Tex was one of those guys right out of a movie—the classic Texan," recalls Mike Smith, the man from Muleshoe, Texas. "He was a good man, a really strong guy, and a good cannoneer. The big deal in an artillery unit was to pick up a projectile—we called them projos, or sometimes just joes—run over to the gun, then use your momentum and strength to shove it way up into the breech, hit it so hard with one arm that it would kind of ricochet up into the barrel. And Tex could do that all day."

On Kate, of course, that didn't happen very often, because they rarely got the chance to shoot.

Not long after Koon's arrival in October, the 1/92 Artillery's S-3, or operations officer, flew in to Kate for a look-see. "Major Riovo told us to build a new FDC, and it had to be entirely underground," recalls John Kerr.

"We had been there for quite a while when the order came down through the FDC officer, Lieutenant Kerr, that we had to dig an underground FDC," recalls Bob Johnson. "An underground FDC was normal; however, this was very unusual because the order was, 'You will do this as quickly as humanly possible; your most urgent job is to dig an underground FDC and we will send reinforcements out from battalion HQ to help.' "

Because things had been so peaceful, with no sign of the enemy, Johnson was taken aback. He was constantly on the radio that linked Kate with its higher headquarters. "I don't know about the officers, but I was the enlisted man in charge of FDC," he recalls. "Neither I nor any of the other enlisted men had any clue that anything was happening anywhere in the area. But these were very strict orders, and that came as a little bit of a shock."

Later that day, reinforcements flew in. "They were base-camp warriors," Johnson recalls. "They brought their shovels and their hands, and they were good guys. We were all digging in the ground and filling sandbags for at least a week."

Johnson took it upon himself to design the underground bunker, and did so in such a manner that when carving a deep hole in hard-packed soil was concluded, the excavation had built-in earthen tables and chairs. "All we needed was to bring in the radio equipment, the charts, the FADAC," Johnson recalls. "We could stand up in that bunker; around the perimeter were different types of tables for charts, radios, for whatever else we needed. The whole thing was about ten by ten feet, or a little bigger."

Johnson and his crew then stacked sandbags three high on the ground around the bunker perimeter, laid steel planks across the space between them, and piled four layers of sandbags atop the planks. "We were impervious to artillery or mortar shells coming down on top of us," explains Johnson. "And we were too low for rocket fire to hit [the top of the roof], so once we got that done, we were immune from attack."

The entrance to the bunker was an outside stairway with a sandbagged roof; at its bottom it took a ninety-degree turn to enter the FDC. This provided a shield against blast and shrapnel.

"It's really wonderful when you're allowed to do the complete design of something like that," Johnson says. "You can make it as safe as you want."

The original FDC, which was vulnerable to flat-trajectory fire from rockets, RPGs, and recoilless rifles, as well as a direct hit by an artillery shell, became the command bunker.

A few days after the FDC was completed, according to separate recollections by Koon and Geromin, a few cannoneers, accompanied by CIDG strikers, descended to the shallow creek below Kate's eastern flank. As they approached their usual bathing spot, the Yards suddenly stopped. The GIs smelled smoke. A half-smoked cigarette was found smoldering on the ground near the brook. The expedition immediately reversed course and silently climbed back to the safety of Kate.

Perhaps because the cannoneers had left base without official permission, nothing about that smoldering cigarette was reported to either Mike Smith or John Kerr. Nor does Barham recall hearing anything about the incident from the CIDG.

• • •

A few days later, on October 27, Sergeant Dan Pierelli, 23, a weapons specialist from Special Forces Camp A-233 at Trang Phuoc (also called Ban Don), arrived to replace his teammate, Staff Sergeant Santiago Arbizo, a demolitions specialist, who returned to A-233.

Like Nelson Koon's and Klaus Adam's, Pierelli's military route to Kate had been long and convoluted. Handsome and fair-haired, he was a lean, wiry man two inches shorter than my own six feet, but weighing about 40 pounds less than I did at that time.

Dan had long yearned to serve his country. Born in New Haven, Connecticut, and raised in nearby West Haven, in 1965 he earned a coveted appointment to the US Air Force Academy at Colorado Springs. Like many before him, however, he found the academy's rigorous academics overwhelming. He left Colorado Springs and, by long-standing custom, was transferred to the Air Force Reserve.

Had Dan done nothing further, he almost certainly would have satisfied his military service requirement without ever serving on active duty. Instead, he enlisted in the Army. After basic and advanced infantry training, he volunteered for the airborne and Special Forces schools.

Dan arrived in Vietnam in March 1969 and was assigned to A-233. He sewed on sergeant's stripes just under two years after joining the Army, about as fast a climb through the lower ranks as was then possible, but also a product of Special Forces' rapid expansion and combat losses.

Situated right on the Cambodian border north of Bu Prang, Camp A-233 at any given time had between 200 and 300 CIDG strikers. To detect and deter PAVN infiltration, frequent patrols, often composed of a company-size force, or about half the available strikers, and led by a pair of Green Berets, patrolled the area of operations for which they were responsible.

"We were looking to make contact," explains Pierelli. "Sometimes we'd get intelligence telling us to go into a particular area because the NVA were coming down. A lot of times they had come down through Cambodia, and they had [something] in mind that they wanted to do."

Special Forces strategy along the border was to make contact with the enemy and force them to either withdraw across the border or to assume a defensive posture inside Vietnam. This would allow us to use our enormous firepower to destroy the invaders.

Most of the enemy formations that Dan's patrols encountered were Viet Cong, rather than the better-equipped and more rigorously trained PAVN. Between March and October, Pierelli went on dozens of patrols, occasionally getting into firefights, and in the process learning how to work with other US and ARVN units. When a patrol needed artillery support, Pierelli could call it in from guns at A-233. He could also make radio contact with an Army pilot flying a 185th Recon Company Birddog. Based in BMT and colloquially known as the Pterodactyls, these pilots called in and adjusted artillery or radioed Air Force forward air controllers to request support from fast movers, the jet-propelled fighter-bombers or attack planes that moved at near-supersonic speeds and carried bombs, napalm, or rockets—whatever was needed.

By October 27, the day he arrived on Kate, Dan Pierelli was comfortable with combat, a solid young Green Beret sergeant who knew what to do when the shooting started. Like me, however, he had never been on the receiving end of PAVN artillery.

"That night, the 27th, we got a radio message from 5/22's operational headquarters in BMT," John Kerr recalls. "They said that there was a lot of enemy activity in our area and that 50 percent of us should be awake all night with our guns. And they said that we'd probably be attacked that night."

Kerr was shocked. "We'd been sitting around here for a month and a half, not hardly shooting anything, and all of a sudden they say we're going to be attacked!"

Kerr told Mike Smith about the message, and word was disseminated throughout the artillery detachment. There is no record of any such warning coming through Special Forces or CIDG channels, and neither Kerr nor Smith recalls telling Luke Barham or Dan Pierelli about the alert message.

The night passed uneventfully.

For several weeks after the new FDC was built, helicopter resupply had been reduced to a minimum, probably to reduce the chance that Kate would attract unwanted enemy attention. "For the most part they just didn't resupply us," recalls Forrest Scott. "We were starving and doing without." Until the 27th, when a giant Chinook landed. "It had ammo, C rations, batteries, all kinds of stuff that had been requested, and they brought in a sling load of water," Scott explains. "They set the chopper down—never stopped the blades—and we unloaded it. I'd been in-country and was scheduled for R&R, so when everything was off-loaded, I jumped on that Chinook."

Scott was flown to BMT, where he caught a plane to Saigon, and from there flew on a commercial charter to Bangkok.

ON the morning of October 28, 1969, the CIDG company on Kate, which had come from A-233 and was based there, was replaced by a fresh company from A-233.

With the hindsight afforded by forty-six years, the timing of this troop rotation strikes me as odd. Staff Sergeant Rocco DeNote, my teammate in A-236 and then the communications NCO at Camp Bu Prang, confirms that at this time "there was a significant enemy presence in the northern part of the area of operations. Units such as the 66th PAVN had been identified, and alert was high at all sites preparing for an anticipated attack."

If an attack was imminent and everyone in Kate's chain of command knew it, why replace men familiar with the terrain and Kate's defenses with a new unit that knew nothing about the setup? Was there a breakdown in communications? Did the honchos at B-23, our higher headquarters, fail to tell A-233 of the expected attack? After all these years, I could find no one who knew or who now recalls the answers to such questions.

For a few hours on the morning of October 28, one Huey after another landed on Kate. Fresh strikers took over the fighting positions of those they replaced. After the last of the newcomers had arrived, however, the flights were interrupted. Sixteen men from the old CIDG unit were left on Kate, along with the replacement company.

In midafternoon, I left Bu Prang for Kate, a flight of less than ten minutes.

PART TWO

I hear the irregular snap! snap!

I hear the sounds of the different missiles—the short t-h-t!
t-h-t! of the rifle balls;

I see the shells exploding, leaving small white clouds—

I hear the great shells shrieking as they pass;

The grape, like the hum and whirr of wind through the trees,

(quick, tumultuous, now the contest rages!)

All the scenes at the batteries themselves rise in detail before
me again;

The crashing and smoking—the pride of the men in their pieces;

The chief gunner ranges and sights his piece, and selects a fuse
of the right time;

After firing, I see him lean aside, and look eagerly off to note the
effect;

—Elsewhere I hear the cry of a regiment charging—

—Walt Whitman, "The Artilleryman's Vision," *Leaves of Grass*

FIVE

From high above, Firebase Kate was a mottled red football with dark laces on a bed of green felt. The pilot put the nose down, and as we descended the felt became jungle, the football resolved itself into sandbagged gun pits and bunkers carved out of red dirt, and the laces turned into curving lines of foxholes.

Although I wasn't expecting to see any action, I had prepared myself for it. I carried the Colt Automatic Rifle, or CAR-15, the rare, short-barreled version of the standard M16. Instead of the Army's standard "load-bearing vest" of suspenders, a fanny pack on a web belt, and small ammo pouches for the M16 magazines, I had a World War II vintage ammo belt made for those who carried the big, heavy M1918 Browning Automatic Rifle. I could put two or three magazines of 5.56 ammo in its big pouches, which were intended to hold much larger, 20-round, 30-06-caliber magazines

In the back left pouch of my BAR belt I carried a "baseball" hand grenade, a "goofy grape" grenade, the purple smoke used by Special Forces in only the most dire situations to tell a rescue chopper that an American was in deep trouble.

The grenade was for when I was out of ammo, escape was impossible, and the enemy was closing in. It was to be my last gasp at taking as many foes with me as possible. I would not be taken alive.

We settled down in a dust cloud, and the crew chief began tossing out boxes of ammo and C rations. I grabbed my CAR-15 assault rifle and rucksack, and as I hopped off, a slender, compact man hopped on from the other side—Captain Lucian "Luke" Barham. "Hey, how ya doing, have a good time," he said, barely audible over the roar of the Huey's engines. Barham gave a little wave and the Huey rose, supported by a cushion of hurricane-force air, rotated to the right, then plunged over the side into the deep valley below, gathering airspeed; in seconds it reappeared, climbing into a high, overcast sky until the sound of its engines faded and the bird disappeared. It was about 1500 local time on the afternoon of October 28, 1969.

I looked around, unhappily noting the high, forested ridge to the southeast. *Why in God's name did they put a firebase here?* I thought. From that ridge, the enemy could shoot down at us with flat trajectory weapons—small arms, rockets, recoilless rifles. It felt like we were in a punch bowl; I flashed on what I'd read of the Dien Bien Phu fiasco, where the French sited their guns in a valley surrounded by big hills, convinced that the Viet Minh could never haul artillery to those heights.

I put those thoughts aside as Sergeant Dan Pierelli came to meet me. As we moved toward the command post, I looked around, noting the two big 155 mm howitzers and the smaller 105 mm, which was pointed north toward Ambush Hill. Not understanding until years later that artillery in Vietnam operated in a 360-degree world, I wondered why the big guns had no overhead cover, only chest-high sandbags. Then I turned my head to take another look at that thickly forested, sharply defined ridge to the southeast. I knew that we were less than four kilometers from the poorly defined border, positioned within a bulge that my map showed jutting into Cambodia, a disputed zone claimed by both countries. It was a reminder that Cambodia was to the north, east, and west, and that even if PAVN troops were not on that forested ridge, Kate was still well within the range of their 82 mm mortars, their 75 mm and 57 mm recoilless rifles, their B-40 rocket-propelled grenades, and of course their big 122 mm rockets.

I shook hands with Lieutenants Smith and Kerr, dropped my gear in the little sleeping hooch that I would share with Pierelli—and got a wake-up call: The roof was a row of sandbags on a sheet of plastic. It would keep the sun and rain out, but it wouldn't stop a rifle bullet, let alone a mortar. The front side, facing away from the hill, was exposed. In short, it was a half-assed attempt at best.

Together we started a slow, thorough inspection of the defensive perimeter. Let's call north 12 o'clock, and south 6 o'clock. Then Kate's 12 o'clock was a gentle slope leading down to a grassy saddle that rose at the far end to Ambush Hill. Between 12 and 1 o'clock it became slightly steeper and grew ever steeper as it progressed to 3 o'clock. By that point, I judged it to be a difficult task to climb, but still traversable. The hill fell down through grass that was two to three feet high and low brush into the valley at the foot of the hill. That was covered with very thick jungle with a small stream at the bottom—all in all, terrain very typical of the region, which was rolling hills and very dense jungle.

From 3 through 6 o'clock the slope was much the same, but grew steeper as it went. The vegetation was about the same, but the slope became extreme through about 10 o'clock and then gentled again as it came back toward 12 o'clock.

With Pierelli, I walked the perimeter defenses, meeting the CIDG strikers and their leaders as we made our way from one foxhole to the next. But here's the thing about CIDG leaders: The guy who presents himself as, for example, a company commander was chosen by a US Special Forces officer, probably because, all things being equal, he spoke the best English—he was the guy we could talk to. But the Montagnards are a tribal society that relies on a high degree of consensus. It was likely that this guy wasn't a top leader, but even if he was, anything of importance, any order that I gave a company or platoon commander that might have severe consequences, would be discussed and confirmed by all the leaders—and often I didn't know who most of them were.

The life of an infantryman in war—any infantryman, any army, any war—is a showcase for privation: little sleep, poor food and never enough of it, less water, an absence of cleanliness and sanitation that turns the human body into a feast for bacteria and fungi that manifest as skin infections, and a total lack of privacy. My strikers had grown up in a preliterate society. Most of their siblings hadn't survived childhood. Western concepts of personal hygiene and labor-saving devices were entirely absent from their upbringing. So they were tough, inured to hardship, and anything but lazy—but like every soldier in every army, they didn't go looking for extra work. CIDG strikers were pragmatists. They prepared for battle in accordance with what they believed was needed. The prolonged absence of enemy contact meant that their predecessors on Kate had been comfortable with foxholes maybe two feet wide by about two and a half feet deep. When in contact with the enemy, however, the well-trained Montagnard striker would continue to dig and improve his position, a little at a time, until his fighting hole was chest-high. Until there was a two-foot-deep grenade sump in the bottom that could double as a piss tube during times when leaving the foxhole was suicide. Until he had overhead cover, built of whatever he could get his hands on, and the more of it the better.

That was not what I found on Kate. I found two-man fighting positions with no overhead cover, nothing to protect the men inside from mortars or grazing fire from, say, a nearby high ridge. A single roll of concertina wire, maybe a hundred meters long, was overgrown with weeds in several places. In strategic locations I saw a few trip flares. Attached to a thin, almost invisible wire concealed at ankle height in the tall grass, they could be triggered by an approaching enemy to shoot a parachute flare a few hundred feet straight up. The flare would burn for half a minute or so as it floated down, allowing us to see who to shoot at. I thought that we could put more of those out on the line and farther down the hillside.

There were also a few claymores, deadly devices that, properly emplaced and maintained, can blow back any approaching skirmish line or night infiltration. One look from above told me that nobody had checked the claymores for weeks. On closer inspection, I found that someone—undoubtedly the previous company of CIDG strikers—had "borrowed" some of the C-4 explosives from inside the mine. C-4 is great for starting fires, as almost every infantryman learns. Removing it from the mine is not so good. Not good for a properly functioning anti-personnel mine. Not good for stopping an attacking wave of enemy soldiers.

Below the foxholes were fifty to a hundred meters of grass-covered slopes, and below that, thick jungle. Kate had been occupied for six weeks, but nobody had gone down to cut fields of fire—avenues to see and shoot through the knee-high grass, or below that in the thickest spots in the jungle. The enemy could hide in that jungle, virtually invisible, and shoot at us. I just couldn't comprehend how this could have been allowed by an infantry officer, much less by one that was Special Forces trained. I still can't believe it.

I understood, however, that Kate had never experienced enemy contact, that there had been no sign of the enemy in the area. They *thought* they were safe. But I *knew* that PAVN was coming—to Bu Prang. I'd read the daily intelligence reports, and they told me that nothing was going on at the three firebases ringing Bu Prang Camp. The enemy would hit Bu Prang, but there was no indication that the firebases were even on the PAVN radar. Barham got the same reports; maybe he believed that PAVN would attack Bu Prang from only one direction, from across the border in Cambodia.

Long before completing my inspection of the perimeter defenses, I realized that I had been totally wrong: I had not been sent to Kate to sit on my ass. There was a lot of work to do, and I was just the man to see that it got done.

I conferred with Pierelli, who had arrived only the previous day, and learned that he too had been disturbed and distressed at the condition of the perimeter defenses. Aware that an officer was coming to replace Barham, Dan had wisely decided not to confront Barham or Arbizo. As we made the rounds now, though, he pointed out most of the shortcomings and deficiencies even as I noticed them myself. He also informed me that until our arrival, while the CIDG troops hadn't found much time for digging, Barham had allowed them time to play cards or bat a volleyball back and forth over a net.

Infantry doctrine calls for patrolling in a four-leaf-clover pattern all around the base. That is to say, taking different routes on different days, patrols explore the area around their perimeter in all four directions by taking a circular route each time.

According to Pierelli, however, and several others on Kate, when it came to patrolling, Barham had pretty much let his Montagnard strikers decide how much and what kind, perhaps on the theory that if there were enemy forces nearby, they would somehow know it, and their patrolling mojo would in some fashion reflect that. Otherwise, all we knew from their frequent hunting expeditions was that there were plenty of game animals in the nearby jungle.

I couldn't, of course, be certain that the enemy knew Kate's location and purpose. But military prudence in a war zone demanded that I assume that they would. The strikers who had departed the previous day, however, had apparently been allowed to behave as if their stay on Kate was some kind of vacation. Rest and recreation on a remote jungle hilltop that was just spitting distance from the PAVN sanctuaries in Cambodia.

Barham's strikers had hunted for game regularly. But hunting translates to avoiding the very dense jungle and steep, treacherous terrain that a PAVN unit would probably use to hide their whereabouts during the days of their approach to Bu Prang. They would move mostly at night, and they would have security or recon units on their flanks and both ahead and behind their main force.

I looked around, trying to see Kate as an enemy commander might. If I had, say, a PAVN battalion, how would I attack this hilltop? What approach would I take? Dan and I discussed this, and agreed that, to a determined enemy, this firebase was low-hanging fruit, to be plucked and eaten at his pleasure. To call Kate's defenses inadequate was to give more credit than was due.

And the more I thought about it, the more certain I was that an attack was coming. Maybe no enemy soldier had yet seen the dark clouds of burning diesel that rose over Kate every few days when they burned shit. Maybe they hadn't yet seen the helicopters coming and going. Perhaps they had no idea that Kate's guns had fired into Cambodia and registered their fire on possible targets near Bu Prang.

But they would.

When the attack on Bu Prang began, Kate's guns would go into operation. We would then become a target. And at the moment, we would be a vulnerable target.

By the time I completed my circuit of Kate's defenses, the sun was low; I expected that the troops were getting hungry. I assembled the striker leaders, such as they were. "First thing tomorrow morning, let's get these guys working on fortifying the bunkers," I told them. "And let's get this concertina area cleaned out."

These strikers were new to Kate. Through the language barrier, I sensed that they shared my concerns, my assessment of the situation. And they agreed: First thing tomorrow, lots of digging. Overhead cover. Cut fields of fire. Clean up the concertina wire and check the claymores. Get ready for a big fight.

"One more thing," I said. "First thing in the morning, let's put a patrol together and go see what's going on around here." And again the striker leaders agreed.

Before it got dark, I asked Smith or Kerr—I've forgotten which one—to get the artillery guys together, and I gave them a little talk. No more volleyball, I said. No more cards. From here on out, we must prepare to be attacked. Right after that meeting, one of the young GIs mentioned that he'd been down to the creek below Kate a few days before and the strikers he'd been with turned back because they found a burning cigarette on the trail. The only problem with this announcement was that he didn't tell *me* or Dan or either of the artillery officers about it.

"Duty on Kate was very, very nice," recalls Kenn Hopkins. "We really liked it—until Albracht got there. From the first day he came around and said, 'You guys have to tighten this stuff up; you're really lax.' And we grumbled, 'God dang it, this guy's taking our fun away now.' Because we were kicking back, enjoying our time there, and he wants us to work. But it's a good thing that he did too, a really good thing."

After talking to the men, I ate something and turned in early, confident that the wheels were in motion. I was pretty sure that in a few days, a week tops, Kate would be in good shape, prepared to resist almost anything the enemy could throw at us.

I could not have been more wrong.

I have fought with gun and cutlass
On the red and slippery deck
With all Hell aflame within me
And a rope around my neck.

—George S. Patton, Jr., "Through a Glass Darkly"

SIX

Half an hour before midnight, I was jarred awake by the rattle and pop of small-arms fire. I opened my eyes, struggling to comprehend, to orient myself in time and space. In the field, we usually slept in our clothes, but on a good night we could take off our boots. That was the last night that any of us slept without boots on.

I rolled out of my tiny hooch and as I hurriedly laced up my footgear, I could see flashes of gunfire around the forested peak on the far side of the saddle to the north called Ambush Hill. I listened for the explosions that could mean RPGs, hand grenades, or mortars, but heard only M16s and AK-47s, each firing with a distinctive sound. I moved across the blacked-out firebase until I found Pierelli and some of the artillerymen.

Pierelli said, "It's Ambush Hill. We put a listening post out there at night."

Meanwhile, the gun crews had leapt to their howitzers and were firing off illumination rounds—big flares, swaying as they descended beneath parachutes, throwing orange, almost otherworldly light, flickering and shifting. A few minutes later, I heard the outpost strikers coming, six or seven men beating feet as fast as their legs could carry them, down steep

Ambush Hill to the nearly flat saddle between the peaks, then up and into Kate—more than a football field expanse in all. At Kate's end, a thick band of dense jungle vegetation ran across the whole saddle; near the middle, someone or something had cut or worn a gap, more than wide enough to drive a deuce-and-a-half truck through.

Gasping for breath, our strikers charged through that gap and up through a narrow opening in our concertina wire and back inside to Kate's relative safety.

They came in yelling, "Beaucoup VC, beaucoup VC!"

They spoke a few words of French, our strikers. And to them there was no difference between the Viet Cong and the PAVN.

"Many enemy soldiers." That was what they were saying.

If this was an enemy probe to determine the disposition of our forces, and what we had available to shoot, it was a roaring success. Not knowing whether "beaucoup" meant an enemy platoon or a regiment, I got on my AN/PRC 25 radio and called Bu Prang Special Forces Camp to request air support. Meanwhile, Kate's artillery began laying high-explosive hell on nearby preplanned targets—avenues of approach, trail and stream junctions, and local landmarks that might be used for nighttime navigation or patrol rallying points. The smaller, 105 mm howitzer began to fire on Ambush Hill and approaches to its flanks.

"We were sitting around in our hooch, just shooting the breeze and listening to the radio," recalls Nelson Koon. "Then we heard small-arms fire, and we got a call to turn our howitzer around and fire illumination, so the patrol could find their way back.

"The Montagnards came running back in yelling, 'Beaucoup VC!' but we sat around the gun acting real cocky. We figured it might have been a squad or a platoon of NVA or something. 'We'll get their asses tomorrow,' we said, and bragged about how we'd take our unit crest and stomp it into some [PAVN soldier's] forehead. We'd sew our unit patch on their ass—all sorts of crazy stuff."

The first AC-47 Spooky aircraft arrived overhead about forty minutes after I made the call, and began laying curtains of fire all around Kate. Kate's artillery had to shut down, lest they hit the orbiting aircraft.

At 0300, with no further sign of the enemy, Spooky departed for its base and I slipped back into my fart sack for a few winks. A good thing, because it was the last uninterrupted sleep I would enjoy for days to come.

WEDNESDAY, October 29, 1969, dawned cool and clear along the Vietnam coast. The highlands had low cloud cover, intermittent high-explosive showers, and flying shrapnel, heavy at times, along the Cambodian border.

Although the PAVN was a modern force, equipped with excellent Soviet-style infantry weapons, it had no air support—by 1969, US Air Force and Navy pilots had shot down most of Hanoi's combat aircraft and forced the rest to hide in underground shelters. So while we and our allies hauled huge howitzers around the battlefield with helicopters and trucks, the PAVN, when it operated in South Vietnam, had so far in this war left its big guns, its captured French 105 mm howitzers and its Chinese- or Soviet-made 130 mm field guns, at home. Instead, it improvised artillery from what could be carried on soldiers' backs. That was why it was so dependent on mortars and rockets—and so damn well versed in their usage.

PAVN also turned the recoilless rifle, developed and deployed in Western armies as an anti-tank gun and bunker-buster, and copied by the Chinese, into a fair substitute for true artillery: Connected to a forward observer or with an unobstructed view of the target, the PAVN had more than once demonstrated that it could fire 57 mm and 75 mm recoilless rifles at ranges up to 8,000 meters—4.6 miles—with surprising effectiveness.

While I slept through the hours before dawn on October 29, PAVN troops hauled recoilless rifles up the heights to Kate's east. Mounted on a light machine-gun tripod, once he had the range, from that distance any half-assed PAVN gunner could put a recoilless rifle's high-explosive warhead into a water bucket with one eye closed.

SOMETHING loud and close jarred me awake at dawn. I opened my eyes. It had to be Mike Smith's gun bunnies firing. Nothing to worry about, I told myself.

Kenn Hopkins was asleep in an underground hooch next to the protective parapet around his 155 mm howitzer when the same blast woke him.

"I thought it was the 105, down at the other end," he says. "That usually didn't wake me up, because it was outgoing. This was similar, but it felt like it had a different sound to it. And then it came again, it was BAM! . . . BAM! . . . BAM! One after another. What they were doing—they didn't know the range, and they'd fire a round, watch where it hit, and adjust their sights. They were walking reckless rifle rounds up the side of our hill until they hit our gun."

Twenty-year-old PFC Bernie Tiranti, blue-eyed, slim, and dark-haired, had immigrated to Chicago with his parents from Germany when he was a baby. An enlistee who was trained as a howitzer crewman, when he arrived in Vietnam, he was offered a rear-area job. Bernie turned it down. Awakened on this morning by the noise of incoming fire, he sat up on the cot in his bunker. Just as he did so, a B-40 rocket punched through the sandbagged wall and struck his lower back. By some miracle, the warhead was a dud, although the force of its impact crunched Tirani's back so hard that he would suffer the effects of this injury for the rest of his life. He refused evacuation because he had not suffered a wound, and felt well enough to continue.

Nearby, the blasts awakened Nelson Koon, who bunked with Sergeant McFarland, a tall, heavyset man who wore glasses. "We were both asleep in our hooch," says Koon. "Neither of us had experienced incoming before, so we thought the blasts were *our* guns shooting—that it was *out*going fire. But then I said to myself, *Who's doing the shooting? And what am I doing in here—I should be out there on the gun!* And then we heard a guy yelling for a medic. McFarland looked at me and said, 'Go out there and get that guy,' and I said. '*You* go get him.' So we *both* went out and the guy was yelling and screaming that he'd lost his legs. He was a blond-haired kid, real cocky the night before, but now he wasn't cocky. We dragged him into our hooch, still screaming that he'd lost his legs. We pulled down his pants, and he didn't have a scratch on him."

Not so Sergeant Tex Rogers's big howitzer, its shiny stainless-steel barrel pierced by a high-explosive anti-tank (HEAT) round from a recoilless rifle and rendered inoperative.

From the hooch I shared with Pierelli, the second explosion felt much closer. And the third even closer. Once I was awake, I realized that it wasn't *our* guns firing.

After the first explosion, Lieutenant John Kerr jumped out of his sleeping bag in the sandbagged CONEX container that had formerly been the FDC. He *knew* that Kate's guns weren't firing, if only because *he* hadn't told them what to shoot at. He pulled on his boots and ran to the new underground FDC, grateful for its good overhead cover.

"Spec 4 Bob Johnson was on radio duty," Kerr recalls. "He looked at me and I looked at him, and he said, 'Better go get your rifle!' I turned around and ran back to get my M16. The rifle was fine, but my sleeping bag was a pile of feathers; a recoilless rifle or mortar round had come through the CONEX roof and landed on my cot."

By the time Pierelli and I were up and out of the sack, it was a drummer's symphony of explosions, *BOOM! BOOOOOM! . . . BOOOM!* Shells from recoilless rifles and mortars and rockets landing everywhere. A muscular black gunner named Rudy Childs burst into our hooch, screaming, "We're taking incoming! I'm hit! I'm hit!"

I called for the medic, and we put Childs on our floor. He was in shock, really freaking out, and his back was peppered with shrapnel and bleeding badly. Dan and I pulled out our field dressings and started to patch him up; as bad as he looked, we tried to reassure him, to calm him down. "Hey, you're going to be okay," I said, repeating it a couple of times. "It's not that bad; you're just bleeding a lot. You'll be fine."

"Oh, am I?" he said, and we both nodded yes, and this had an almost immediate effect. Childs calmed down a lot, allowing us to bandage him. Meanwhile, I'm thinking, *Holy shit! This guy is really shot to pieces.*

Like almost everyone else on Kate that dawn, Lieutenant Mike Smith was asleep in his bunker when the barrage began. A veteran of several previous firebases that had survived extensive mortar and rocket attacks, he'd built a sandbag "blast wall" in front of his bunker entrance. "About 7:00 a.m., I awoke to this *KAWOOMP!*—which, it turned out, was a HEAT round going through the sandbags to get the first gun," he recalls. "We realized that it must be incoming, so I grabbed my [steel] pot, my rifle, and all that business to head out and see what's going on. My radio operator was right behind me.

"I came out of my bunker looking around, and in that little clearing across the valley [from which, a few weeks earlier, he had taken a photo of Kate], I saw movement—men, a flash! And then, all in the space of a second or so, an explosion and I'm back inside the bunker. Later, I wrote my wife that I'd seen the guys who shot me."

Smith believes that *he* was never the target. "The old FDC was at the very top of the hill, set up high, a well-protected box with a helluva bunch of sandbags around it. My bunker was slightly to the left and sort of low-slung. I think they just missed the FDC and hit between that, my bunker, and the pit where we put all the generators."

Smith was blown back into his bunker along with his radio operator. The RTO was unscathed, but a jagged piece of shrapnel more than an inch long buried itself in Smith's head, just above the hairline. "It didn't go all the way through my skull. I guess the angle it came at wasn't enough to do me in, but I was bleeding like a stuck hog," he recalls. "All I remember after that was taking the radio over to the FDC to get more [antenna] height," so he could report Kate's status.

In the FDC, the unit medic rendered first aid. "I was all bandaged up and looked kind of wild," Smith recalls. "I had the sense—and the medic shared this—that the wound was more serious than it would later turn out to be. I also believed that this wasn't [a prelude to] a major attack. I don't think that I would've left Kate if I had known the magnitude of the situation."

THE barrage lasted only ten or fifteen minutes. Before it was over, I was on my radio calling for air support, but by the time the shelling stopped, there was nothing overhead. I did a damage assessment, and checked on the strikers. None had been killed, but a few had shrapnel wounds.

As I mentioned earlier, below the northern tip of Firebase Kate was a flat, grassy gap in the jungle big enough to drive a deuce-and-a-half through. A footpath led through that gap and into the open, grassy saddle leading to Ambush Hill. In hindsight, I now realize that had the enemy waited until

Spooky departed, then climbed back up Ambush Hill and slipped fifty or sixty well-armed men into that band of jungle, they could have moved into position while we were pinned down by the dawn barrage. When the artillery stopped, they could have assaulted right into the firebase, rolled up the strikers on both flanks, and thrown grenades into our bunkers. In other words, they could have wiped us out in ten minutes.

The reason they didn't, I think, is that the previous night's probe was the leading edge, the recon element, of a much larger force moving through our area toward Bu Prang. Since the arrival of US combat troops in 1965, the PAVN had been outnumbered and outgunned by US and Allied forces. Their salvation was Cambodian and Laotian sanctuaries, and their demonstrated expertise in moving unseen through very difficult terrain. They were definitely in South Vietnam to fight, but they always wanted to choose the time and place of an encounter, usually at a moment when, even briefly, they had numerical superiority. PAVN company and battalion commanders operated with minimal tactical autonomy: Instead of allowing, say, a company commander to seize and exploit an unexpected opportunity, PAVN commanders preferred to plan and rehearse every attack. On that late October night, they didn't have time to scout the terrain and then organize a ground attack. Instead, they laid hot steel on us, seeking to neutralize our big guns.

And that they did: One of Kate's howitzers was permanently out of action and the other two were damaged.

LESS than twenty minutes after the barrage stopped, I assembled about two dozen strikers armed with M16 rifles, grenade launchers, and a couple of M60 machine guns. We left the circle of foxholes, threaded our way through the gap, and moved across the grassy saddle and up Ambush Hill.

"I brought an M79 grenade launcher, carried a radio, and brought up the rear," recalls Dan Pierelli. "Bill was up front, and he had another radio. Special Forces standard operating procedure: Anytime an American went on an operation, a patrol, anything where he might make enemy contact, he carried a radio."

Ambush Hill was about the same elevation as Kate, or perhaps a few meters less. Unlike Kate, it offered a somewhat gentler slope in three directions down to the jungle below. The summit was much smaller than Kate's, maybe thirty meters across, and topped by a copse of tall trees surrounded by a veil of thick brush offering good concealment.

We reached the hilltop without drama. In the tall grass we found a PAVN pith helmet and numerous blood trails—evidence of last night's firefight. I realized that we were fighting the big boys: PAVN regulars, not Viet Cong guerrillas.

Aside from that, I had no sense of the game board. All I knew was that our outpost was probed the previous night, followed by this morning's mortar, rocket, and recoilless rifle greetings. Obviously, there must be more bad guys in the neighborhood; I thought that it would be much better to find them before they found us.

I sent a point man down Ambush Hill toward the jungle. The rest of us followed, single file, through waist-high grass down a slope that grew steeper as we descended.

About thirty meters from the tree line, the jungle turned into the Fourth of July and Bastille Day: at least one machine gun, and several AK-47s.

We went prone and returned fire, and a shit storm of flying lead came right back over our heads. The grass was high enough to hide us, but offered no protection. I called to Dan and he blooped a few M79 grenades into the tree line. That quieted them down until we could pull back to a sort of berm, a long knee-high mound of soil covered with grass, that offered, at least for a few minutes, both cover and concealment. Three of my men were wounded but still ambulatory.

For just a second or two, I was back in OCS. One of our tactical officers is speaking. *Gentlemen,* goes his voice in my head—a hundred times faster than in real life—*a lot of you are new to the Army. You're young guys with no experience. We're training you to be infantry officers, leaders of men. When you become a new second lieutenant, you* will *be tested. You'll be the butt of jokes about being green and inexperienced. But when your men hear their first shots fired at them, they're all going to look to you. Your privates, corporals, and sergeants, even your senior platoon sergeants, they will* all *look* to you—*that's how the Army works. They're going to look to you, and you'd better goddamn well be ready to make the right decisions.*

Sure as shit, soon as the shooting starts, my strikers said, "What do we do?"

I'd been an officer for two years. Special Forces trained, I'd been around many senior noncoms, and they had taught, tutored, and mentored me. I wasn't afraid. I knew what to do—and I was pissed about being ambushed. I couldn't tell whether it was a squad down there or a regiment, but if they wanted to dance, Arthur Murray was my middle name, and I was ready to rumba. I laced up my dancing shoes and called for air support music.

Ordinarily, my first move would have been to have half my men lay down a base of fire while the rest maneuvered into position, and then switch off. That's Infantry 101: Fire and maneuver. But we were very close to the tree line, and the grass was so high that from the prone position we couldn't see anything. The berm was covered with the same tall grass; the only way to see what we were shooting at was to stand up.

If we must be targets, best be *moving* targets.

So I pulled my troops into a staggered skirmish line, two-deep, and we swept down the hill, firing as we went. Soon we were in thick jungle; as we started our sweep on what I thought was their flank, an OH-6 Cayuse, a light observation and cargo helicopter known as a LOACH, appeared overhead. He was from the 7th Battalion, 17th Cavalry. Normally, they're part of a hunter-killer team: The LOACH hunts for the enemy, and an AH-1 Cobra, bristling with guns and rockets, kills them. But this LOACH was alone. Unarmed.

The pilot called on our tactical frequency to say that he was in the neighborhood, heard my call, and here he was. "Let me see what's going on there for you," he said, hovering just off the treetops. He rose to maybe twice treetop level and called back, "Get out of there, man! I see you, I see where you're going, and they're mounting a force to flank you, a whole shitload of guys coming—a lot more than you've got."

I told everybody to pull back up to the berm; as we moved, I heard the LOACH pilot flying over the enemy, meanwhile hollering on the tactical frequency for more help. This was one crazy dude; it takes two hands and two feet to fly a helicopter, but while he slid sideways, an eyeblink off the trees and talking on the radio, he was also shooting out the window with his .45 sidearm, and the enemy, of course, was shooting back with automatic weapons. He ran out of ammo, put in his second, and last, magazine—an act that required two hands!—and resumed firing.

He called to anyone listening that he was almost out of ammo, and then Pterodactyl 10, also known as Captain John Strange of the 185th Recon Company at Gia Nghia, slid in overhead in his tiny O-1 Bird Dog. Strange saw what was going on, saw the PAVN massing for attack.

"Hey, you got to get out of there!" he called.

By then we were moving back toward the berm as rapidly as possible up that very steep slope. At the berm, I checked around—I had three wounded but still walking. Then my strikers said that a man was missing. I called Strange and asked him to fly over the grassy area below us and see if anybody was there.

Half a minute later he was back on the air: "You've got one down in the tall grass."

It was the point man. I wouldn't leave him, dead or alive. I took three men and we charged downhill—catching the enemy by surprise—and fortunately we didn't have far to go. He was hit in the head, barely alive. Then it was Rice Krispies time, all snap, crackle, and pop as the PAVN opened up with dozens of rifles. My strikers fired back.

I reached down, picked the wounded striker up, put him across my shoulders in a fireman's carry, and grabbed his weapon. Just like in the movies. Then I discovered that this is a lot effing harder in real life. We moved as fast as we could back up the hill, steel-jacketed hornets buzzing and whining all around us, and somehow got back behind the berm unscathed.

Later, when I had time to think about it, I realized that as the only infantry officer on Kate, I probably should have sent a couple of men to get the wounded man. Covered them with fire instead of going myself. What if I'd been killed? That would have imperiled everyone else on Kate. In truth, however, that's not in my nature. I would never ask my men to do something that I hadn't done or wouldn't do. I lived by that, then and now.

It's wonderful that God takes care of fools and drunks. Usually.

A couple of strikers took the wounded man, and I paused ten seconds to think. Strange had said that we had to get out of there because they were closing in on us; as we were moving back uphill, he had added, *They're going to cut you off at the gap.*

That meant that they were moving southward, using the jungle to mask their progress, and were planning to take us off as we came toward the narrow passageway leading into the firebase. The one and only thing to do was beat them to it—hi-diddle-diddle, right up the middle, the most direct route: straight across that grassy saddle—and hope to hell that we got there first. We took off, moving as fast as we could, two guys carrying the head-shot man, and others helping our ambulatory wounded, and we ran like the devil was on our heels.

Safely back at Kate, I learned that the striker I rescued, the one with the head wound, had died.

There is a Reaper, whose name is Death,
And, with his sickle keen,
He reaps the bearded grain at a breath,
And the flowers that grow between.

"Shall I have naught that is fair?" saith he;
"Have naught but the bearded grain?
Though the breath of these flowers is sweet to me,
I will give them all back again."

—Henry Wadsworth Longfellow, "The Reaper and the Flowers"

SEVEN

Everyone on Kate heard the shooting; there were plenty of questions about what was going on. I told them that I wasn't completely certain, but apparently the new neighbors were a sizable PAVN unit. They'll probably want to visit, I added, so we should prepare a suitable welcome.

Around 1000 hours, almost before my strikers were back in their foxholes, PAVN 82 mm mortars, B-40 rockets, recoilless rifles, machine guns, and small arms slammed Kate with a typhoon of steel and fire. Most of this, but not all, came from those easterly heights. The 105 mm howitzer guarding our northern and most vulnerable quarter was knocked out, its tires flattened so that it couldn't be aimed. Nevertheless, its crew disregarded the mortars and rocks to remain at their gun. They manhandled it around to where they could fire at the ridge, and started shooting.

The previously damaged 155 mm howitzer was hit again.

The only bright spot was that Air Force Major George Lattin, a forward air controller based in Gia Nghia, was now circling high overhead in his Bird Dog to serve as our primary aircraft traffic manager. He was our lifeline, the only thing that could save everyone on Kate from certain death. Lattin, call sign "Walt 20," was on his way to becoming a legend in his own time—but, like me, this was the first engagement of his first day of combat in Vietnam.

Outnumbered and outgunned, effectively surrounded by a vastly superior PAVN force later estimated at between 4,000 and 6,000, we would have been overrun that very day had not Lattin vectored fast-mover help to our tiny outpost. First in were the burly but surprisingly agile F-4 Phantoms from the 559th Tactical Fighter Squadron, call sign "Boxers," out of Cam Ranh Bay. Lattin then brought us swift and deadly F-100 Super Sabres from the 35th Tactical Fighter Wing, call sign "Blades."

We heard them coming before we saw them, but the Phantoms' banshee shriek bounced off so many hills that it was impossible to gauge the direction of their approach. I stood in the open with John Kerr and Kenn Hopkins, watching them swoop in, one or two at a time, barely off the jungle treetops, pale curlicues of water vapor dancing off their wingtip vortices, great metallic darts traveling at impossible speeds, the unearthly howl of their engines battering our ears, the wild wake of their passage bending and snapping the foliage—and then the elongated silver teardrops of napalm canisters tumbling end over end into the ravine below us. At once the fighter's nose rose and his afterburner boomed to life, shooting him skyward and battering us with earsplitting sound.

The tumbling napalm canisters exploded, spilling liquid fire to boil across the dark green jungle. The heat warmed our exposed skin and the wind wafted the sharp, metallic taste of charred petroleum to bite deep in our throats.

When the Phantoms were done, the Super Sabres appeared, low and fast, flitting seemingly almost close enough to touch, sweeping across the ridge to our east. Black tail-finned bombs seemed to break loose of their own volition, slanting downward. The blasts, perhaps a rifle shot distant, hurled a concussion wave that seemed to bend the air before staggering us with invisible force.

It was great theater, truly an unforgettable performance.

After a few bomb runs, however, it seemed like someone higher in the Air Force food chain needed help with their paperwork. "Bill and I were on the east slope of the firebase," recalls Kerr. "I stood right next to him while he was on his little handheld radio talking to these fast-moving jets that were dropping 750-pound bombs up and down this ridgeline—and the whole side of this hillside just blew up.

"Then the [pilots of the] jets demanded that Bill give them a body count. 'We can't stay on station without a body count,' they said.

"Bill said, 'This is extremely steep terrain going down into this gully, triple-canopy jungle—we're not going to go down and count noses.'"

Undaunted, the Air Force pilot insisted on his body count. The Pentagon needed numbers to keep score in what they viewed as a war of attrition. Secretary of Defense Robert McNamara held an almost religious view of systems analysis, which demanded that every action be quantified; numbers from the battlefield convinced him that if we killed enough of their troops, the North Vietnamese would back off and end the war. There was, therefore, constant pressure from the top to get bomb damage assessments after every air strike. Decades later I would learn from one of the FACs who flew in support of Kate that while they were responsible for filing a BDA after every strike, they were rarely, if ever, able to get anything approaching a reliable body count. So they usually omitted it completely. If forced, they merely made something up.

"Bill kept saying, 'I can't give you a body count. We're not going down there to count bodies—it's too dangerous,'" adds Kerr.

Meanwhile, the enemy was still shooting at us.

Then and now, I presumed that it wasn't actually the pilots who needed the body count. Evidently their higher-ups wanted a number that would justify so many aircraft remaining on station to help a very small firebase. Despite my inability to furnish the Air Force with quantitative evidence of effectiveness by inventing a number of dead bodies, Lattin, flying low and slow with a bird's-eye view of the situation, interceded for us. He elevated our air support priority to first among all US forces in Vietnam. After half an hour or so, the Boxers and Blades were out of ordnance and their tanks were running dry. After a final strafing pass, they climbed away and disappeared into the midday sky.

It was about 1100 hours; I called for medevac choppers to take out our wounded. This proved to be a dangerous procedure, not only for the pilots and crew who flew through fire to land on Kate, but also for the man who was obliged to stand in the open while directing the chopper to a safe landing on our small, crowded hilltop.

That was me. As the medevac slowly hovered in, both pilots had their eyes riveted on me. Seconds from touchdown, from the corner of my eye I saw a B-40 rocket's fiery launch from the hillside to our east. I was poised to dive behind something—but the pilots didn't see the rocket. Frantically milling my arms, I waved them off, but the bird kept coming. In my mind's eye I saw rocket and helicopter arriving simultaneously. Finally, the pilot realized what was happening, and started to peel off.

The rocket landed with a fiery explosion.

Something red-hot slammed into my upper left arm, staggering me.

Jagged holes appeared in the medevac Huey's underside as it shuddered upward. It dipped from sight into the valley below, and then climbed back into the safety of the clouds.

My arm was on fire—the worst pain I'd ever felt. Dark blood soaked my fatigue jacket as I ran to Kate's makeshift aid station. Doc cleaned the entrance and exit wounds—it seemed that the shrapnel went all the way through. He wrapped my arm in a big bandage, what we had dubbed an elephant Kotex. The red-hot steel and prompt disinfectant ensured that there would be no infection.

Doc told me that I was very lucky.

Then he said another medevac chopper was inbound and asked if I wanted to get on it. Until then, I hadn't even thought about leaving. I shook my head. I wasn't going anywhere.

Meanwhile Huey and Cobra gunships had peppered the jungle around Kate's flanks with their 7.62 mm miniguns and rockets. Then a second Dustoff chopper came to take our wounded out, including a few strikers, gunner Rudy Childs, and the blond gunner who thought that he'd lost his legs. I don't know if he still believed that, but he had to be carried to the aircraft. After everyone else was loaded, Mike Smith, his head wrapped in a bloody field dressing, climbed on the chopper.

Watching him go, Kerr was of two minds—he empathized with Smith for what appeared to be a serious wound, but also struggled against feelings of apprehension and anxiety. "I had only been in Vietnam for about two months," he says. "I was still green—and now all of a sudden I'm an artillery firebase commander? I was scared—I didn't have much experience on the guns. I'd been in the FDC, mostly handling the radio and fire direction for the battery. I knew how to do that, but with Smith gone, that left just me and Albracht, and I didn't know if I could handle it."

Spoiler alert: John Kerr handled everything that came his way over the next few days, and he did so about as well as anyone could ask of any man, and always with dignity, good humor, and courage. He was a rock.

BY early afternoon, Lattin's little Bird Dog needed more smoke rockets and puppy chow; he headed back to base. His departure was celebrated almost immediately with a hard rain of yet more mortars and rockets. From the shelter of my bunker, I tried to establish radio contact with Lattin's temporary replacement. I heard a new voice and a new call sign on the FAC frequency. An FAC, call sign "Mike 82," was attempting to contact call sign "Chicken Hawk." The FAC called again and again, but there was no answer. My call sign was "Chicken *Wolf*," and after a few minutes, it came to me that it was odd, not to mention confusing, that two similar call signs were being used in the same area of operation.

The incoming lessened slightly, which is to say that the interval between explosions lengthened. I waited for Mike 82 to contact Chicken Hawk, but he couldn't seem to raise him. Slowly it dawned on my befuddled mind that the FAC might be trying to contact *me*. So I called and asked if he was trying to contact Chicken *Wolf*.

"Sorry, I thought your call sign was 'Chicken *Hawk*,'" replied Mike 82.

Like today's best computer passwords, Army call signs of that era were always two words, compiled from lists of nouns and adjectives that when selected at random and put together produced a nonsense phrase, something that would be difficult for anyone to guess. I've heard such phrases as "Splashy Tiger," "Splendid Anvil," "Angry Elbow," and "Juicy Marble." "Chicken Wolf" didn't make sense, but that was the Army's intent.

But none of that interested me just then.

"You can call me Chicken Hawk, Chicken Wolf, or Chicken Shit," I growled into my microphone. "Just get some air support in here *now*!"

Despite our signal operating instructions, from that moment, my call sign became "Chicken Hawk." After a while I dropped the "Chicken"; I was known as Hawk for the rest of my Army career; to this day, I still answer to that.

Mike 82 was Air Force First Lieutenant Will Platt, 25, a Michigander attached to Company D, Fifth Special Forces, flying his Bird Dog, on this occasion, out of Gia Nghia. He was one of six forward air controllers assigned to the Mike Force. Working almost nonstop, these aviators were now focused on supporting the six firebases around Bu Prang and Duc Lap. Without direct supervision, Platt managed himself, relying on intelligence from Special Forces camps and Army airfields to learn where he was most needed. And on that day, he knew exactly what was going down around Kate. "The men on Kate had every asset in the Air Force pulling for them," recalls Platt.

From the duration and intensity of enemy shelling just then, I began to suspect that our PAVN pals' activities schedule included a ground attack. The bombing, I hoped, would delay that, but for how long I couldn't predict. I judged our defensive posture difficult, but not impossible. On three sides, our foxholes, most getting a little deeper by the hour, were about fifty meters above the surrounding treetops, and the slope below I estimated as very difficult to climb while remaining erect; it might take both hands and feet to reach the summit. To the east, however, the slope was less extreme and the jungle closer. I had only about 120 able-bodied strikers—too few, I thought, to defend the perimeter against a determined attack. I sent a coded message to Camp Bu Prang, asking for reinforcements and resupply of ammunition and water. My requests were passed to B-23 headquarters, and I was promised another CIDG company of 120 men from A-234 at An Lac.

LATE that afternoon, SP4 Warren Geromin left the safety of the FDC bunker to refuel the generators. "All of a sudden the NVA decided to try and knock out the 155," he recalls. "I heard some whooshing sounds and about ten

RPG rounds landed in and around the gun bunker. One of the gun crew said, 'Shit, let's get them before they get us.'"

McFarlane, Hopkins, Koon, Tiranti, and some of the other gunners had decided that they would no longer put up with being targets. "We said, 'This is a bunch of BS—we've got to get going,'" Hopkins recalls. "*My* gun got hit in the tube, so there's no way that we're going to fire that thing. The other gun had been hit, but not in its tube. So we went over to the other gun, set it up to fire, loaded it with a regular H-E shell, and fused it to explode on contact."

They aimed the piece by peering up the barrel from the open breech, a procedure known as bore sighting. Fearing that their gun might blow up when fired, the gunners improvised a twelve-foot lanyard and attached it to the firing lever. Then they crouched behind the parapet's sandbag wall. "So we pulled the lanyard, the gun fired—and we got a secondary off that, *BOOM*, *BOOM*, a huge explosion, twice or three times the flash of a regular 155 going off," Hopkins says, still proud and surprised. "We picked a spot randomly and just happened to hit an ammo dump. Talk about luck being on our side!"

Not *all* the luck. "I heard the gun being loaded and turned," adds Geromin. "They fired one round that exploded, but then there were a whole bunch of incoming RPG rounds that went towards the gun." The RPGs further damaged but did not knock that 155 out. With a little ingenuity and a crew willing to brave plunging fire, the gun could still be fired at the source of most of Kate's incoming—the ridge across the ravine to our east. As was virtually every M-114 howitzer in the Army inventory, that gun was built by my neighbors and friends at the Rock Island Arsenal. I come from a tough town, a place where people build the best for the best.

A little later, a CH-47 Chinook swooped in to drop sling-load gear, then flew away. It took Sergeant Houghtaling's gung-ho gun crew only about ten minutes to wrap their disabled 105 mm howitzer for pickup. The Chinook returned, hovering low over the gun pit. Inside, on his belly and looking through a small window in the floor, the flight engineer called out directions to his pilots over a headset. When the big bird was close enough, an artilleryman standing on the gun snapped the fifty-pound hook through the thick, tempered aluminum loop under the Chinook, then jumped down. Slowly, the chopper rose, taking slack out of the heavy slings until they were taut. Then he ascended almost vertically before climbing away with the damaged gun.

Just before dark, the Chinook was back with a new 105 mm howitzer dangling from its belly. In a remarkably short time it was in the empty gun pit. The hook was removed, the sling gear pulled off the gun, and as the Chinook vanished into the sky, the gun crew went to work, relaying their piece and then aligning its sights.

Hopkins and PFC Michael R. Norton, from Eskdale, West Virginia, a short and stocky 21-year-old gunner on the 105 crew, each carried a bloop gun, the M79 grenade launcher, as their sidearm. "We got together to look at the higher ridge facing the side of our LZ," Hopkins recalls. "[Norton] saw movement, so both of us fired our M79s. All movement stopped after the rounds hit. A few seconds later, Norton fired again, and as the projectile sailed through the air, we both saw an NVA low-crawling. A second later, the M79 round struck the guy and we both jumped up yelling, 'Got you.'

"We went down to Norton's gun to tell his crew what happened and to receive congratulations," Hopkins continues. "As I was coming back up to the top [of the hill] I heard a whooshing sound overhead. I looked up and saw a red object going over my head. I remember watching war movies and what you were supposed to do when being fired at, so I started running up the hill, zigzagging all the way. I thought to myself, *Man you probably look silly running like this*. But it did not matter; I made it up to some of my guys and the protection of some sandbags. They told me it looked like the movies with me running up the hill."

By this time, Bu Prang Camp was itself under intermittent mortar and recoilless rifle fire. The skies between Bu Prang and Kate were full of all sorts of flying machines, including Captain Strange's Bird Dog. He was coordinating all the Army aviation around Bu Prang, including Kate.

A little after the Chinook departed, a line of five UH-1D Hueys—the flying delivery trucks known as slicks and armed only with door-mounted machine guns—approached low and fast from the west. They were escorted by two Huey gunships; all seven aircraft were from the 48th AHC out of

BMT. In the right-hand seat of the leading gunship was Chief Warrant Officer Ben Gay, age 20, of Richmond, Virginia, serving as aircraft commander and leader of this two-ship fire team.

Across the valley to the southeast, our PAVN neighbors had been planning a big reception in our honor. When the party committee saw that we had invited more friends to share the fun, they were furious. As the first slicks approached, the neighbors began shooting at them with 12.7 mm heavy machine guns, small arms, and RPGs. My strikers were in their fighting positions shooting back, but it didn't seem to have much effect. I told Geromin, the generator man, as well as Hopkins and Koon and whoever else I could lay hands on, to find spots and fire at the enemy positions. The 105 crew cranked their gun around to the east and opened up in direct-fire mode.

"There was still green jungle out there then, so I was shooting into the trees where I saw puffs of smoke, hoping that it was a bigger gun because I couldn't see small-arms fire in there," recalls Geromin. "I hoped that I was shooting at something, but basically I was just shooting into the jungle."

Invoking the law of unintended consequences, the handful of men firing rifles at the enemy drew the attention of a PAVN 75 mm recoilless rifle crew. Not the sort of weapon that would be fired at a fast-moving aircraft. Several rounds hit a few feet in front of the sandbagged wall that Geromin was using for cover while he fired. "If it had been one degree higher, we wouldn't be here, because the wall couldn't have taken it," says Geromin. "After that, I thought, *They're trying to kill me*, so I got really mad and ran off about seven magazines on full automatic."

Even so, the ground fire was too fierce for the slicks. The two gunships, one firing rockets and the other both rockets and miniguns, made pass after pass, shooting at those automatic weapons and getting shot at in return. For ten minutes it was the Wild West.

Then came a brief lull; the incoming seemed to slacken a bit, and the slicks returned for another landing attempt.

Not so fast. As they descended into range, the enemy opened up with everything it had. Again the slicks were turned away. Gay and his wingman came down for another run, laying curtains of 7.62 fire and high-explosive rockets on that ridge and the hillside below it. While the PAVN gunners were thus occupied, the slicks slid back in for a third pass. This time they made it in; by the time the last Huey dropped its strikers, the rain of rockets and mortars was almost continuous.

That was the end of my reinforcements. I would have to make do with just forty.

KENN Hopkins is a brave man and, from what I saw on Kate, a true warrior. But he was not your typical young cannon cocker. Mike Smith, who had been among the officers in the Fort Sill unit that trained Hopkins, knew him much better. "At that time, he dressed like guys dressed when they wanted to sort of assert that they didn't like the Army—they'd wear these little bracelets and necklaces and things that they knew would aggravate [higher-ranking] people, sort of like aggravating your dad, I guess. But he was basically a good soldier . . . just kind of a hippy-dippy guy."

While Hopkins was in training at Fort Sill, he'd met a Vietnam veteran who warned him about taking refuge in his hooch during a ground attack. "I was pulling guard duty, and there was a sergeant there . . . and he was telling us war stories," Hopkins recalls. "The sergeant said, 'If you get hit, and you stay inside your hooch, you're dead. *You never want to stay inside your hooch.* You cannot see what is coming at you and it ensures you will be overrun. They'll just come in, they'll walk right over you, throw a satchel charge inside, and you're dead.' "

It was good advice, but Hopkins, I think, misunderstood what the sergeant meant. He meant that during a *ground* attack, those defending a firebase or other fixed position should actively participate in its defense, not hide in a hole. When there was no ground attack, however, but bombs, mortars, rockets, or other artillery fire was landing on the position, the only sane reaction was to take cover, wait for the incoming fire to stop—and *then* get out of your shelter and into position to help repel a ground attack.

Before he came to Kate, Hopkins served several weeks on a firebase near Ben Het that took a steady pounding from PAVN rockets and mortars. This base, however, was dug in exceptionally well, with deep bunkers.

Moreover, its howitzers were emplaced to fire only within a 180-degree arc, instead of the usual 360. Because of this, each gun was protected by a thick, high parapet with dense overhead cover that would stop even a direct hit.

"I felt safe at Ben Het because we had the gun protected, and we'd actually sit outside and watch the incoming," Hopkins recalls. "I remember, at Ben Het, we're sitting in front of the hooch door. We had a little blast wall, and we'd just sit out there smoking and watching the incoming and OMIGOD! One hit real close—probably about 100 meters away! Oh, jeez, there's a piece of shrapnel—I've got to get down, down, down. I couldn't go fast enough, damn, and they hit me.

"Stupid. Don't go out there and watch the incoming. It hit me on the belt buckle, and bounced off . . . a piece of spent shrapnel about so big, [like] a big marble."

He wasn't hurt. And Hopkins's fear of incoming artillery—an entirely rational fear—lessened a bit.

On Kate, Hopkins had dug a sleeping shelter, or hooch, about waist-deep. "We had pierced-steel planking over us, with four sandbag layers," he recalls. The roof was about three feet above the surface. He shared this space with another cannoneer.

Because of his previous experiences, however, Hopkins feared incoming artillery fire less than the possibility of being trapped in his hooch during a ground attack. "Because if a piece of artillery hit at the door, and we were on the ground, no harm, no foul; concussion, maybe, shrapnel, no harm. I wasn't afraid of that, and I wasn't even thinking of small arms because they kept hitting us with artillery. I don't think we ever, except for ground attacks, got small-arms fire. It was mostly artillery pelting us."

Then there was the time that he zigzagged up the hill to avoid an incoming B-40 rocket, believing it was aimed at him. I think it unlikely that Hopkins or any other individual was the target of those rockets. The B-40 could carry one of several different types of warheads and was usually fired at vehicles, bunkers, troop concentrations, crew-served weapons, and occasionally low-flying aircraft. I think this episode served, on some level of consciousness, Hopkins's need to feel invulnerable to artillery fire. And I think *that* need was fueled by the fear of taking refuge underground, in a place where he could not escape an enemy grenade or satchel charge, a place where he feared he would be defenseless and would die.

And so, instead of taking cover behind or under layers of protective sandbags, during the worst of the shelling, when PAVN mortars, rockets, recoilless rifles, and even heavy artillery were pounding Kate, Hopkins remained aboveground. Time after time, with explosions and flying steel all around him, he went prone next to a sandbagged bunker or a steel CONEX container, or crouched behind a blast wall. It is nothing less than a miracle that he was not killed. When we came under ground attack, Hopkins, usually joined by Koon, Tiranti, and sometimes a few others, roamed the perimeter, supporting the strikers by sharing their fighting holes and shooting at the enemy with their rifles or grenade launchers. Koon often had their platoon's M60 machine gun, and he obviously knew how to use it.

When things were relatively quiet, Hopkins sometimes dropped in on his neighbors. "I remember going around all the time, giving people information, telling them what's going on. The FDC crew's job was to stay inside, and our job, in my mind, was to stay outside, see what's going on, and keep the FDC informed, which I did. Bob Johnson told me that he always appreciated me coming around and telling them what was going on outside."

Johnson concurs. "One day during the siege he came into the FDC bunker," he recalls. This in itself was very unusual: "I don't remember [anyone] . . . from the guns *ever* coming into the FDC bunker before," Johnson adds. "He was very friendly, very talkative, and he was describing what was happening aboveground, all around the firebase and the perimeter. For those of us hunkered down in the bunker, it was fascinating to hear all this firsthand information. He spoke very calmly, as if he were the anchor on the nightly news relating events from the war zone. I was thinking, *This is a very impressive individual*, because of how collected he is [while] relating all of this rather dispassionately, with all the hell that was going on. We were very grateful to be brought up-to-date on the action aboveground."

In fact, Hopkins's visit caused Johnson, by then in his twelfth month in Vietnam and the veteran of many firebases, to reevaluate his personal assessment of Kate's situation. Until then, he had not realized the significance and immediacy of the enemy threat. Following Hopkins's recitation of the disposition of PAVN troops surrounding Kate, he began to appreciate the great danger that he and everyone else on Kate faced.

"The only time I ever got any sleep," Hopkins continues, "about three hours, was when Spooky was above. Other than that, it's rattling. When we're getting hit, oh, make sure you're not over in the area that's getting pummeled right now. I'd be up *here*; if we were getting hit *there*, I would be someplace else. I never went inside my hooch until the very last day. I couldn't keep myself inside a hooch; it just freaked me out. I was staying away, like I said; I wasn't necessarily afraid of the incoming killing me—concussion maybe—and as long as we're getting hit on *that* side of my house, I would be over here on *this* side of my house. And as soon as the first round hit, I was up and running just so I wouldn't be in that impact area."

Hopkins's odd behavior did not go unnoticed by the artillery chain of command: "One of the gun chiefs came to me and said that . . . a member of his gun crew . . . was irrational, delirious, out of control, and needed to be airlifted out," recalls Kerr. "I suspect that individual was Hopkins. I'm pretty sure it was, but don't know it for a fact. I said no. I didn't want a mass exodus of people going out by helicopter; at that point in time we didn't know but that we were being hit by a half dozen snipers. We didn't know we were up against 4,000 PAVN troops. So I said no."

FROM my perspective as ground force commander, the best thing about getting the 105 mm howitzer replaced was that it was the only weapon that could fire something called a "beehive" round, which was devastatingly effective when used in a direct-fire, anti-personnel role. Beehive rounds didn't exist for the bigger-caliber guns on Kate.

Formally called the M546 anti-personnel tracer shell, the beehive round was fired directly at enemy troops, with the gun's muzzle close to parallel to the ground. Before firing, a fuse was set to explode at a given distance from the gun, from a hundred meters to a few miles; the warhead would explode into a cone-shaped cloud of 8,000 inch-long finned steel flechettes. Upon impact, the fins break off, often causing a second wound. Just one flechette was capable of causing a lethal wound.

With hundreds of enemy troops attacking us, no weapon could have been more welcome. And needed. While my reinforcements were still sorting themselves out, digging new holes or helping enlarge existing ones, up our very steep southeastern slope—an incline so radical that, like Barham before me, I had decided it was too difficult a slope to worry about—up that lightly defended slope came a PAVN assault force.

As it happened, this wasn't the big neighborhood block party that I'd been expecting. It was merely the welcome wagon, a platoon or so, with rifles and machine guns. This opening move lasted perhaps ten minutes, and then they withdrew. Now they knew where our M60 machine guns were sited, at least on that side. Like the nosy neighbors in every community, they'd be back. As soon as it was dark, I had my strikers relocate their M60s on the side that was attacked.

Then I asked Kerr to take my radio and a pair of battery-powered strobe lights and climb down into the generator pit, about four feet deep. On the pit floor, he put one strobe at either end on a north–south axis and pointed them at the sky before turning them on. The pit was deep enough that this strobing light could be seen only from almost directly overhead. This established our position to friendly aircraft. He could then direct fire as needed, using the lights as a reference point.

After sunset, the wind died. A cloak of darkest cobalt settled over our battered hilltop. Soon it was quiet enough to hear the faint clank of metal meeting earth—the sound of men digging in the surrounding ravines. For an instant, my blood ran cold.

On guard near the north end, Nelson Koon and PFC Dennis Nadine, a powder man, "heard the enemy cutting down trees in the darkness, apparently to reinforce their positions," Koon recalls. "It was eerie."

The digging noises continued until the faint drone of twin Wright Cyclone engines was heard from high above. Shadow 51, an AC-119G gunship, descended from the clouds and began a slow, counterclockwise orbit; within minutes, from somewhere to our north, green tracers spouted from a PAVN 12.7 mm, searching the sky for Shadow. Shadow 51 responded with a fountain of *red* tracers, painting the hillside where the greenies had issued. The nightly fireworks show was on.

"And when he gets to heaven,
To Saint Peter he will tell;
One more Marine reporting sir,
I've served my time in hell."

—Marine grave inscription on Guadalcanal, 1942

EIGHT

By the time US combat troops were committed to Vietnam in 1965, the Viet Cong had perfected a battlefield tactic that allowed them, at a time of their choosing, to overcome ARVN's overall superiority in numbers and firepower, and thereby to inflict many casualties. The grift went like this: A battalion-size force—about 500 men—would infiltrate an area over a few days, quietly dig in, and then lay siege to some small ARVN or US Special Forces post. First they'd bombard it with rockets, recoilless rifles, and mortars, and then they'd maneuver a small force close enough to trade small-arms fire with the outpost, with the objective of forcing the defenders to expend their ammunition. Usually, the VC were capable of capturing this outpost at any time—but that wasn't the game. Instead, they punished it, killing as many of its defenders as possible, and meanwhile shooting at low-flying aircraft and helicopters that were bringing in supplies and reinforcements, or evacuating the wounded.

The VC objective was to draw a relief column. When the situation at the besieged camp reached the crisis point, the ARVN usually dispatched a modest force, perhaps a company or two, by road. This relief column would be ambushed by a second and larger Viet Cong force. If a second relief column was dispatched, then it too would be ambushed. Thus ARVN commanders were lured into committing their forces piecemeal, allowing the enemy to kill and wound far more soldiers than if they had attacked a larger force. That accomplished, the enemy either melted back into the jungles, swamps, or mountains, or they joined with previously positioned reinforcements to mount an attack on the now diminished parent unit of the relief force. In this fashion, from time to time they were able to take over provincial capital cities, hold them long enough to inflict still more ARVN casualties, then slip away to fight another day. The strategy was to wear down as many ARVN units as possible while fostering the notion that eventually the ARVN would fold. When the PAVN entered the picture, they took over this game.

By 1965, even the dimmest ARVN commander had to know this con well enough to beat it—but no. They continued to piecemeal their forces into meat-grinder ambushes. Some ARVN commanders refused to send any relief force at all, because they feared inviting an attack on their own location.

Thus it was that almost exactly four years before I arrived on Kate, in October 1965, a regiment-size PAVN force besieged the Plei Me Special Forces camp forty kilometers south of Pleiku. This triangular-shaped jungle fort was defended by an "A" Team and a CIDG battalion. PAVN pounded the camp with mortars and rockets, ringed the hills around it with 12.7 mm anti-aircraft guns, and, after shooting down two Air Force attack planes and an Army Huey, effectively shut down the airspace. An elite Delta Force team under Major (later Colonel) Charles Beckwith made their way into the camp and for a time held off the attackers, though at the cost of many American and Montagnard lives. When the situation again grew dire, the ARVN II Corps commander, Major General Vinh Loc—a cousin of Bỏ Đại, Vietnam's effete emperor-in-exile—ordered a reinforced company to take the road south from his headquarters in Pleiku and rescue or reinforce Plei Me.

This was, of course, exactly what the PAVN commander wanted and expected. Major General Harry Kinnard, West Point Class of 1939, commanded the First Air Cavalry Division at An Khe, about forty miles east of

Pleiku. Kinnard held no royal pedigree—although he had been knighted by Queen Wilhelmina of the Netherlands—but in 1944 he'd jumped into Normandy in command of an airborne infantry battalion. Before deploying to Vietnam, Kinnard had read ARVN advisers' after-action reports and boned up on Viet Cong tactics. To head off Vinh Loc's stupidity, he flew to Nha Trang to ask Lieutenant General Stanley "Swede" Larson, commander of Task Force Alpha (later renamed I Field Force Vietnam), to intercede with Vinh Loc. Vinh Loc apparently understood that PAVN was running a scam and that he was the pigeon—but nevertheless feared that Pleiku would be imperiled if he risked the two battalions that might be required to effectively break the siege of Plei Me. So Kinnard offered to move two battalions of his cavalrymen to Pleiku to guarantee that city's safety. He also offered the ARVN relief convoy artillery and air support from First Cav assets, which included four artillery battalions and hundreds of helicopters.[3]

At Kinnard's urging, Vinh Loc dispatched a heavily armored ARVN convoy, including tanks, personnel carriers, field artillery, and two infantry battalions, to rescue and evacuate Plei Me. These troops fought their way to Plei Me and overcame a first ambush twenty miles south of Pleiku and a second, much larger one only four miles from Plei Me. Supported by the Air Cav's aerial rocket artillery, the rescue force turned the tables on PAVN by beating back both ambushes with minimal casualties.

I mention this here because, four years later—just before I went to Kate—something much like what had been used to relieve Plei Me had been ginned up in anticipation of a PAVN attack on Bu Prang: Major General Donn R. Pepke, commanding the US Fourth Infantry Division based at Pleiku, created Task Force Fighter, a battalion-size force composed of an air cavalry troop, a ground cavalry troop, and an infantry company, along with command and control elements and logistical support. He positioned Fighter at BMT's larger airfield. "Task Force Fighter was to serve as the command and control element of two [Fourth Division] infantry battalions

---

3 My coauthor, then an Army combat correspondent in the First Air Cav's Public Information Office, was involved in the preparation of a "backgrounder" press briefing that described these negotiations.

that would deploy, if required, to BMT to replace two battalions from the ARVN 23rd Infantry Division," wrote Pepke in his after-action report. These two ARVN battalions, based at BMT, were committed to reinforce or relieve Bu Prang, as the situation required.

All units in Ban Me Thuot's TAOR, including Bu Prang, were under control of the 23rd ARVN; a division forward command post was established at Gia Nghia.

Unlike the relief of Plei Me four years earlier, however, this deployment would be dictated not by tactical necessity but by US domestic politics. To demonstrate that Nixon's "Vietnamization" strategy was on track, the 23rd, regarded as second only to ARVN's First Airborne Division in combat capabilities, would be handed a tailor-made showcase to display its prowess.

At the time, I was aware that Bu Prang and its supporting firebases were under the 23rd ARVN's operational control. But no one on Kate knew that Task Force Fighter had been created to eliminate any plausible excuses for the 23rd not taking the field against PAVN. Personally, I expected that if the Americans and their CIDG infantry on Kate needed help holding it, I would get not only air support but infantry reinforcements from the 23rd ARVN or the US 4th Infantry Division.

If your officer's dead and the sergeants look white,
Remember it's ruin to run from a fight;
So take open order, lie down, and sit tight,
And wait for supports like a soldier.

—Rudyard Kipling, "The Young British Soldier"

NINE

One of the many things that aviators of all US military services share is that, in a cockpit, the command pilot, sometimes called the aircraft commander, is the one with the most experience and demonstrated aptitude for the job, but he is not necessarily the ranking individual.

One of the things that makes Army aviation unique is that, starting with the Vietnam era, most of its pilots are warrant officers.

During World War II, before the Army Air Corps broke off to become the Air Force, a separate service with its own uniforms, force structure, and chain of command, almost all Army combat pilots were commissioned officers. After the separation into two services, the Air Force continued that custom. To this day, virtually every Air Force pilot is a commissioned officer. Likewise, except for a handful of chief warrant officers, all US Navy aviators are commissioned. During the Vietnam era, the Marine Corps employed so-called naval aviation pilots—enlisted men in the highest enlisted grade of sergeant major flying their H-34 helicopters and O-1E Bird Dogs.

After the creation of the Air Force, fleets of bombers, transport aircraft, attack planes, and fighters were shifted from the Army to the Air Force. The

Army retained a relatively small number of aircraft for battlefield observation, liaison, command and control, and medical evacuation. Until the late fifties, nearly all were flown by commissioned officers. Congress limits the size of each service and fixes a ratio between its officer corps and its total manpower; during the early sixties, when the introduction of helicopters brought explosive growth to Army aviation, the decision was made to open flight training to warrant officer candidates. While a junior warrant officer earns only a little less than a junior commissioned officer with a similar length of service, they are considered specialists, not commanders. They are not trained to lead large formations of troops, plan elaborate operations involving thousands of men, or manage complex logistical problems. They are trained to fly, fight, and survive. Thus it is also cheaper and faster to train a warrant officer pilot than to mint a new second lieutenant and then teach him to fly: a warrant officer candidate completes flight school in only four months, with most of that time devoted to developing his aviator's skill set. After graduation, most serve two years or less on active duty. This allowed the Army to put literally thousands of helicopter pilots into the air within a relatively short time without requiring congressional authority to fund an expansion of the officer corps.

The result was a flock of young, eager pilots, many still in their teens, flying a multitude of aircraft, but mostly helicopters, that supported the fighting in Vietnam. The Air Force and Navy put college graduates with a year or more of flying time in the cockpits of their multimillion-dollar jets. We had high school grads with four months of training and less than a hundred hours in the sky to jockey our helicopters, which went for $25,000 a copy, guns, radios, and paint job extra.

One of our Army pilots—a good one, but also very much a typical Army aviator—was Harold Benjamin Gay, a short, powerfully built Virginian. As a boy he was known as "Butch." As a young adult, he chose to go by his middle name. Ben Gay grew up in Norfolk, Virginia, and as his high school graduation approached, he signed up for delayed entry into the Army's flight school program. He entered basic training in October 1967 at Fort Polk, Louisiana, then reported to Fort Wolters, Texas, for flight school. "There were about 225 in my basic class," he recalls. "The first couple of weeks were very intense; our drill sergeants were constantly on us in an attempt to weed out people who couldn't perform under pressure."

Flight school began with four weeks of academics: basic military protocol, officer subjects, and such fundamentals as navigation, aircraft systems, flight theories, and tactics, students meanwhile absorbing aviation's special vocabulary. On March 1, 1968, Gay climbed into a Hughes TH-55 Osage, a tiny, two-place helicopter with a reciprocating gasoline engine; it was the first aircraft of any type that he had set foot in. "My concern was whether I was going to pass out, throw up, or both," he says.

With an instructor pilot at the controls, Gay took off from the main airfield and headed to a small outlying airstrip called a "stage" field. Minutes later, Ben witnessed a midair collision; both helicopters exploded. "I still remember the flaming fuel tank from one of [the helicopters] doing loops as it fell to the ground," says Gay. "My instructor pilot called the tower and said that they needed a medevac and two body bags. He kept on going, and there wasn't much expression or response from him, so my feeling was, *Maybe this happens all the time.*"

Welcome to Army aviation, Cadet Gay.

Like OCS, flight school was highly demanding on many levels. Even with a big dose of daily classroom instruction, Gay and his fellow aviation cadets were expected to solo with only ten to twelve hours of in-flight instruction. "If we couldn't solo—take off, fly three patterns, and land safely—we were out," he explains.

Gay pinned on aviator's wings and warrant officer's bars on October 21, 1968. Twelve days later he was in Vietnam, assigned to the First Aviation Brigade's 155th AHC in BMT. The unit's 24 troop-carrying "slick" Hueys and six Huey gunships flew in support of US, ARVN, and Allied infantry and artillery units in southern II Corps. "A typical mission was assignment to a particular commander for the day," Gay explains. "We might take him or his XO out for a recon of an area, or bring food, water, mail, or ammunition to a firebase, or take an infantry unit to the field, or carry troops to the rear area so that they could go on R&R or sick call—what we called 'ash and trash' missions, which was whatever they needed us to do," Gay explains.

[Before most Americans heated their homes with oil or gas, stoves or furnaces required periodical cleaning, which entailed removing coal or wood ash and carrying it outside for disposal. The colloquial phrase "ash and trash" refers to mundane but necessary housekeeping chores.]

"We flew every day," Gay went on. "Probably once a week we had either a small-scale or large-scale air assault, primarily South Vietnamese soldiers. Occasionally, we worked with the [US] Fourth Infantry Division."

Flying in the Central Highlands was challenging. The dry season brought almost talcum-fine dust that got into everything and caused severe visibility problems during landings. In the rainy season, that fine dust turned into the most icky-sticky red mud that most GIs would ever see. The region's saving grace was daytime temperatures in the nineties, compared with triple digits at sea-level elevations.

Nevertheless, nineteen-year-old Gay took to combat flying like a salmon to the sea. "We were up in the mountains. It was absolutely gorgeous and the scenery was breathtaking," he recalls. November in the highlands is cold at night and warm and pleasant during the day. "We built little wooden hooches and dug very large underground bunkers; our airfield was somewhat isolated, and we came under mortar or rocket attack maybe once or twice a week—not very intense, but if even round one lands, it's enough to get your attention."

Soon he was logging twenty-five to thirty hours a week in the air. In April 1969, Gay was transferred to the 48th AHC. He continued flying slicks; after a short time he qualified as an aircraft commander, and two months later, on the cusp of the summer rainy season, he was invited to join the unit's gunship platoon, known by their call sign, "Jokers." Flying a gunship is more difficult than piloting a slick, and gunship missions were of a very different and far more demanding character. For these reasons, joining the Joker platoon was by the platoon commander's invitation only.

Soon after Gay became Joker 73, the 48th traded in their UH-1B gunships for the new UH-1C. "The Charlie model was a lot faster; it had the [bigger] L-12 engine instead of the L-11 or L-9 like the Bravo model," Gay explains. The two airframes were much the same: the main differences were that the Charlie model had a redundant hydraulic system—if one system was hit by ground fire, the second would continue to operate—and its main rotor blades were about 50 percent wider than those on the Bravo. "This gave it a lot more maneuverability, and a lot more speed—but it also made it more difficult to get into the air," he recalls.

"Right about then is when I decided to extend," Gay adds. "I was 20 years old, single, flying a helicopter, I'm an aircraft commander, I'm in Vietnam, I had great friends; it was a very exciting time."

The job was not without hazard: By halfway through his first year in combat, Gay had already lost several friends. "Most of them died due to accidents, from flying in bad weather, or while flying at night—especially in the 155th," he recalls. "There were no navigational aids like back in the US. There was no one to call who could get you on radar and direct you in. We were purely on our own up in the mountains, and with poor maps—a bad combination that took a lot of lives. We also lost some to combat."

Gay was shot down twice. "Shot down, as in the aircraft was coming out of the sky because pieces and parts were coming off," he explains. The first time, flying a slick southeast of BMT, he autorotated into an open field and was extracted; his aircraft was recovered. The second was a far more harrowing experience: flying a gunship, he autorotated into dense jungle near the Duc Lap Special Forces Camp. He and his crew left their ship in a tree, and evaded the enemy to reach the camp. The aircraft was lost.

One of Gay's closest friends was Chief Warrant Officer Nolan Black, who before coming to the 48th had served with Gay in the 155th and before that was in the 101st Airborne Division. Slim, with a swimmer's shoulders but a head shorter than most of his brother aviators, Black was 27, older than most of his peers. Born into an impoverished Missouri farm family, he narrowly survived a childhood bout with polio. After World War II, his family moved to Rockford, Illinois, then a booming manufacturing hub. While in high school, Black joined the Civil Air Patrol and became enchanted with flight. Dreaming of becoming an Air Force pilot, he earned a private pilot's license, and came in second to another boy in a fruitless quest for a senatorial appointment to the Air Force Academy. During high school,

Black became a lifeguard and pool manager at a resort hotel. There he met 17-year-old Carol Marks; after high school, she enrolled in Rockford's Swedish American Hospital School of Nursing.

Student nurses then lived in dorms that were much like convents. They were not allowed to marry. The Air Force Academy's cadet corps was restricted to single men. In 1962, Carol and Nolan gave up their career dreams to marry each other. They moved to Beloit, Wisconsin, the following year so that Nolan could accept a job in a furniture store. Carol found work as a hospital nursing assistant, and Nolan discovered that his friendly, low-key personality was perfect for selling furniture. As their childhood dreams of nursing and flying faded, the couple slipped into a small-town life that revolved around work, church, community groups, and neighbors. They bought a small house and hoped to fill it with their children. Alas, after four years of marriage, Carol learned that she would never conceive. The couple began looking for a baby to adopt.

Their lives were interrupted by the war in Vietnam. Although he was married, and past the age when most men were drafted, Black was also childless and therefore vulnerable to the draft. In 1966, after learning that he would soon be called up, he enlisted in the Army. After basic training at Fort Leonard Wood, Missouri, he went to Fort Rucker, Alabama, for training as a helicopter crew chief. After graduation, with Carol in tow, he went to Fort Hood, Texas, for duty. Several months later, Nolan was accepted for flight training and the couple moved again, first to Fort Wolters and then back to Fort Rucker, where in June 1968 Black graduated as a helicopter pilot and warrant officer. On that same day, the post chaplain notified the couple that a young, unmarried expectant mother had decided to give her baby up for adoption.

A few months later, while at Fort Bragg, North Carolina, their quest for parenthood was realized by the adoption of Laura Kristina, their new daughter.

In January 1969, Black shipped out for Vietnam for duty with the 4th Battalion, 77th Artillery, in the 101st Airborne Division. Four months later, he was transferred to the 155th AHC, where he and Gay first became acquainted. Later, he followed Gay to the 48th.

"Blackie was a good man, a good pilot, and a real family guy," recalls Ben Gay. "When he first got into gunships, he flew with me a lot as copilot. When he took his helmet off, there was a picture of his wife and daughter in there."

Another 155th pilot was tall, slim, fair, movie-star handsome Les Davison, an Illinois farm boy. He was born into a family of fliers: "My dad flew off carriers [in World War II] and my uncle flew fighters in the China/Burma/India Theater. Another uncle became a pilot but just at the war's end." After graduating from high school in 1965, he went to college for two years before he realized that he was wasting his time. He was 20, the draft was conscripting almost all able-bodied men his age, and he realized that without a student deferment, he was going to Vietnam. "I didn't want to walk through the jungle," he says. "I thought that flying *over* the jungle would be a better idea, so I talked to the Air Force, Navy, and Army. The Air Force and Navy required a degree to fly." He graduated flight school "the day after Joe Namath won the Super Bowl" in January 1969. After more training at Fort Rucker, he left for Vietnam in March with around 200 hours of helicopter flight time.

His tour with the 155th began in March 1969 by flying slicks, as most new pilots did. By September, thanks to a couple of pilots getting wounded and sent home, he flew gunship copilot for only a month before becoming an aircraft commander. After a couple of months of flying the trail ship in a two-bird fire team, he became a team leader in the gunship platoon, call sign "Falcon 2." He was still a Warrant Officer One, the lowest grade. And at dusk on October 29, at what he supposed was the end of a long, hard, day of flying, Davison was at back at BMT, refueling his gunship for the fifth time that day—he had been in the air since dawn, landing only to refuel and rearm. "Our asses were dragging," he recalls. "The last thing I wanted to hear was my call sign on the radio."

The act followed the thought: His radio crackled to life, and minutes later Davison was back in the air, trailed by Falcon 9, with WO2 Jack Coonce on the stick, and headed for an aerial rendezvous with Dustoff 63, the aerial ambulance that I hoped would take out some of my wounded. Hoped, because while the Geneva Conventions specified that ambulances and their crews were noncombatants, PAVN gunners used the big red cross on a white background adorning each side of every Dustoff bird as an aiming point. Hoping to give Dustoff some breathing space, I requested a Spooky, but it would not be on station until 2230.

"Dustoff 63 was flown by WO2 Denny Harrell, a good pilot and a good friend," Davison says. Twilight was long gone by the time Davison, Coonce, and Harrell flew past Duc Lap. "There was a little horizon, but not much," Davison recalls. "It happened so gradually we didn't notice—and then it was just all gray outside and the rotating beacon [on top of each Huey] was flashing off the gray back into the cockpit."

Startled, Davison called to Coonce to move away. "Break left Falcon 9, we're in the soup," he radioed. "We're coming around to the right on instruments." He told his copilot, Bob Maddox, to turn off the beacon and watch the instruments with him. "I hadn't done this since flight school," he said, and told Dave Nachtigall, his crew chief, and door gunner Cal Serain to watch for ground reference. After a long, nervous minute or so, the flight broke out of the fog. "I never knew you could start sweating so quickly," he says.

After climbing above the clouds, Davison's Falcon 2 rejoined Falcon 9 and headed west. "Now we started to see patchy ground fog forming, and it was getting thicker as we flew on. I can't speak for the others, but I was certainly . . . on edge," Davison recalls.

Twenty minutes later, the Falcons and Dustoff were orbiting Kate. From my bunker I could hear them, but we couldn't see each other: Kate was shrouded in fog. I called the Dustoff pilot and told him that it had been fairly quiet since sundown—just a few mortars and some sporadic small arms, mainly from the west. A little earlier, our listening post on Ambush Hill had been hit, and our strikers were bringing in a badly wounded man. It would take a while to get him in; with that man we had five wounded for pickup.

By the time he was back with us, however, Davison's fuel was so low that he was almost ready to abort. Instead, Davison and Coonce put Dustoff between them, Dustoff blacked out, the Falcons lit up their beacons, and all three birds swooped down through the fog toward us. The Falcon gunships leveled off and Dustoff continued its descent.

"Denny hovered down Kate's [landing pad] light! The stuff those Dustoff guys did was unbelievable," Davison adds. "We listened as a Special Forces type talked the Huey in to the LZ.

"A few seconds after touchdown, we heard [the Special Forces man] scream into the radio, 'Incoming mortars! Get out, Dustoff!'

"Bob [Maddox] flipped our Master Arm switch to 'Hot' and over the intercom confirmed that we were ready to shoot," Davison says. But after a quick radio check, it seemed that no one on either of the gunships had seen a tube flash through the fog. Without targets to attack, they could only wait.

Fearing that the mortars would hit at any moment, Davison silently urged Denny to take off. Davison's radio blared: "Dustoff 63 coming out to the east!" Denny's usual mellow baritone had somehow been transformed into a squeaky soprano.

As Denny cleared Kate, three mortar rounds landed at the south end of the hilltop, orange flashes biting back the darkness for an instant.

Nelson Koon was just then standing near the wire at that end of our perimeter, unbuttoning his fly. But let him tell it: "I had to take a whiz real bad, so I stood up and three mortars landed maybe ten meters away in a perfect triangle formation. It was like the war had stopped—I was peeing and watching the mortars explode. I didn't get hit—and I'm thinking, *WOW, that's kind of cool.* Then the medic threw me on the ground, and I'm pissing all over myself, and I say, 'What the hell are you doing?'

"He said, 'Are you trying to get yourself killed?'

"I said, 'No, I'm trying to take a leak.' "

High above this earthy comedy, the aerial drama continued.

"Falcons are at 2,500 feet directly overhead, watching for you," Davison called.

"We're breaking out, 2, coming up bright flash," Denny replied.

"Contact," Davison came back. "Are you going to try again?"

"Don't have to. We got 'em."

"You picked up five in that time?" Davison was incredulous.

"Yep, those guys down there have got their sierra together. Let's go home."

As the shriek of three jet turbines faded to silence, I radioed my thanks to Denny and his crew. The mortars continued for a bit. Koon changed his pants.

By the time the Falcon gunships made it back to BMT, they had been flying for twenty minutes with the "low fuel" light on, expecting their engines to quit at any moment: There was probably more moisture in Koon's shorts than in Falcon 2's fuel tank. But both gunships landed safely. I never got a chance to thank those Falcon gunship crews, so I do so now.

Do not stand at my grave and weep,
I am not there; I do not sleep.
I am a thousand winds that blow,
I am the diamond glints on snow,
I am the sun on ripened grain,
I am the gentle autumn rain.
When you awaken in the morning's hush,
I am the swift uplifting rush
Of quiet birds in circling flight.
I am the soft starlight at night.
Do not stand at my grave and cry,
I am not there; I did not die.

—Mary Elizabeth Frye

TEN

"I spent the night of the 29th in the generator pit, on the radio with Spooky and Shadow, the gunships," John Kerr recalls. "I enjoyed that; we had really good support that night. At dawn on the 30th, as soon as the last gunship left, incoming fire resumed. Then it was Albracht and me sitting in his foxhole and kind of staring at each other, as if to say, *What are we going to do now?*"

As soon as that barrage began, I started preparing to defend against a ground attack. The night before, I had sent a coded message requesting more reinforcements, lots of ammunition, and water; we were running low on everything.

The incoming paused again about 0930—and the shit hit the fan: I was with Hopkins walking the perimeter, and as we approached the very steep southeastern quadrant, I saw movement below.

"We saw some people down there, and he called in air support," Hopkins recalls. "I remember watching the bomb going down there and the concussion wave coming back—wow! That is really something to see!"

I didn't know it at the time, but some of the digging noises we'd heard the two previous nights were PAVN troops cutting steps in the hard-packed clay of the steep hillside. Now several hundred PAVN burst out of the jungle and started up toward us, firing rifles and machine guns—the big block party I'd been expecting was on. We responded with our own small arms, but plainly the three dozen CIDG riflemen on that flank would soon be overwhelmed by what looked to be at least a PAVN battalion.

I called our FAC, and he vectored some F-100 Super Sabres in to work over the ridge and the ravine between us with 500-pound bombs.

After a few passes, the fast movers pulled out; instantly the tree line was ablaze with fire. With Hopkins, I jumped into a hole occupied by a couple of strikers and our medic, Doc. In a few minutes a quartet of Huey gunships arrived.

"Gunships would come in, they would strafe, we would pop up, we would shoot, they would come in, we would go down," Hopkins says. "I got my timing off and I got peppered with some shrapnel on my arm. Some of the [fragments] bounced off, and the Yard next to me said, 'I'm sticking with you, you numbah one!' And I thought, *If he knew how scared I am, he wouldn't want to be close to me at all.* And then Doc said, 'Oh, you got a Purple Heart there,' and I said, 'Bullshit.'"

I called for more gunships to help stop the ground assault; with each passing minute, it seemed more and more a threat. My strikers fought bravely and well, but we were heavily outnumbered and soon my men were getting killed or wounded in their holes.

Our PAVN neighbors were really dug in on the east ridge. They'd also emplaced 37 mm anti-aircraft guns; as far as I've been able to tell, this was the first such deployment of that weapons system inside South Vietnam. Some of our aviator pals reported being hit by flak at 10,000 feet near Kate—well above small-arms range. It made their approaches to Kate even more hazardous.

Among the gunships that answered our call were two from the 48th AHC, the Jokers. With First Lieutenant Ken Ryder, a newly arrived replacement, as his copilot, Ben Gay, Joker 73, flew the command ship with twin rocket pods, each carrying 19 supersonic rockets with high-explosive warheads. His wingman was Nolan Black, Joker 85, with a seven-rocket pod and a minigun on each side of his ship. Black handled the weapons, while in the left seat WO2 Maury Hearne, 22, out of Norwalk, California, had the flight controls. Fair-skinned, athletic, and boy-next-door handsome, Hearne was outgoing, likable, and highly respected as an aviator by his fellow pilots. Behind them, each manning an M60 mounted in a side doorway, were Sergeant Clyde Canada, 21, of Canoga Park, California, and SP5 Douglas Hugh Lott, Jr., 23, of Columbus, Georgia. Black had trained as a crew chief before starting flight school—his copilot was trained as a helicopter mechanic. There was probably no better-trained or more capable Huey crew anywhere in Vietnam.

By the time they responded to my call for help, however, Gay and Black had already had a harrowing morning flying around Bu Prang Camp, which was under mortar attack. While refueling on the small strip outside the camp, their gunships were targeted—their cue to leave. Heavy with ordnance and fuel, Gay attempted takeoff from Bu Prang's short, unimproved strip, but as he neared the end, his main rotor RPM dropped and his transmission oil temperature light glowed red, indicating that both transmission and engine were dangerously stressed. Gay aborted takeoff and tried twice more, each time with the same result. As he was revving his engines for a fourth attempt, his UHF radio crackled to life with a call from our FAC: Kate was under ground attack by a massive PAVN force and his fire team was needed at once.

"I made another takeoff run down the strip," Gay recalls. "As we neared the end, our RPM dropped again, but I continued anyway; at the end of the strip was a low cliff, and as we fell off that, our airspeed rose, boosting rotor RPM." That was enough to get airborne. Seconds later, using the same maneuver, Black followed. Together they flew toward Kate as fast as their redlined engines could haul them.

"When we came around the side of the hill, we were maybe fifty to seventy-five feet off the deck, which is almost touching the ground; they probably could've thrown a stick up into the rotor blades and taken us down," Gay recalls.

"But I couldn't believe what I was seeing: a huge mass of enemy troops, hundreds of guys swarming out of the jungle. Guns on the firebase were pumping beehive rounds out. This was World War II–type combat, not a guerrilla war with three or four guys shooting bolt-action guns. This was a toe-to-toe, eye-to-eye brawl."

He immediately opened fire with rockets—momentarily forgetting that, as a safety measure, each must travel about a hundred meters before its warhead arms. "Normally when you fired a rocket, there were two bangs—the rocket breaking the sound barrier, then the warhead exploding. But my rockets did not explode—they simply hit the enemy soldiers," Gay recalls.

Behind him, Black opened up with his miniguns, joined by Gay's door gunners and his own, to bring down some of the attackers. Both ships circled back for a second pass, this time keeping enough distance to let their rockets arm. "We probably took three or four rounds, most of them through the rotor blades, one to the synchronized elevator, and one round went through the tail boom, but nothing in the cockpit area and no injuries," Gay recalls.

That pass, and several that followed, saved our bacon, saved everyone on Kate, by breaking the back of the PAVN attack. The survivors withdrew and the shelling resumed, though not as heavily as earlier.

I took stock of our ammo and found that we had very little left. And we had fired off all our claymore mines, usually to good effect. Even if we were to get more of these anti-personnel mines, there was so much incoming that I didn't see how my men could leave cover to emplace them a safe distance below their fighting positions.

Several aircraft tried to bring us ammo, but each was driven off by intense fire.

Around noon there was a little break in the action. By now we were virtually out of water, and many of my strikers had only a couple of 20-round magazines left. While we redistributed what little ammo we had, I called again for resupply.

A 155th AHC slick loaded ammo and water on the Bu Prang airstrip, took off, and headed toward Kate. As it approached, it was riddled with small-arms fire, wounding two crewmen. The pilot wisely aborted the mission and limped back to Bu Prang.

Meanwhile, a 189th AHC UH-1H "H model Huey" slick flown by Jim "Herbie" Matlock, 21, and copilot Wilbur Guthrie, 27, had left BMT after picking up SP4 Pete Olsen, a Special Forces radio operator who needed a lift to Bu Prang. Tall and lanky, a volunteer from Tennessee, Matlock was only a few months out of flight school but by all accounts a superbly gifted pilot—and not a bit shy about it. He was not, technically, a command pilot as he hadn't yet been so certified, but he was nevertheless in charge of this aircraft. Quiet, short, and dark, Guthrie had already completed a combat tour in Vietnam as an enlisted door gunner; during the Tet Offensive, he'd manned an M60 from an airfield bunker. After rotating Stateside, he reenlisted for flight school. Returning to Vietnam in early October 1969, he joined the 189th at Camp Holloway, Pleiku. Three weeks later, on extended loan to the 155th, he and Matlock were flying ash-and-trash missions in support of Special Forces camps.

Flying out of Pleiku and BMT, Guthrie experienced the war as distant; he looked forward to getting some easy stick time: "I thought that this would be a good mission for me; we would be flying long days and seeing a lot of our company's area of operation," he wrote. "I would get an opportunity to do hover-down landings through a hundred feet–plus of triple canopy mountaintop jungle terrain. [Matlock] was reputed to be great at these kinds of landings. He had the smooth control touch and confidence to safely perform any kind of difficult landing. He was also a patient teacher and had the nerve to let a new guy put the rotor blades so near the trees and hover there with little to no extra power available in the event of trouble."

The first few days of their temporary duty were mundane: hauling the wives and children of Montagnard strikers in CIDG units to a BMT hospital or back to their villages. "We flew dogs, hogs, and kids," wrote Guthrie. "[Matlock] was in the habit of taking a small kid in his lap and [letting] them play with the flight controls, get a thrill out of 'flying' a helicopter."

There were no kids, dogs, or hogs aboard on October 30. On the 45-minute flight from BMT to Bu Prang, they listened to three radios—VHF for communicating with other aircraft in their platoon, UHF for an assortment of common aviation channels monitored countrywide by all aircraft, and Fox Mike (FM) to contact ground units. All three radios sprang to life with the sounds of aircraft in heavy combat. "It sounded like there was a hell of [a] war going on somewhere," Guthrie wrote.

Upon learning that Bu Prang was under attack, Matlock diverted to Gia Nghia to refuel in safety. While JP-4 was being hand-pumped into his bird, Guthrie and Matlock chatted with Gay and Black and their crews, who told them that Kate was under heavy attack and that all available air support had been summoned.

With full tanks, Matlock and Guthrie took off and headed for Bu Prang. From altitude they saw a swarm of aircraft buzzing around Kate a few miles away, filling the airwaves with essential chatter. "I could never explain what it sounds like listening to three radios at once and everyone is yelling and talking simultaneously, men under heavy fire trying to give instructions and duck bullets at the same time," Guthrie wrote. "We heard aircraft call that they were taking hits from all directions . . . I could not help but give thanks that this was not our fight, that we were only taking a radio operator to his camp, then going back—a simple little mission, thank God."

Matlock set the Huey down on Bu Prang's airstrip and Olsen jumped out and ran for the gate. As the aviators were ready to leave, "a helicopter from the 155th out of BMT landed, shot all to hell and back," Guthrie wrote. "They had been trying to take water and ammo in to the troops on Kate. [The pilot] said that nobody could make it through that kind of fire. After assessing the damage to their aircraft, they aborted the mission to return home for repairs," wrote Guthrie. "Do not misunderstand me. These were brave men and they had tried their best to deliver the ammo. But the fire was too intense and they had sustained a lot of damage and some casualties. We could hear the radio operator on Kate, call sign 'Chicken Wolf,' begging for water and ammo. They were almost out of everything, and with night coming on, they were sure to be overrun."

(I worked with the Air Force FACs running the fast movers, and with helicopter gunships. Kerr had another radio on the same frequency; he worked with slicks, using my Chicken Wolf call sign instead of the artillery call sign he would use in the FDC.)

Watching the fighting from three miles away, Guthrie recalled that he had never seen so many gunships in the air in one place, and they "didn't seem to be making a dent in the effort to drive the enemy away."

That's pretty much what it looked like from Kate too. I spent much of the day dodging from one foxhole or bunker to another, drawing heavy fire each time I moved around the perimeter. I had to position myself to see specific enemy positions that required a gunship's rockets and guns or Air Force bombs and napalm. I began using tracer ammunition to precisely direct the FAC. I would lay down a stream of tracer fire from my CAR-15 to the exact enemy position that I wanted hit. I had my radio, and when the FAC knew where I wanted it, he radioed, "Got it!" and dropped down, using my tracer stream to aim a marking rocket. Then the fast movers would roll in and bomb on his smoke marker. I did this the first time without incident, but the enemy quickly figured out what I was doing. I was thereafter a marked man. I was out in the open a minute to maybe two, two and a half minutes at a time, and then I had to dodge whatever rockets or mortars were coming and get to cover. To me, the benefits of pinpoint bombing outweighed the risks—but remember, I still thought that I was bulletproof.

Back at Bu Prang, to Guthrie's shock and horror, Matlock casually volunteered to brave the tempest of flying lead and steel around Kate and bring our ammo and water in.

Meanwhile, Joker 73 and Joker 85—Ben Gay and Nolan Black, respectively—had reloaded their rocket pods and miniguns at Gia Nghia and were headed back to Kate.

Considering it unwise to set down on Kate, Matlock had the ammo and water loaded in two rows in each cargo doorway, and got two volunteers from the camp to kick the stuff out as he slowly overflew our hilltop at six feet off the deck.

It didn't quite work out that way. When Matlock's aircraft came into sight, Kerr radioed to ask him if he'd take some of our wounded out. Matlock agreed.

Black and Nolan arrived over Kate in their gunships at almost the same time as Matlock and Guthrie in their slick. The Jokers' guns gave them cover on their approach. Then our FAC directed Gay's fire team to find and finish a suspected PAVN anti-aircraft site with at least one 12.7 mm heavy machine gun.

"I located the area of the AA site and began an attack run at about 150 feet above the jungle, followed by Blackie and Hearne in the second aircraft," Gay wrote in his after-action report.

Matlock and Guthrie in Ghostrider 12 were just then hovering into Kate. "As we passed over the wire and bunkers, the men in the cargo compartment kicked out the water and ammo," wrote Guthrie. "[Matlock] flared the Huey and stood it on its tail to stop it."

"The medevac helicopters came in like a shot," recalls the slightly built Geromin. "They were so amazing. They came in at full speed just above the treetops, and as soon as they got to the base of our hill they would gun it to get up the slope and then circle around at what seemed like full power. Then they'd stop and hover just a little above the ground so that they didn't have to build up the momentum to lift off; it seemed like it took just a couple of minutes to come in, reload, and take off because the enemy was constantly shooting at them."

"I landed on the *H*, for 'helipad'—it should have been an *R* for '[mortar] registration point,'" says Matlock.

Geromin manhandled a wounded striker toward the landing Huey—neither the first nor the last time that he would do so on Kate. "He was shot up so bad that when I lifted him he could barely hold his head up, and he was so bloody that I had to put my arms under his armpits and grab my [other] hand or he would have just slipped right out of my grasp," Geromin says.

Covered with the wounded man's blood, he put the striker on the Huey's cargo floor. The crew chief beckoned Geromin to come aboard, but he shook his head. "I'm not hurt! It's not my blood!" he yelled over the engines.

A beat behind Geromin, more than a dozen strikers mobbed the aircraft. "A Yard, unharmed and carrying his weapon, jumped on. The gunner yelled to us, 'Is he supposed to be going?'" says Geromin. *"If he isn't wounded, he's not supposed to go,"* Geromin yelled. "The gunner aimed an M60 at the Yard and told him to get off or he would blow him away. So he jumped off, another Yard grabbed and disarmed him, two more Yards took him away, and a few seconds later, I heard one shot, and then the two Yards walked away without the guy they'd pulled off the chopper."

Geromin believes the striker was executed for desertion.

Matlock now tried to hover off the helipad, but the overloaded ship, with wounded men standing on the skids and clinging to the side, couldn't rise. "We shooed the excess away, and lifted off just as an 82 mm mortar round landed under us, right on the *H*," Matlock recalls. "The blast wave blew [the helicopter] off the LZ, doing some structural and sheet-metal damage to the bird. We also took a few rifle rounds coming out."

In fact, the mortar's steel tail fins were driven almost completely through the aircraft's hardened aluminum fuselage.

Working to Kate's north, Gay had made several passes, each time followed by Black and Hearne, all firing rockets at the PAVN machine gun. "[As] I turned in behind Blackie, I observed AA ground fire from a *second* 12.7 mm gun hidden about ninety degrees from the first one," Gay recalls.

It was a flak trap—the second gun had remained silent and hidden until the first had lured a gunship into range. "I saw [Black's] ship getting hit," says Gay. "The bottom of the aircraft was struck in the fuel cell by 12.7 mm rounds and immediately burst into flames. I called immediately: *8-5, this is 7-3. You're on fire; you need to put it down.*"

Both aircraft were so low that they couldn't see very far. Black replied, "Where's a field?" Before Gay could respond, the stricken Huey's tail boom separated from its fuselage, and the ship flipped upside down, plunging fifty feet into the jungle and exploding on contact with the ground.

The aircraft was so close that I felt the blast's intense heat on my face and arms—a spectacle that haunts me to this day. As the reality of what I had just witnessed sunk in, I felt hollow. Fighting nausea, I struggled to focus my attention on the multitude of other urgent issues confronting me: Where would the next ground attack come from? Did I have enough men to hold that flank? Enough ammo?

Meanwhile Matlock and Guthrie were fighting gravity and blast damage, nursing their overloaded Huey up from the trees and out of small-arms range. To them, and to many on Kate, it appeared that Joker 85 had been hit by an RPG. "We were taking off to the west and they crashed just to the north of our flight path," Matlock recalls. "As we passed over the wreckage, I saw [PAVN] troops shooting into the cockpit."

Gay began to circle the flaming wreckage, but immediately came under heavy fire; the FAC ordered him to leave the area.

I thought about mounting a rescue for any survivors; after a few seconds, I realized that no one could have lived through that explosion. And that it would have been suicide to venture among the hostiles swarming around the crash site.

Every man on Kate who witnessed this horrific event was damaged in some way for the rest of his life. None of us had met those aviators—Black, Hearne, Canada, and Lot—didn't, then, even know their names. But they were our brothers, American soldiers who had repeatedly risked their lives for us, and now they were dead. The thought was overwhelming. Even now, thinking about it is painful.

Later, making my rounds of the perimeter, I spotted a lone PAVN soldier about 450 meters away, moving through a relatively open area below the ridge. I went prone and began firing at him. I'm a good shot, but this guy was a little past my carbine's effective range. Never mind: After my fourth or fifth tracer, the 105 crew took their turn. First shot: a direct hit. The PAVN flew straight up at least forty feet.

Despite that tiny triumph, our situation was deteriorating. Two more gunships, several slicks, and a Chinook were hit by small-arms fire around Kate. By nightfall, the powers that be would decide that sending gunships on close support missions into and through relentless PAVN ground fire from every direction was suicidal. While Air Force fast movers could still work in close proximity to our hilltop impact zone during daylight, after that day Kate could no longer expect close support from helicopter gunships.

When I had time for an accounting of the rifle and machine-gun ammunition that Matlock, Guthrie, and their crew had risked their lives to bring us, I was furious: Some moron—as it happened, Captain Whiteside, an operations officer at B-23—had cut my requisition in half. "No one needs that much ammo," he said. All that blood and fire, all that fear and angst getting it in to us—and if PAVN attacked again in force, I wasn't sure that we'd have enough ammo to stop him. I got back on the radio and demanded more.

I have known the call to battle
In each changeless changing shape
From the high souled voice of conscience
To the beastly lust for rape.
I have sinned and I have suffered,
Played the hero and the knave;
Fought for belly, shame, or country,
And for each have found a grave.
I cannot name my battles,
For the visions are not clear,
Yet, I see the twisted faces
And I feel the rending spear.

—George S. Patton, Jr.

ELEVEN

Handsome and fair, First Lieutenant Ronald A. Ross was 23. Very short and slender, he was an almost elfin man, with surprising agility and upper-body strength. He grew up in Muskego, a Milwaukee exurb, lettered on his high school wrestling team, and after graduation spent two years studying marine biology at the University of Wisconsin in Madison. He earned good grades, would almost certainly have graduated, then probably would have gone on to grad school, but in 1966 he decided that his nation's needs outweighed his own ambitions. He enlisted in the Army, and upon completing basic training at Fort Leonard Wood, Missouri, was awarded the Outstanding Trainee Trophy. He was then trained in signals intelligence and posted to Vint Hill Farms Station in rural Virginia, the Army Security Agency's oldest base. He graduated from Artillery OCS at Fort Sill in December 1967. A year later, after completing jungle warfare school in Panama and troop duty at dusty Fort Irwin, California, he was assigned to the 5/22 Artillery, near BMT. Like most lieutenants in wartime, he served in a variety of roles within the battalion and made several good friends, among them First Lieutenant Reginald Brockwell. "Everybody liked Ron. He was a funny guy, personable, a wonderful human being," Brockwell recalls.

When Ross came due for R&R, he requested Hawaii, and let it be known that he would meet his wife and newborn son there. When Lieutenant Colonel Elton Delaune, the 5/22's ambitious new battalion commander, learned that only a few months earlier Ross had taken emergency leave to marry his pregnant fiancée, he apparently decided that Ross was morally unfit for the officer's uniform he wore. Delaune seemed to develop an abiding dislike for Ross; some battalion officers recall that Delaune thought that Ross was a screwup.

"I got along well with Delaune," recalls Brockwell. "I liked him. He was a nice man, but I think he was there for his six-month [command] tour and he was going to do the most he could do to promote his career."

I have no direct knowledge of the internal politics of the 5/22 Artillery, or of Ross's activities in that battalion, so it's possible that Ross in fact was a screwup. On the other hand, during my brief Army career, I more than once observed how easy it was for a noncom to allow personal prejudices to fuel a strong dislike for a particular soldier under his control, and then to ride him, looking for any excuse to harass or punish him. It also sometimes happens that a senior officer will decide to lean on a junior one, criticizing his every misstep. It might have been that Delaune was something of a bluestocking who frowned on premarital pregnancy. Whatever it was that drew Delaune's ire, it is a fact that young men make mistakes. Lieutenants make mistakes: I certainly did, as did pretty much every lieutenant I ever met. For that matter, I'm sure that lieutenant colonels also make mistakes. Not everyone who's tagged a screwup deserves that label.

On October 30, with Mike Smith in a field hospital, First Lieutenant Tom Klein, a 5/22 battery XO then at Duc Lap, was told to prepare to go in to Kate to replace Smith. Brockwell was told to be prepared to replace Klein at Duc Lap. Instead, despite Ross's scheduled R&R in Hawaii, Delaune ordered Ross to Kate. I find it strange that Delaune sent an officer that he had labeled a loser to an embattled firebase that was then functioning as not much more than a PAVN impact area.

Ross landed under fire on a resupply chopper in midafternoon. Officially, he was Mike Smith's replacement; the first men he met were Koon, Hopkins, Tiranti, and McFarland; the gun crew welcomed Ross to Kate, and they chatted for a few minutes. "He said that he was supposed to be on his way for R&R to see his wife," recalls Hopkins. "He told us that he'd pissed off some colonel, that's why he was sent to Kate," he said. "But then he said, 'Hey, you guys need help, I'm here.'"

When the mortar barrage resumed, the men took cover inside a gun revetment. With little understanding of what life had been like on Kate during the preceding days, or of how long these men had been in combat, Ross decided to use the incoming fire to teach his new troops about dealing with mortars.

"He said, 'Gentlemen, if you hear the round leaving the tube and then hear it coming in and explode—that's mortar fire,'" recalls Nelson Koon. Ross went on to explain that this meant that after the mortar was fired, there were a few seconds in which to take cover.

"We'd been taking incoming for two or three days," says Koon. "We knew what the hell mortar fire was."

Our medic showed Ross to the FDC, where he met John Kerr. "Ross reported to me, and he asked, 'What should I do?'" recalls Kerr. "I said that I pretty much had the FDC under control, and that our guns were no longer operational. I told him to find Captain Albracht and see if he needed some help."

When I found time to sit down and brief Ron Ross, he seemed like a very nice fellow, smart and well-spoken. I told him that except for the 105 crew, most of the artillerymen on Kate were either hiding in their bunkers or fighting as infantry—there wasn't much he could do with the guns. I suggested that he could spell Kerr so he could get some rest. Ross should then work the FDC radios with Johnson, and in the morning I'd give him the grand tour of our perimeter. After that, he could help with the infantry.

Bob Johnson spent most of his waking hours monitoring FDC radios and handling anything else that came up when Kerr wasn't present. With one 155 out, the other damaged, and the 105 in direct-fire mode, there wasn't much artillery radio traffic. Johnson recalls that Ross had an extended radio conversation with one or more 5/22 Artillery officers. "From the nature and tone of it, he was obviously talking with very good buddies," recalls Johnson. "There was at least one person very concerned about Ross's welfare. He urged [Ross] to take care of himself, not to take any chances, just get the mission done and get back to them. Lieutenant Ross was respectful of their concerns, so I assume that they were officers, and as was typical of most young men of that age, including myself, he seemed to feel that he was immune from harm. He said that although he would take all precautions, he wasn't concerned and that he would be back with them soon. He was an extremely upbeat type of person."

As sundown approached and the fast movers could no longer operate safely at low levels, Kerr left the safety of the underground FDC, where since the start of the fighting he had handled such essential tasks as coordinating artillery fire from Susan and Annie, and working the radios to bring in gunships and medevac and resupply choppers. He found a partially exposed location where he could adjust Susan's guns on known or suspected PAVN positions.

"I adjusted [Susan's] fire on the ridge to our east. Because range errors are more probable than deflection errors, and Susan was about eight miles away—right at the 155 howitzer's maximum range—it was risky having Captain Adam's guys shoot over us at that ridge," recalls Kerr. "But they put their fire where I wanted it, and with no short rounds. It seemed like it was working."

Kerr probably didn't know it, but that day, while he was attempting to adjust Susan's fire, *Cheap Thrills*, one of Susan's two 155s, had to be taken out of service. "From the time I got in-country in January until the end of October, I'd say we were firing it all the time," explains SP4 Francis "Butch" Barnes, the assistant gunner. "That day, when we couldn't hit our coordinates, someone checked our tube, and we'd shot our gun out. We'd shot so many rounds that the tube was worn-out."

Our PAVN neighbors decided that fire from Susan's remaining 155 was an annoyance that couldn't be tolerated. They couldn't reach Susan, so they directed fire from recoilless rifles, rockets, and mortars at Kerr, the forward observer. A mortar shell blew shrapnel into the inner part of his left thigh. Not that close to the family jewels, but close enough.

Running on adrenaline, Kerr felt no pain for several minutes; he did not even notice that he'd been hit. "So much incoming was landing that I immediately ran down into the FDC bunker," he says. "One of the soldiers there said, 'Look at your leg, Lieutenant,' and I saw that it was soaked in blood."

Doc patched him up, but Kerr refused evacuation. He would tough it out, continue to work as best he could. As the shock of his wound wore off, however, he began to feel pain on a scale that he had never before experienced. He said nothing about it, continued to do what he had been doing. The medic offered him morphine, but Kerr declined. "We didn't have a lot of that, and it did not yet hurt real badly," he recalls. "I figured somebody would soon need it more."

I cannot say enough about the courage, selflessness, and cool professionalism of that medic. He was only a few days from the end of his tour when the shit hit the fan. He was told to leave Kate, return to BMT, and begin out-processing. Instead, he told his first sergeant that he would make it back to the world with the rest of Charlie Battery or he wouldn't make it back at all.

Kerr's wound was far more serious than it had first appeared. Soon he was unable to walk, and dragged himself around on one leg until it was too dark to adjust artillery.

As twilight fell, several strikers observed flashlights across the ravine on the opposing hillside. The 105 crew fired high-explosive and beehive rounds at them. A little after 1900 hours, someone spotted movement in the wood line below our northeast perimeter: the NVA were massing in the jungle there. I moved to the perimeter, but remained in the open so I could effectively direct both the air support and my strikers. Almost immediately, about 500 PAVN troops poured out of the jungle and started up our hill.

The strikers opened up with all they had, but I could see that it wasn't enough. What I came to think of as my mobile reserve—Koon, Hopkins, and Tiranti—rushed to that section of our perimeter and moved up on line. Koon, who had gone to such stupefying lengths to serve in Vietnam, brought his M60. "I fired at this one [PAVN] soldier and I hit him," he recalls. "He kept coming and I just kept firing and he finally dropped about five feet in front of me. And I said to myself, *Well,* you *wanted to see what Vietnam was like.*"

We held them long enough for the fast movers to return with 500-pound bombs. Then it was dark, and an AC-119G Shadow came on station to lay a curtain of minigun fire just below us, cutting the attackers off from their reinforcements. We took a few more casualties, but our perimeter held; by 2100 hours the enemy had backed off.

I knew they'd be back. As always, I kept Bu Prang informed, and they passed our status to B-23 in BMT, and then up the line to the ARVN 23rd.

It seems to me, all these years later, that if ARVN was supposed to demonstrate their battlefield chops, this was a pretty good time to do it. We were surrounded by all the PAVN troops you could ever hope to find in one area.

But the 23rd ARVN remained in its BMT garrison.

If you can keep your head when all about you
Are losing theirs and blaming it on you,
If you can trust yourself when all men doubt you,
But make allowance for their doubting too;
If you can wait and not be tired by waiting,
Or, being lied about, don't deal in lies,
Or, being hated, don't give way to hating,
And yet don't look too good, nor talk too wise;
. . .
Yours is the Earth and everything that's in it,
And—which is more—you'll be a Man, my son!

—Rudyard Kipling

TWELVE

I was running on adrenaline and the tiny dextroamphetamine pills that Special Forces provided for extended combat situations. Late that night I was back on the radio with Spooky 61, orbiting overhead since full darkness, firing at any light they saw around us, and at anything that we heard from the darkness outside our stronghold.

Earlier in the day, Dan Pierelli had discovered that the artillery platoon had their own 81 mm mortar, which was primarily for firing illumination rounds—parachute flares—as a defensive measure. Expert in the use of both light and heavy infantry weapons, he asked around in the artillery community and was rewarded with several boxes of HE rounds. So that night, and on those that followed, when Spooky or Shadow was on station, or during the day when there was no incoming fire, he began laying harassment and interdiction mortar fire on the enemy.

"I fired a lot of HE during the day, in between mortar and rocket attacks," he recalls. At night, while Spooky or Shadow was circling overhead, he waited until they cleared a certain area, then began firing at tree lines, hillsides, and ravines where we had heard digging sounds. "We could hear the North Vietnamese digging in, heard rustling off in the distance, so I was dropping rounds, and as Spooky or Shadow flew over, once I knew they were out of the line of fire, I'd start popping a bunch of rounds from about 300 out to about maybe 400 meters," Pierelli adds. "We knew they were down there."

A little after midnight, Spooky 61 departed; the mission commander said that their replacement, Spooky 41, would soon be on station. Spooky 41's navigator and mission commander was USAF Captain Al Dykes.

AL Dykes was a part-time student at the University of Colorado when he got a draft notice. It was 1961, a time of peace, long before more than a handful of Americans had even heard of Vietnam. Rather than face induction into the Army, Dykes decided to enlist in the Air Force. "I wanted to fly," he recalls, but "the only program open was for navigators."

After completing a yearlong navigator program at Connelly AFB in Waco, Texas, Dykes was commissioned a second lieutenant. He remained at Connelly as an instructor until 1966, when the school relocated to Mather AFB, near Sacramento, California. Dykes began looking for another job, and learned about a hush-hush project called "Phyllis Ann" in Alexandria, Louisiana. Although no one could tell him anything about it, Dykes nevertheless volunteered for what he thought would be six months of temporary duty.

He joined a small group of pilots, engineers, loadmasters, and gunners. "They took us to a big, long building without offices. It was just tables and chairs, with some temporary partitions," he recalls. "They said, 'You have two weeks to figure out an instructional program for the flying phase.'"

That was when he learned that Phyllis Ann was a C-47 transition program. Dykes and his fellow instructors were to teach pilots, navigators, and crewmen how to fly an aircraft that had been developed in the 1930s. Based on the Douglas DC-3, the first practical commercial airliner, but with reinforced floors and wider doors, the C-47 "Gooney Bird" went into Army Air Corps service in 1941. Thousands of these sturdy and dependable aircraft flew for the Air Corps and the Navy, and for many Allied nations. As supreme commander of Allied forces in Europe, General Dwight D. Eisenhower described the C-47 as vital to winning the war. And to winning the peace: Thousands of C-47 sorties brought food, fuel, and other essentials into Berlin to break the Soviet blockade of 1947–48.

As newer and bigger cargo aircraft entered service, however, thousands of Air Force C-47s were sold as surplus or scrapped. By 1966, there were few remaining in active service and most of those were off-the-books aircraft used by various fighter and bomber squadrons for administrative chores. For Phyllis Ann, aircraft were taken out of storage and from National Guard and Reserve units, then refitted with new engines and sophisticated, off-the-shelf civilian electronics. Some became EC-47s and flew electronic reconnaissance missions. HC-47s were modified with loudspeakers and other equipment for psychological warfare. The rest became AC-47s—gunships. When the Air Force ran out of Gooney Birds, they took dozens of Air Force Fairchild C-119 "Flying Boxcars" from Air Force Reserve units. Because they had more internal cargo space than a C-47, the C-119s were armed with miniguns, 20 mm cannon, sophisticated radar and infrared sensing devices, and spotlights. These "Shadow" gunships were intended to do everything that the AC-47 Spooky could do, but also to hunt blacked-out trucks hauling supplies and reinforcements by night down the Ho Chi Minh Trail.

If Shadow was supposedly the more capable aircraft, Dykes was much happier to be in a Gooney Bird. "One night some of us were eating dinner at the Phan Rang Officers' Club," he recalls. "There were some C-119 pilots and navigators at the next table. We looked down the runway and watched a 119 taxi into position for takeoff. The pilot wound the engines up, then gunned it and took off down the runway as fast as he could. He saw that he wasn't going to be able to take off, so he aborted. Too much ammo and flares, and the ship is underpowered to begin with. Well, he turned around, taxied back, and tried to take off again, and couldn't. Then he tried it a third time, and failed again.

"So I casually said to my friends—just loud enough for the guys at the next table to hear—'You know, I had to bail out of a C-119 *five* times!'

"The 119 guys looked like they were scared to death. 'What happened, what happened?' they asked.

"I went through the Army jump school at Fort Benning, and that's what we jumped out of."

That's Al—always good for a laugh.

Dykes and his fellow instructors drew up training routes and flew their C-47s to learn their quirks. Two weeks later, the first trainees arrived. "We had people in their 20s and early 30s in all positions except pilots," Dykes explains. The Air Force had scoured its rolls to find pilots with C-47 experience. Most were World War II or Korean War veterans.

"We trained more than sixty crews. They ferried sixty-three airplanes to Vietnam. Some went through Hawaii, and some through Alaska, then the Aleutians, and down to Midway Island and across the Pacific to Vietnam."

The bottoms of these AC-47s were painted black and they were outfitted with a trio of 7.62 mm General Electric SUU-IIA/A Gatling guns, originally designed for use in pods under the wings of an A-1 Skyraider. The SUU-IIA/A's two-speed motor drove a six-barrel gun capable of delivering 3,000 or 6,000 rounds per minute, depending on need.

Because the AC-47 was to fire on narrowly defined ground targets, and to do so at night while flying at low altitudes, navigators and pilots required special training. "Spooky fired, usually, between 2,500 and 3,000 feet above ground level," Dykes explains.

Above the battlefield, higher is safer, and the 7.62 mm bullet can pierce a filled sandbag more than a mile distant. As an aid in aiming, however, Spooky's miniguns fired one tracer in every five rounds; tracers burn out at half a mile, and their ballistic characteristics are slightly different from armor-piercing bullets. By limiting Spooky to low altitudes and taking fire direction from ground units in contact with the enemy, gunship crews could apply its enormous firepower with almost pinpoint accuracy. But, operating within range of ground-based small arms, Spooky and Shadow were strictly limited to night activity.

While Dykes was gaining experience with Gooney Birds in a Stateside training environment, the first squadron of AC-47s, with only five operational aircraft, deployed to Vietnam in November 1965. By the time Dykes arrived in 1969, there were two AC-47 squadrons, one at Tan Son Nhut and one at Phan Rang, each with sixteen aircraft. Dykes flew out of Phan Rang.

"We flew Spooky without a rear door, so the loadmaster could throw out parachute flares," Dykes explains. "They'd float down slowly and light up an area that would help show where the good and bad guys were before we started firing." Spooky also carried another type of flare, dropped on or near a target to serve as a reference point for adjusting its fire. These flares burned for up to thirty minutes.

The AC-47 crew included two gunners to maintain and reload the miniguns.

"If we were firing all three guns at once, we were firing 18,000 rounds a minute," Dykes says. Normally, however, Spooky did not use "fast fire."

"If a target was real hot, we might fire all three, a three- or four-second burst, just to make sure they were all working," Dykes continues. "Then we took one gun off, to keep it loaded, and cut the other two to half fire, or 3,000 rounds a minute. If it was unnecessary to fire two at once, we'd work one gun at a time, firing for a few seconds at a time. That way we could spend all night with the guys down there—that Gooney Bird would fly for hours and hours. It just didn't burn much gas."

Each Spooky aircraft carried as many as 40,000 rounds of 7.62 mm ammunition, and if conditions permitted, it could remain on station for up to ten hours. It fired while cruising at 120 knots in a left-hand orbit.

"We took a lot of gunfire from the ground," Dykes explains. "We lost an airplane near Saigon because he came home one morning in daylight; a Viet Cong 12.7 mm shot him down. So our hard-and-fast rule was that we didn't go *to* a target until it was dark, and we were back over home station before first light," Dykes explains.

Nevertheless, during the course of the war in Vietnam, between the USAF and the VNAF, a dozen AC-47 gunships were lost in combat.

Paradoxically, Spooky's high-tech weaponry was aimed with a crude improvised device. "We didn't have all this GPS and electronics and all that stuff back in the sixties like we do nowadays," Dykes says. A handmade instrument was mounted on the pilot's side window. In it was a bulb from a Christmas tree ornament positioned to shine up through a glass with an *X* painted on its center. A mirror reflected the *X*, referred to as a "pip" or "pipper," at an angle on the pilot's front window, and the aircraft was maneuvered to keep the *X* on the target.

Dykes explains that the pilot usually didn't adjust fire with this aiming device only; he also adjusted it by banking the plane. "The guns were mounted at 12.5 degrees below horizontal. Circling at a 25- to 30-degree bank put the guns at about 40 degrees below horizontal; we could see where the tracers hit and know where we were firing."

With the aircraft in motion at 120 knots, engineers had calculated that a three-second burst from one gun would put a bullet in every square foot of a space the size of a football field. "Spooky aircraft held the best Air Force record ever established," says Dykes. "When we were winding the program down, a general, one of the group that created the AC-47 concept, came out from the Pentagon and told us that we had defended more than 6,300 targets and that any target that we attacked with somebody alive on the ground to guide our fire, they got out alive. It was 100 percent successful. He said it was the *only* program in the Air Force that had ever had a 100 percent success rate. That was partly because if we couldn't talk to the guy on the ground, we didn't fire. We had to know that we were never shooting at friendlies. But if he could talk to us, we got him out."

When Shadow took Spooky's place over Kate, Pierelli would go into the generator pit; he had an infrared strobe that Shadow, unlike Spooky, could see. "I was talking to Shadow one night and told them that I was going to put the infrared strobe in the center of the hill," Pierelli recalls. He told Shadow that from there he could estimate where we were and where the enemy might be. "Shadow also had spotlight capabilities," Pierelli continues. "One night, as he was about leave us, he said, 'Watch this!' He turned on the spotlight and all I could see was one huge circle of light going across the jungle. It was beautiful, for lack of a better word."

Both Shadow and Spooky communicated on UHF, VHF, or FM radio. "The pilot had the radios taxiing out, during takeoff, and coming back and landing," recalls Dykes. "As soon as we were off the ground, all communi-

Courtesy of Warren Geromin

For the first weeks of its existence, Kate was peaceful enough to allow helicopters of all sizes to land with cargo and passengers.

Courtesy of Mike Smith

In the weeks before the shooting started, everyone on Kate could expect a delivery of hot food about once a week.

Courtesy of Mike Smith

Before I got to Kate, my predecessor allowed the Montagnard strikers to hunt. Here they return with an enormous wild pig.

Courtesy of Nelson Koon

One of few times when Kate's 155 mm howitzers fired, in mid-October 1969.

Courtesy of Kenn Hopkins

Projectiles, which the gun crews called "joes," for the 155 mm howitzer. The projectiles on each end have fuses attached. The two center joes have shipping plugs.

Courtesy of John Ross

Short, slender, almost elfin in appearance, Ron Ross had surprising agility and upper-body strength and lettered on his high school wrestling team. He studied marine biology before enlisting, and was an honor graduate of his basic training company.

This is me after Kate with the II Corps Mike Force at the Battle of Dak Seang.

Courtesy of William Albracht

Courtesy of William Albracht

When I joined the Mike Force, I became a hunter instead of prey.

The interior of a fire direction center on a firebase like Kate.

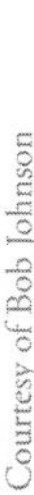

Courtesy of Bob Johnson

Courtesy of Mike Smith

Lt. Mike Smith (*right*) adjusts artillery fire on Kate in September 1969. At this point there was no sign of the enemy near Kate.

Courtesy of Mike Smith

Things on Kate were so peaceful that the defenders enjoyed afternoon volleyball games—until the day that I arrived.

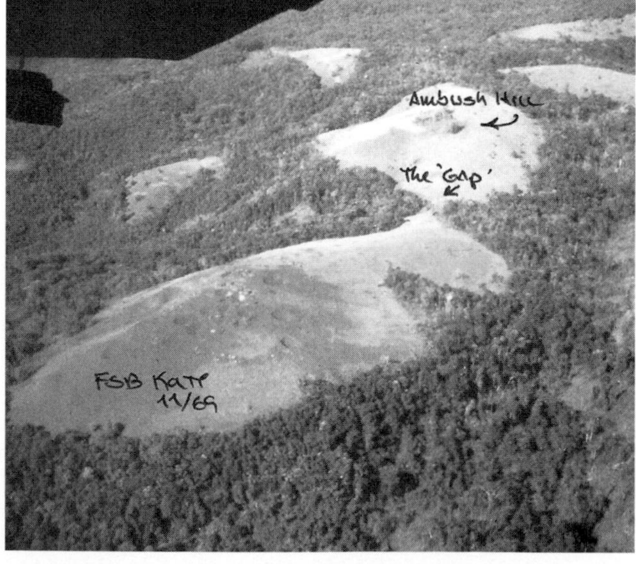

Courtesy of William Albracht

I snapped this photograph from an airplane shortly after I left Kate. Ambush Hill's proximity to Kate can be seen clearly.

Close air support on Kate, as well as on other Vietnam firebases, often meant bombs falling on the very edge of the base.

Courtesy of Ke[illegible]n Hopkins

Courtesy of Bob Johnson

Ambush Hill (*left*) as seen from Kate.

Courtesy of Warren Geromin

The view from Kate's southern end.

Courtesy of Mike Smith

From this clearing some 200 meters east of Kate, the enemy repeatedly fired RPGs and recoilless rifles, ultimately destroying all three of our howitzers. This photo was taken a month before hostilities began.

Courtesy of Mike Smith

A shallow stream at the bottom of the deep ravine east of Kate. When the fighting began, the enemy mounted many attacks from this ravine.

Courtesy of Mike Smith

A giant Chinook helicopter delivered supplies to Kate in September 1969. When the shooting started in late October, few pilots dared land on the base.

Sgt. Tex Rogers performs maintenance on his howitzer.

Courtesy of Misty Rogers Templeton

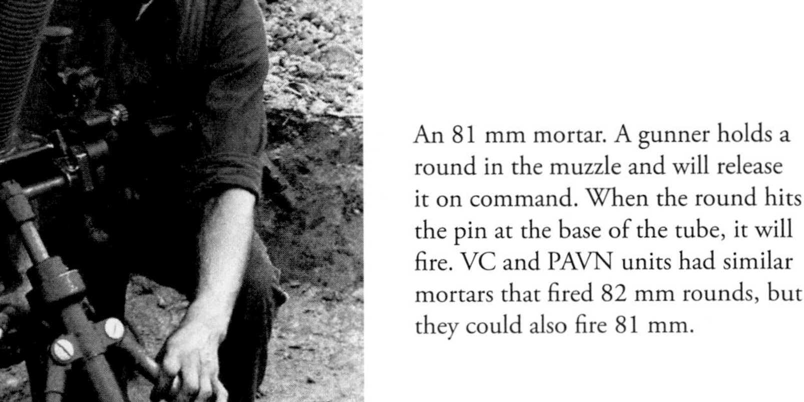

Courtesy of Marvin J. Wolf

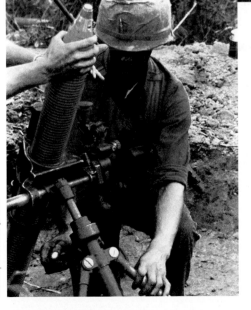

An 81 mm mortar. A gunner holds a round in the muzzle and will release it on command. When the round hits the pin at the base of the tube, it will fire. VC and PAVN units had similar mortars that fired 82 mm rounds, but they could also fire 81 mm.

Courtesy of Kenn Hopkins

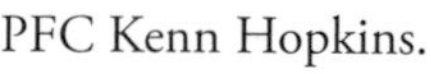

PFC Kenn Hopkins.

Courtesy of Bob Johnson

Specialist Four Bob Johnson.

Courtesy of Reginald Brockwell

First Lt. Reginald Brockwell.

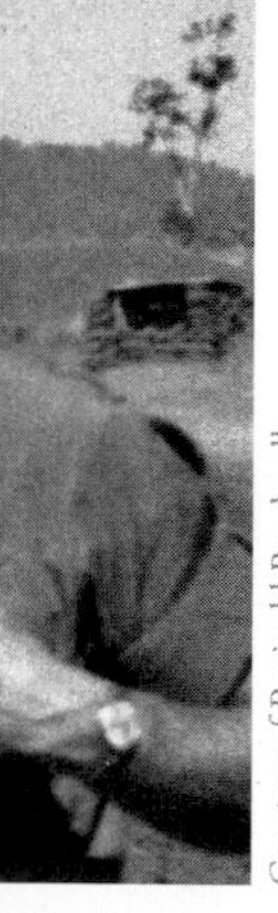

Courtesy of Reginald Brockwell

Lt. Col. Elton DeLaune.

Courtesy of Misty Rogers Templeton

Tex Rogers holds the luckless deer shot by a passing helicopter gunship. Tex dressed and butchered the animal, providing the men of Kate with a welcome meal of fresh venison.

Specialist Four Warren Geromin.

Courtesy of Warren Geromin

Courtesy of Kenn Hopkins

Sgt. Dan Pierelli, a consummate professional and my right hand. Without Dan, Kate could have had a different ending.

Courtesy of Nelson Koon

Specialist Four Nelson Koon.

Courtesy of Mike Caldwell

Specialist Four Bernie Tiranti.

Courtesy of Carol Black Fredericks

Chief Warrant Officer Nolan Black.

Courtesy of USAF

Major Gerald R. Helmich.

Courtesy of John Davison

Warrant Officer John "Les" Davison, also known as "Falcon 2."

Courtesy of Ben Gay

Chief Warrant Officer Ben Gay.

Courtesy of Al Dykes

Air Force Major Al Dykes, also known as "Spooky 41"—our nighttime lifeline.

Courtesy of Mike Caldwell

Sgt. Mike Caldwell.

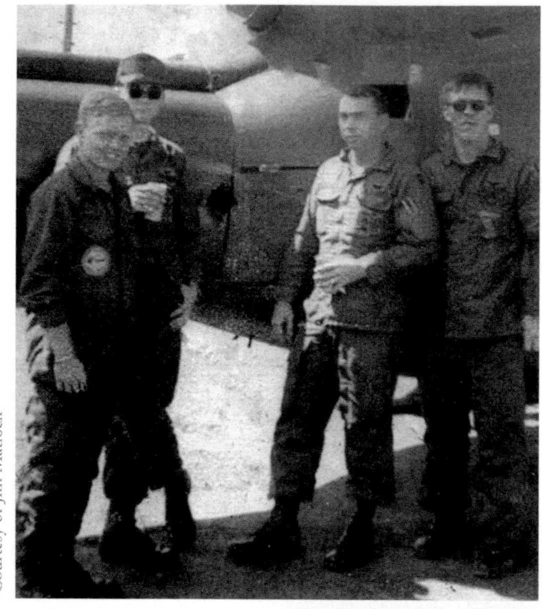
Courtesy of Jim Matlock

The crew of Ghostrider 12 (*left to right*): unidentified, pilot Jim Matlock, copilot Wilbur Guthrie, unidentified. Note the damage to the fuselage near Matlock, caused by mortar landing during takeoff from Kate.

Courtesy of Mike Smith

An OH-6 LOACH flies over Kate.

Courtesy of Kenn Hopkins

A B-52 strike (Arc Light) on targets near a firebase in northern II Corps.

Courtesy of Mike Smith

Capt. Klaus Adam (*left*) with one of his battery officers.

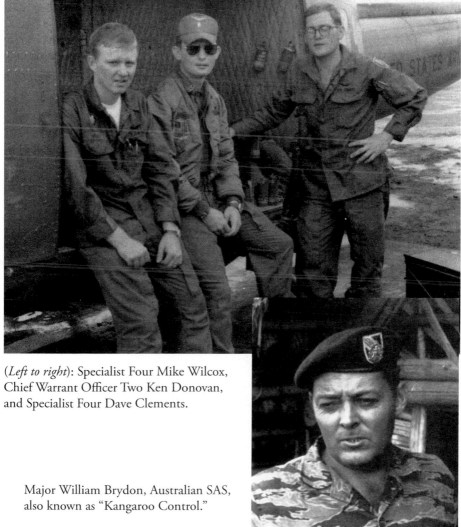

Courtesy of Ken Donovan

(*Left to right*): Specialist Four Mike Wilcox, Chief Warrant Officer Two Ken Donovan, and Specialist Four Dave Clements.

Major William Brydon, Australian SAS, also known as "Kangaroo Control."

Courtesy of Steve Sherman

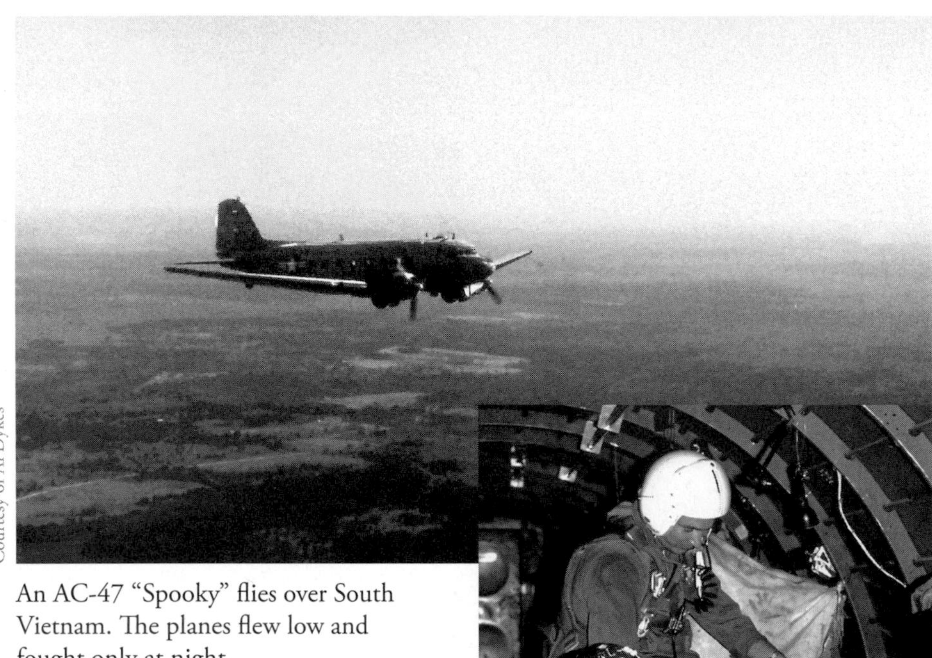

Courtesy of Al Dykes

An AC-47 "Spooky" flies over South Vietnam. The planes flew low and fought only at night.

Spooky aircraft gunners load and arm a 7.62 mm minigun.

Courtesy of Al Dykes

Courtesy of Al Dykes

Tracer fire from a Spooky aircraft circling over Kate can be seen in this time-exposed photograph.

Courtesy of Steve Sherman

(*First row, right*): Lt. Col. Franklin Collins, commander of II Mike Force, at an awards ceremony in Pleiku. Collins was the overall commander and planner of the MF unit that attempted to reinforce Kate.

Courtesy of Mike Smith

The impact ceremony at Ban Me Thuot at which several of Kate's survivors were decorated.

Courtesy of William Albracht

(*Left to right*): SFC Don Simmons, me, and SFC Lowell Stevens at a 1996 Mike Force reunion. Simmons and Stevens led the Mike Force unit that we linked up with in the early hours of November 2. This photograph captures the first time I'd seen them since that night.

Courtesy of William Albracht

In 2012 I was awarded a third Silver Star, this one for my actions on Kate. I am grateful not only for the award but for the closure that it provided.

cations were handled by the navigator. We had to record every mission's conversations; we sent map coordinates and everything. So I had a tape recorder on my desk behind the pilots at the NAV station. When someone called us, we'd mash the button and record the conversation.[4] And so the navigator did all the talking while airborne on a mission."

Spooky and Shadow aircraft were assigned targets by a special air controller. "If you needed air support, you'd call your command post. Those people would call a controller we called 'Ragged Scooper' and give him the coordinates. He'd alert the nearest available Spooky, wherever it was—sometimes we were flying combat air patrol over Nha Trang, for example; sometimes we'd stay airborne so that we could take off and be gone in a hurry; give us the coordinates and we go right to the target . . .

"I was just out of Alabama, not too many years before, and I had that good ol' Southern accent," Dykes remembers. "The second time we approached Kate, there was another aircraft in the area, and someone in it noticed my accent and asked, 'Where are you from?'

"I said, 'Gadsden, Alabama,' which is halfway between Birmingham and Chattanooga.

"Hawk picked up on that, and from then on I was no longer Spooky 41. I was Alabama."

Al Dykes's second mission to Kate was around midnight on October 30. "I called Kate up on the radio and said, 'Hawk, this is Spooky 41. We're about five minutes out from your position.'"

I called back and told him where we were. We were running out of batteries for our strobe, so I turned it on just long enough for Spooky to get a fix, and then turned it off. I told him where the enemy was located—pretty much all around us, but especially to our east and north. I liked the sound of Spooky 41's voice—he sounded calm and avuncular, a rich baritone with a distinctive Old South accent.

Our conversations were in the clear: My Signal Operating Instructions, a little set of laminated cards that gave us frequencies and call signs and authentication tables, were current for only one month. They expired at

4 See Appendix.

midnight on the 31st; as that date approached I was told to continue using what we had been using. It didn't much matter: PAVN knew exactly where we were, and they were zeroed in on every inch of the firebase.

I was always worried when neither Spooky nor Shadow was overhead at night. Like me, Dan Pierelli, and the artillerymen who were fighting as infantry, the strikers were exhausted from days of fighting with almost no sleep. I had them on 50 percent alert—one guy in each hole awake—but between their fatigue, the ground fog that sometimes settled over Kate, and the nearness of the jungle below our positions, more than once we caught enemy sappers who had crept within a few meters of our perimeter. With Spooky or Shadow orbiting overhead, just the sound of their engines was a deterrent. Several times a night, we'd ask them to fire for a few seconds into a tree line a little below us, just in case PAVN was massing for an attack.

When each Spooky or Shadow aircraft appeared overhead, I usually went over what we needed that night, and I usually added, "As long as they hear you up there, you put out [minigun fire] a little bit here and a little bit there, they're not going to try a hell of a lot, because they know what you people can do; they know you can shoot [them] up every time they move."

"Roger that," Dykes returned on this night. "And by the way, Chicken Hawk, Happy Halloween, the Spookies are out!"

BUT this night was different. Even with Spooky above, spreading the gospel of lying low to every PAVN trooper within earshot of its engines, we observed flashlights on the heights to our east periodically throughout the whole night. The 105 crew fired several HE rounds at them, and so did Pierelli with the 81 mm mortar. Moreover, even the sound of Spooky's engines could not mask the digging noises that came from all sides, or the racket made by large numbers of troops moving through the jungle, especially around our south end. I directed Alabama to saturate these areas with fire, but its effects on what sounded like a large force were unknown, and in any case temporary.

About an hour before dawn, Sergeant Houghtaling, the young noncom in charge of the 105 howitzer crew, was in his hooch, a half culvert of corrugated steel that sat on a couple of layers of sandbags and was covered with more sandbags. The cannoneer who shared his shelter had reloaded his M16, but forgot to set the safety. As he crawled in, his rifle discharged and hit Houghtaling in the right elbow; the bullet went up his arm and exited his shoulder. The medic came over and patched him up, but he was in great pain.

"A guy came up to me and said, 'Sarge, Houghtaling wants you,'" recalls Pierelli. "I went over there and got down on my knees next to him; he was in and out of consciousness, and every so often he would say, 'Sarge, it hurts, it hurts!'

"I asked if they had given him morphine, which can make you crazy, and someone said that they did. I asked when they last gave him a shot, and I told the medic to give him another one. Then I painted a big *M* on his forehead with iodine," he adds.

The continuous troop movements during the night had me worried more than usual. When the sky was beginning to lighten in the east, about when Spooky usually packed up and left, I called Alabama.

He told me that he had to go, that he had to beat the sunrise home.

I asked if there was *any* chance that he could stay until the sun came up. And I told him about the PAVN located on the ridgeline across from us, and that every time, as soon as the sun rose, they fired rockets and then mortars at us.

Dykes said, "Hang on a minute."

Lieutenants Crites and Resquist, Spooky 41's pilots, listened to our conversation.

Dykes said, "Well, crew?"

Crites, the pilot, replied, "You don't even have to ask; you know that we're going to stay."

"I had that kind of a crew; we're going to stay where we have to," says Dykes. "I called Hawk back and said, 'We're going to go out to the east and just orbit until the sun comes up, and then we'll cruise back in.'

"We had a little more than 2,000 rounds of ammo left," he continues. "We started back in just as the sun popped up over the horizon. Hawk was right: We saw four rockets launched from that one position. I told the pilot, 'Just open up on 'em and give 'em all of it.' We were on them in half a minute—

dropped in with the sun behind us, rolled up on our left wing, and fired all 2,000 rounds," says Dykes.

Spooky 41 then climbed to about 6,000 feet and turned for its base at Phan Rang.

"I was not a troublemaker, but everybody I worked with knew that I was headstrong about certain things, and that I wouldn't back down," recalls Dykes. "The sun was well up when we landed [at Phan Rang] and taxied in. The squadron commander, a colonel, was standing there waiting while we climbed out of our ship. He didn't call to the pilots. He waved me over. Just me.

"He said, 'Do you know that I could have you court-martialed? You broke all the rules!' I stood there at attention for about five minutes and all I said was 'Yes sir' and 'No sir,' and he went on and on and on. I'd never been chewed like that in my whole career, before or since. I've had a few people say, 'Now, Al, you don't do that,' for something, but not like that, standing at attention getting chewed out. When he was finished, the colonel looked at me and said, 'If he asked you to stay again, you would, wouldn't you?'

"I said, 'Yes sir.' And he turned and left."

Dykes felt that he had made a connection with me and everyone on Kate. "I don't know, I can't explain it, but [that morning] I got back to my base and I went in to the duty officer and I told him to put my name down to fly every night. As long as Hawk needs somebody over there, I'm going back," Dykes explains.

"The duty officer signed me up," Dykes continues. "I didn't fly with the same pilot each time, but I was the NAV every night. I felt a connection with them; I didn't know what it was then, but I do now: When I was ten years old, we lived south of Gadsden, Alabama, in a place where there were no real houses or buildings, and you could look up and see five or ten hawks flying around all the time. I collected their feathers to make my own arrows to play bow and arrows. So the hawk has always been my favorite bird, and then I go over to Vietnam and there was Hawk . . . It might sound strange, but I felt that connection to him."

FUNERAL FIRES

Gun fire and fear
Grew bigger
With each moment
We laid there,
Covered by an umbrella of terror.
Where not even the blue sky
could touch us
or give us courage.
We lay there
Listening to the rhythmic bombings of Elysian Fields
By angels flying B-52s while
We dreamed of voyages beyond
This corpse-filled moment
But I also knew, for sure, I was not ready
For any funeral fires.
I just had too many more desires!

—Anonymous, War Zone C

THIRTEEN

About the time that Al Dykes was getting his ass reamed by his squadron commander, twenty-seven American airmen were sitting down to morning chow in an Air Force mess hall about 400 miles east of Kate, in Utapao, Thailand, a resort city on the north rim of the Gulf of Siam. After eating, they would walk over to a makeshift briefing room, where they would learn the details of that morning's mission. They would be looking at aerial photos of the area east of Bu Prang, closely examining our battered and cratered hilltop and the surrounding terrain, especially to the east.

As those airmen emptied plates heaped with cooked-to-order bacon and eggs, as they buttered their toast and stirred cream and sugar into their hot coffee, I was picking my way around the west side of Kate's perimeter with Ron Ross, giving him the lay of the land, helping him to see our situation through an infantryman's eyes, and sharing my most immediate tactical concerns with him. By then, I had been forced to consider what might happen to Kate if I went down, and it wasn't pretty: Kerr was wounded and needed a hospital. So did Houghtaling—from what I had seen, probably the most effective of Kate's artillery noncoms, and the ramrod of a small crew of determined cannoneers who for days had stood their ground, loading and firing even under heavy fire. Pierelli was a solid guy, but he had no experience working with the controllers who brought in the fast movers for close air support. And he wasn't an officer; some of the artillery sergeants, the ones who mostly hid in their holes, outranked him. If I was gone, it would be up to Ross and Pierelli to hold things together. And despite Spooky 41's presence and excellent gunnery, PAVN had been moving troops around us all night. I was pretty sure they weren't planning a parade.

About this time, 23-year-old Warrant Officer John Ahearn, call sign "Stagecoach 11," a former engineering student from New York, climbed into a 155th AHC slick and took off from BMT for Gia Nghia. During the previous week, he had flown almost continuously between Gia Nghia and Dak Lak, east of Kate. "I vividly remember seeing almost continuous air strikes on Kate. I'm a couple of miles away at 4,000 feet and I see an [Air Force] F-100 come in to attack; as soon as it breaks off, I see all these ants swarming out of the jungle and running up the hill—North Vietnamese troops. Absolutely astounding."

Ahearn's Halloween mission was to pick up a replacement for Ron Ross, so that Ross could go to Hawaii for R&R. First Lieutenant Maurice "Moe" Zollner, a 1/92 Artillery fire direction officer, was waiting at Gia Nghia; Ahearn was to fetch him, then fly to Bu Prang to load ammo and supplies, bring both to Kate, then pick up Ross and take him to Phan Rang so he could go on R&R. All these years later, I have to wonder which bonehead had decided to send Ross out to Kate for one day and then replace him. Whether that was Lieutenant Colonel Delaune or one of his underlings, he *had* to know that the most perilous part of serving on Kate was simply getting there or getting out of there. How many Kate-bound helicopters had turned back because of the hellish ground fire in the neighborhood?

Ahearn had never flown into our perilous little heliport. "Bu Prang—I knew it like my backyard," Ahearn says. "I also flew frequently into Susan and Annie." But not Kate. With copilot Marlin Johnson of Decatur, Illinois, in the left seat, Ahearn climbed to 4,000 feet—just out of small-arms range—and headed west.

Meanwhile, those Air Force aviators were on the Utapao flight line, going through long, detailed preflight checklists on each of their three B-52D bombers. These airmen were on temporary duty from one or another of the Strategic Air Command bases scattered around the world. Their usual duty was flying a B-52H long-range heavy bomber configured for delivering thermonuclear bombs on targets thousands of miles distant. Their STRATCOM training missions involved flying great distances to drop such bombs on city size targets from high altitudes. So far, they've never dropped an actual nuclear weapon.

Before arriving in Thailand, these crews completed an intensive two-week training course in the B-52D. The aircraft they would fly this morning was configured to bomb troop concentrations and other live targets from below 26,000 feet, the altitude at which exhaust from their eight jet engines is likely to create telltale streamers of ice crystals—contrails—that are visible from the ground from as much as fifty miles. The B-52D "Big Belly" fuselage has been modified to carry eighty-four 500-pound bombs; each will also hang a dozen 750 pounders under each wing—all told, thirty tons of explosives per aircraft.

About the time when the B-52 aircrews were poking and prodding their aircraft systems in Thailand, PAVN stepped up to Kate for another dance: Accompanied by melodious but deadly mortars and rockets, they launched another full-scale attack at our southeast quadrant, the steepest slope of our fortress hilltop—by far the most difficult to climb.

For that reason, I didn't have many men there. Several hundred PAVN infantrymen surged out of the jungle and up that slope, shooting as they came; many dropped, but some rolled right over my strikers.

I was on the radio, trying to get more air support, when a runner appeared and told me what was happening. I ran to the fight, found some sandbags for partial cover, and began directing the counterattack. PAVN had punched through the wire along a twenty-yard section; some were now through the wire, some still in the midst of it, others firing at us from around our own foxholes. Nearly every Montagnard striker I ever met was a good fighter. He became twice as bold, twice as brave, twice as aggressive, when an American was fighting alongside him. My presence in the middle of that firefight bucked them up, and they leaned into the battle.

Strikers from other parts of the perimeter left their positions and joined me to hit the invaders on their flanks. After a short, vicious firefight—it seemed like a long time, but it was actually only a few minutes—PAVN broke contact, dragging their dead and wounded back over the crest and down the slope. They left behind several satchel charges; I presumed they had expected to destroy our bunkers. We set the fuses and hurled them over the wire, down through the trees, to explode in the jungle below.

A couple of Falcon gunships made passes at the slopes and the jungle below our wire, which served to discourage the rest of the attackers and drive them back.

The gunships soon exhausted their minigun ammo and they returned to Bu Prang. In the few minutes before the enemy attack resumed, I had our wounded moved to our makeshift aid station, and reinforced that section of the perimeter by thinning out the other parts—but now I was running out of able-bodied infantry. Aside from the strikers wounded during that little episode, a few others had been hit by fragments from "friendly" bombs—the Air Force, praise the Lord, dropped their napalm and bombs very, very close to our lines.

Meanwhile, Ahearn was landing at Bu Prang with Zollner. He was there to load our desperately needed small-arms ammunition. "Our Falcon gunship pilots were waiting," Ahearn recalls. "They wanted to tell me something that they didn't want to say [in the clear] on the radio: that they were out of [7.62 mm] minigun ammunition. They could cover me with rockets," Ahearn recalls. "I would have much preferred the miniguns, [but] all I said was, 'Fine, let's get this done.' "

Before taking to the air, Ahearn warned Zollner that if the ground fire was too intense and he couldn't risk a landing, the lieutenant should be prepared to jump into Kate; the pilot would tell him when to go.

Ahearn knew that his best hope for a successful in-and-out was speed. "As I took off from Bu Prang," he recalls, "I flashed on an experience the previous April, when Major Moore taught me that, in an emergency, I could fly my UH-1H up to 20 knots over the indicated red-line speed for a short time. I don't know that I hit *140* knots getting to Kate, but I sure pegged 120."

His RPM indicator redlined, Ahearn flew straight east. "I stayed low, and as I flew over the jungle close to Kate, I saw many trees that had been blown away by air strikes. Huge craters were everywhere! Everything was brown where the foliage had been blown away," he says.

As Kate loomed up in front of him, "I did what's called a cyclic climb, where you pull the control stick back and trade airspeed for altitude, just climb right up the side of the mountain."

He arrived as we were beating back PAVN's third ground assault of the day.

"It was a terrible approach—I didn't know where the helipad was. I just popped over the ridge and hovered over a revetment with a howitzer in it. We're getting fired on, and Zollner has to jump from about five feet. The crew chief and the gunner push all the supplies off, and I put the nose over and fly down the hillside in ground effect [riding on a cushion of air, rather than true flight using rotor-blade lift]. I stay in the trees and finally turn northeast . . . remaining just off the trees for ten minutes or so, scared shitless. It was a terrifying experience, but we did what we had to do."

By then, the three B-52s of the 486th Bomb Squadron were rolling down the long runway at Utapao Royal Air Base. Arc Light Mission Golf 476 would climb to 25,000 feet as it flew south and east at 525 knots over water. In half an hour they would approach Vietnam's watery Ca Mau Peninsula, a Viet Cong stronghold.

Zollner was about Kerr's age, as I recall him, perhaps an inch under six feet and 190 well-muscled pounds, with wavy light brown hair. Although both Kerr and Zollner were from the 1/92 Artillery Battalion, they had not met previously. They huddled in the FDC while Kerr gave Zollner a cursory situation briefing. Minutes later, as incoming rockets and mortars resumed, a Dustoff helicopter dropped out of the overcast. Kerr dragged himself to the helipad, and then helped the heavily medicated Houghtaling get aboard. A few seconds later, dodging a renewed rain of rockets, they hovered off Kate and flew directly to the well-equipped 71st Evacuation Hospital in Pleiku. "Coming out, we were lucky that we didn't get hit by a rocket," recalls Kerr.

Zollner was not so lucky. Soon after arriving on Kate, he was hit—

mortar shrapnel pierced the bridge of his nose. It was painful but not life-threatening, and Zollner proved himself a trooper: He refused evacuation, and afterward, when he was on the radio with Spooky or other close-support aircraft, he used the call sign "Beak" as his private joke. I was glad to have him; he did absolutely everything I asked of him, and he did it well.

About the time Dustoff left with Kerr and Houghtaling, the three command pilots of Arc Light Golf 476, now at 25,000 feet over the Ca Mau Peninsula, turned north by northeast. They throttled their engines back to 400 knots. Bombardiers on each aircraft began pre-bomb-run checklists. Navigators reminded their respective aircraft commanders that they were programmed to turn west just before overflying Dak Som and, as a backup, provided the preplanned turn time and compass heading for the move.

A little before 1000 hours, warning messages were received almost simultaneously on the FDC radio and on mine: *Take cover immediately*. Recall that I had been in the field less than a month, that this was my first time in combat, and that I had never seen a B-52 strike. A day earlier, I had requested heavier bombing closer to our perimeter. But this was my first inkling that my request had been granted—and I didn't know exactly what was coming. I passed the word, and we buttoned up Kate as best we could. With everyone deep in their hole or bunker, if PAVN had hit us right then, they could have washed over us like a wave. But several minutes before I got the take-cover warning, the mortars and rockets had stopped, and for a short while it was actually quiet around Kate.

Ahearn had refueled at Gia Nghia and was back in the air. "A FAC pilot radioed me to position myself north of Kate, circle, and await a B-52 strike," he recalls. This put him over Cambodia, but he didn't regard that as a problem, because nearly every 155 AHC pilot who flew from Bu Prang to BMT took a direct route that took them over a part of Cambodia's supposedly neutral territory, a salient jutting into South Vietnam.

But the prospect of circling over territory that he knew was crawling with PAVN troops made Ahearn cautious. "Because I was going to be in a relatively fixed position, I climbed to a higher altitude," Ahearn recalls. "We flew race tracks and figure eights for twenty or thirty minutes."

I never saw the B-52s. I never heard their engines. At 1011 local time, thirty-six seconds after the first bomb was released, as it reached a velocity of just over 800 miles per hour, it slammed into the ground and detonated. It was followed by 323 more bombs. Ninety tons of high explosives packed in steel landed half a kilometer or less from Kate.

Not knowing what was coming in, I glanced eastward and beheld the first few massive explosions—for a fleeting moment, I thought they were the back blasts from some indirect-fire weapon. Recoiling, shocked, I thought, *Oh my God! If that's the back blast, how in God's name will we ever survive the impact?* Then the incredible shock waves and deafening sounds rolled over me and my nose went in the dirt.

From his perch over Cambodia, Ahearn had the catbird seat: "I'm looking south at Kate from around 6,000 feet and all of sudden, my God in heaven, an ugly brown zipper opens in the green jungle right along the narrow, east/west ridgeline just south of Kate," reports Ahearn. "The entire hillside erupts from east to west on a continuous line westward, toward Bu Prang."

On Kate, it was like being camped out on the road between Sodom and Gomorrah while fire and brimstone rained from the heavens. An unearthly roar assaulted our ears. The earth bucked and dipped and shook for a minute that seemed like an eternity.

Although they slept on clean sheets, showered daily with hot water, ate in an air-conditioned mess hall, and nobody was shooting at them, I've got to applaud those airmen for putting their bombs just where I wanted them. If any *one* of those 500-pounders had landed on Kate, I'm certain that it would have killed me and everyone else on our hill. As it was, one bomb landed in the gully to our east, close enough for shrapnel to kill one of my strikers and wound two others.

Immediately after the strike, Air Force FAC Will Platt—Mike 82—swooped down in his Bird Dog to do a bomb damage assessment. "There was nothing left. Nothing moving. Nothing standing," he recalls.

When the explosions stopped, I went outside. An enormous cloud of dust and smoke hovered over the ridge to our east. I was pretty sure that not many PAVN could have survived something like that.

Unless, as we would later learn, they had been warned. As early as

1967, Russian trawlers bristling with antennas had been spotted off the north end of Guam, exactly beneath the flight path of B-52s taking off from Anderson AFB and headed to Vietnam. Ditto for the waters near Kadena Air Base in Okinawa. In May of that same year, recently declassified documents revealed that US intelligence knew that the VC had some kind of early-warning system that broadcast alerts from twenty-four to four hours before B-52 strikes. The rest of the mystery was explained in 1985: Truong Nhu Tang, a French-educated lawyer who served as a high-ranking Viet Cong political functionary, published his memoirs, which includes this passage: "B-52s flying out of Okinawa and Guam would be picked up by Soviet intelligence trawlers plying the South China Sea [*sic*]. Their headings and air speed would be computed and relayed to COSVN headquarters (Communist headquarter in South Vietnam), which would then order NLF (National Liberation Front) or Northern elements in the anticipated target zones to move away perpendicularly to the attack trajectory. Flights originating from the Thai bases were monitored both on radar and visually by our intelligence nets there, and the information similarly relayed."

So it was that ten minutes after the devastation of that B-52 strike, the shit storm battering Kate resumed: rockets, mortars, recoilless rifles, and small-arms fire smashed Kate from every direction. Our last functioning howitzer, the 105, took its second direct hit from a recoilless rifle and was finally knocked out.

A little later, as I made the rounds of the perimeter with Ross, we took advantage of a lull in the action to chat about personal things. He was from a small town in Wisconsin, I grew up less than 150 miles away, in neighboring Illinois; our backgrounds were similar, although he had been to college and was a bit older.

During our conversation, I noticed that he wore a wedding band, so I asked about his wife. Ross replied that he was due to meet her and their newborn son, John—a child that he had never seen—in Hawaii when he went on R&R.

Ron continued to talk about his son, and how proud he was to be a father, about how he could not wait to hold the infant, about his hopes and dreams for his little family's future.

Then the shooting resumed. In a moment we were pinned down on the northwest side of the perimeter. We were safe for the moment, but I couldn't run the show from there.

When things slowed down, around 1120, and after a few minutes with only occasional incoming, I decided that we had to risk moving. We were high on the military crest; as soon as we stood and moved to the top, we'd be silhouetted against the sky.

I pointed out the sandbagged command bunker and told Ross that was where we were headed. I described its L-shaped entrance and blast wall in front to protect it from the near misses of flying explosives. I told Ross, "We're going to run to that bunker. When you get there, enter from *that* side."

Ross nodded his head to show that he understood.

"There is no point in giving them two targets," I continued. "I'll go first. *Let me get to cover behind the blast wall before you follow.* Understand? Got it?"

Ross nodded again. "I've got it."

It was fifty or sixty feet to the bunker, the first part uphill, but altogether no more than a four-second sprint. I took off, running as fast as I could. The enemy was only about 125 meters away on the opposite hillside; when I was about halfway to the bunker, I heard Ross's footsteps behind me, a few steps back and closing. Then I saw the rocket. Time seemed to slow down as I heard the B-40's distinctive scream. From the corner of my eye, I saw its fiery red tail heading right at me. I hit the entrance behind the blast wall and the exploding warhead's shock wave blew me inside the bunker to safety.

Behind me, Ross lay crumpled in the doorway. One more step, and he would be telling this story. Instead, a jagged hole in his neck pulsed a fountain of blood. I slapped my hand over the wound. Someone from inside the bunker moved up behind me to help—I have no earthly idea who that was—but despite my hand clamped over his throat, Ross was still squirting blood. In half a minute, the fountain slowed to a trickle. Deathly pale, Ross was not breathing, and I realized that he would never see his new son.

I had told him to wait until I was in the bunker.

He said that he understood.

Why the hell didn't he wait?

I felt rotten. Empty. I needed time to come to terms with his death—but I didn't have even a few minutes. I tucked the thought away and returned to the urgent work of getting more air support and preparing for yet another ground attack.

An hour later, as I zipped Ross into a body bag, I noticed that he'd neglected to button the top of his flak vest, leaving his throat exposed. Had it been closed, would that few inches of layered Kevlar have saved him? It's very hard to know.

You may talk o' gin an' beer
When you're quartered safe out 'ere,
An' you're sent to penny-fights an' Aldershot it;
But if it comes to slaughter
You will do your work on water,
An' you'll lick the bloomin' boots of 'im that's got it.

—Rudyard Kipling, "Gunga Din"

FOURTEEN

We needed more men to plug the gaps in our perimeter. We needed ammunition. I needed to lie down and sleep for a week. I needed a cold beer. Most of all, we needed water. By the afternoon of October 31, we were out. Every canteen was dry. Even the canteens of the dead had been drained. Forty-eight hours of fighting under the sun and moon, and no water since the previous night. I was learning the hard way that when you're out of water, when you can no longer sweat, when peeing is out of the question because there's no fluid left in your kidneys, when you grow lethargic and there's nothing left in your body core to draw energy from, when even standing up and walking around is hard—then you're literally starting to die from dehydration. The only thing that you can think about is water. *God, I wish I had some water.* And this was where I was, and where pretty much everyone on Kate was.

I had been on the radio asking for water several times, and none came. I had prayed for rain. Yes, prayed to God to send us water. It was that horrible.

You don't forget that kind of thirst. It's been more than forty-six years, and I haven't.

I radioed yet again, and told Bu Prang that we *must* have some water.

Staff Sergeant DeNote, the communications honcho for Team A-236 and my constant companion over the FM radio lifeline, told me not to worry.

Late in the afternoon, low on the horizon to the west, I saw two Chinooks, call sign "Freight Train," escorted by a couple of Falcon gunships. A pair of Cobra gunships, call sign "Undertaker," were already on station, and they gave the ridge and hillside a good going-over; the first drop was completed without incident.

Warrant Officer Les Davison was ramrodding the Falcon gunship team: "When we arrived, two Undertaker Cobras happened to be on station, and together we covered the first CH-47 in and out without incident. But that had expended the Snakes [ammunition], and our two Charlies just couldn't put out enough firepower to cover the second Hook as well. He made it out OK—but not without taking several hits. The area was definitely HOT!"

The first load was our water.

The second was our ammunition. As the Chinook closed on us, it was taking heavy ground fire from several directions. The Falcon gunships deployed on either side of Kate, moving around and firing at what I can only describe as a highly target-rich environment. It didn't seem to help much—there were just too damn many enemy guns. As the Chinook approached, it descended until it was perhaps fifty feet above Kate's summit, closing on our south end doing maybe thirty-five or forty knots. The pilot released his load and the Chinook leapt into the air, turning left as it clawed for altitude.

The big rope basket with our ammo dropped a few meters short of our foxholes. It tumbled down the slope, crashed through the treetops, and then disappeared into the jungle below.

It took me a few seconds to realize that I had might have witnessed the first successful PAVN aerial resupply of the war. Down in the jungle, the boys in pith helmets would soon be celebrating. There was nothing to do but hope that we could hold off another ground attack until we could get more ammo. Until then we would have to make do with what little we had. And then I realized that we might yet see some of our lost ammo, but not until the neighbors fired it at us.

At least we had water. Four hundred gallons in an M-149 water trailer, the venerable steel "Buffalo." Five thousand pounds of water and trailer, dropped from twenty feet off the deck, the impact breaking two wheels and both axles.

But the tank held.

Water! Safely on Kate, and ours for the taking.

Oh, shit.

Dozens of strikers left their holes and rushed the trailer. Ran for their water. Ran for their lives. Danny and I ran after them, screaming at them to stay away, dragging them away from the trailer, throwing them back, trying to stop the riot. Too late: Attracted by the crowd, the nasty neighbors began walking their mortars the length of Kate. Mortar bombs exploded all around the trailer. *Mirabile dictu,* by God's grace, no shard of shrapnel pierced that rotund steel trailer. Our precious and holy water was saved.

Not so my strikers, several of whom were hit, a few seriously. Also hit was Sergeant Mike Caldwell, a tall, thin, bespectacled 22-year-old draftee from West Sacramento, California, universally known as "Red" for his flaming red hair and freckles. When the first mortars landed, Koon and Tiranti jumped into his sandbagged hooch. "We sat down on a cot, me and Bernie on either side of Red, and then a mortar round landed right inside the doorway," recalls Koon.

"We were getting hit pretty hard, and I had just put both hands over my helmet," Caldwell recalls. His forearms were peppered with shrapnel; he bled profusely. Koon was unhurt. And for the second time in three days, Tiranti was miraculously unscathed.

Meanwhile, Danny and I drove the thirsty strikers back to their holes. Then we dragged or carried the wounded to our makeshift aid station. When everyone had calmed down, we had an orderly distribution of water, one man from a squad at a time.

• • •

AT 1520 that day, while I was in my bunker talking to Major Lattin on the radio, I heard a door slam. And then two more, one after the other.

There were no doors on Kate.

A series of tremendous explosions rocked the hilltop—large-caliber artillery shells landing nearby. The earth shook as several rounds slammed right into Kate. A few bunkers partially caved in. One round landed near the corner of the FDC. Three feet closer and it would have blown the roof off.

When the explosions stopped, I popped out of my hole. Kate was high enough that we could see the muzzle flash of big guns firing from a few miles to the northwest.

I got back in my hole just before the shell buried itself in Kate's side and the hilltop rocked from the impact. Evidently, PAVN had obtained conventional artillery pieces—perhaps they had taken a few of their big guns apart and hauled them piecemeal down the Ho Chi Minh Trail, then reassembled them at Cambodian Army Camp La Rolland, a base used, I am told, to train PAVN replacements. Or maybe they'd captured some ARVN 105s.

"The North Vietnamese had 130 mm guns and 105 mm howitzers, probably captured from the French," explains Reg Brockwell. "So they had the same artillery capacity as we did—except that we operated under rules of engagement that said we couldn't attack [across the Cambodian border] unless it was under exceptional conditions."

The PAVN respected no rules of engagement.

It made no difference where they came from or if it was 105 mm or bigger. Another round landed near Kate. Another. Two more, almost together.

If this didn't stop soon, we would all die. Our defenses simply could not take a direct hit from that kind of artillery and survive. I called—screamed, actually—for Major Lattin to call in the fast movers to silence those guns.

He flew northwest, circling low over the Vietnam side of the international border. After a few minutes, he called back.

"Can't do it, Hawk," he said. "They're on the other side of the fence."

I got back on the radio and told Lattin in no uncertain words that I didn't care where they were. I wanted them hit.

"The only way I can do that is if the ground commander declares a tactical emergency."

No sooner had these words caressed my ears than I said, "I declare a tactical emergency," in the same tone of voice that I might have used to order a cold Tiger Beer at the officers' club.

"Roger," returned Lattin. The next thing I knew, the fast movers were screaming eastward to bomb the bollocks out of Camp La Rolland. A week later there was a blurb in *Newsweek* to the effect that US Air Force planes had bombed a neutral Cambodian Army base. John Kerry mentioned it in his Winter Soldier rants. So let me set the record straight for all time: That was me. *I* did that. If I hadn't, my bones, and those of everyone else on Kate, would probably be rotting in the bottom of a big ravine below Kate's ghost.

The cross-border strike triggered formal protests of outrage from Phnom Penh and all the rest of that bull. I still chuckle when I realize that my name was probably on President Nixon's desk the next morning, the rogue officer who had created an international incident by directing a "neutral" country to be bombed.

But as soon as that heavy incoming artillery was stopped, PAVN attacked from four sides, hundreds of enemy soldiers running, walking, or crawling up at us, firing. Thanks to Major Lattin and the fast movers he brought in, we held our hilltop. A little later, however, when I got the casualty reports and ammo status, it was clear that we were losing this battle. The next time PAVN attacked in force might be the last.

Later, as I did every night, I radioed a casualty report to Rocco at Bu Prang. When I had concluded, Rocco asked if that was it.

"One more thing," I said, thinking about the big bag of M&M's peanut candy that I had stashed in my rucksack. Shrapnel from the PAVN artillery had holed my rucksack and pierced the half-empty bag.

"I took a direct hit in my M&M's," I added, going for the laugh.

"Do you want a medevac?" he replied, concern in his voice.

"Nope. That's it," I said, and signed off.

Not until days later did I learn that Rocco, and the rest of our team at Bu Prang, had mistakenly understood my reference to M&M's as code for testicles.

BETWIXT and between all my other chores, I'd been back and forth to Bu Prang on the radio and, reading between the lines, I was given to understand that there would be no help coming from the 23rd ARVN or the US 4th. The former, I am now certain, because I challenge anyone to show me ten ARVN officers who would have given a rabid rodent's rectum for the life of one Montagnard, let alone a hundred or so who knew how to fight and didn't much care for their kind either. The latter, I am now equally certain, because the Pentagon was crooning "Vietnamization," music by Richard M. Nixon, lyrics by Department of the Army, arrangement by Military Assistance Command, Vietnam.

In plain English, the Fifth Special Forces request for assistance from the ARVN high command had been met with stony indifference. The ARVN would never say no to an American general, but they had a dozen ways to avoid saying yes: They would "study the request." Or "seriously consider it." They would "explore the ramifications." They would try to "reorder their priorities." They would apologize for communications difficulties.

What they wouldn't do was fight for us.

On the other side of the table, US commanders were under strict orders to implement Vietnamization. Most of the warm bodies on Kate—and most of the cold, stiff ones in body bags stacked like cordwood on our landing pad—were South Vietnamese Montagnards, members of the CIDG, whose chain of command ran through the ARVN Special Forces. Recall that the yellow-and-red South Vietnamese flag flew over Camp Bu Prang, as it did over all Special Forces camps in Vietnam. Note also that there was not then, nor had there ever been, so much as a single ARVN soldier on Kate. Nevertheless, whoever was running the US Army in our part of Vietnam would not allow his subordinates to commit troops to a rescue, since relieving Kate's garrison was to him so obviously an ARVN responsibility.

Bottom line: If we could hold Kate, fine. If the ARVN 23rd's commanding general changed his mind and sent some of his precious troops to help us, woo-hoo! Another win for Vietnamization!

And if not—them's the breaks. Shit happens. It's a war, y'know.

We were pawns in a political poker game in which neither side would call the other's bet.

So we'd been written off. Sacrificed for the greater good of forcing the Saigon regime to take responsibility for its own war. By then, almost 47,000 American soldiers had died in Vietnam. What were a couple dozen more corpses if it would speed the day when Nixon could declare victory, bring all Americans home, and win a second term?

All that aside, I didn't believe for a minute that my Special Forces brothers would abandon me and Pierelli, along with more than a hundred Montagnard strikers, and of course all the artillery boys, if there was anything at all that could be done.

KATE'S perilous situation was not unique. By this time, the IFFV Artillery commander's pipe dream that small hilltop firebases along the Cambodian border would protect Special Forces camps at Duc Lap and Bu Prang had become a catastrophic nightmare. Duc Lap's Firebase Helen was the first to fall. "It was overrun on October 28th," recalls Reg Brockwell. "There were quite a few causalities, and [PAVN] then made it their own firebase."

Nearby to Helen was Firebase Martha, evacuated the next day, the day that Kate had first come under attack. Despite those defeats, and what was all too apparent at Kate, no senior IFFV artillery officer was disciplined or relieved of command for sticking indefensible firebases on PAVN's doorstep.

Describing these tragedies in the February 1970 edition of the IFFV troop magazine, *The Typhoon*, Colonel Francis Bowers, commander of the Provisional Artillery Group, would say that "the important thing is that the artillerymen on those three [firebases] had already *done their job of supporting the troops* [emphasis added]. There wasn't any need for them any longer on the hills. The operation on the ground were completed. And these firebases would have been evacuated soon anyway. They were sitting ducks."

All credit to Colonel Bowers for the sitting-duck metaphor. As far as

I have been able to tell, however, Kate's artillery hadn't supported any ground troops except themselves. Kate was emplaced to support Bu Prang, but never got the chance to do so. While I hate to disagree with a colonel, the balance of Bowers's statement in *The Typhoon* was equine road apples:

"General Abrams eventually blamed Special Forces for all firebase failures in this campaign," explains Brockwell, forty years after the fact. "I have no idea why. I heard that the tactical zone commander of the 23rd ARVN refused to support [the firebases]. He said, 'We're not going to risk any Vietnamese troops. They're Americans; it's your problem.' Plus there were Montagnard tribesmen out there, whom the Vietnamese detested and called savages, so basically, they had no skin in the game."

So I was greatly cheered when I got an encrypted message from my "B" Team commander indicating that a rescue/reinforcement operation was in the works.

"The overall Special Forces commander for the Bu Prang operation was Lieutenant Colonel Collins, sharp as a needle, a really, really, really good man," recalls DeNote. "Simmons probably could've stayed in BMT, if he wanted, but he chose to come right into the camp. He's the guy who called in the relief Mike Force."

DeNote is dead right about Collins. I would have followed him through the gates of hell, and that sentiment was shared by everyone else in B-23.

"The plans for Kate's rescue were drawn up in our TOC," DeNote continues. "Collins stayed inside it and operated off our map. The Mike Force had their own radios, so [for the duration of the operation] we had two sets; if one [failed], the Mike Force radios would still be operational."

While I was on the radio, Hopkins had wandered into the FDC, and he sat on one of the desks, listening. For as long as we'd been under fire, he'd been one of our best fighters. He was good with his bloop gun, the M79, and with an M16. Sometimes he paired with Koon on the M60. And always, even under the heaviest incoming, he was moving around the perimeter, helping out in a dozen ways, from bucking somebody up, helping a wounded man, to jumping in a hole to fight alongside a striker. But just then, at that moment, he looked different. Somehow not quite right.

"I went in [to the CP] primarily to see what was going on because I can't be outside anymore. That artillery fire is going to kill me. So I went in there to *get* information instead of to *give* information," Hopkins recalls. "Doc was there, and Albracht was talking to somebody about needing more support, because they were beating us up. And whoever he was talking to, they came back and said something that amounted to 'We're not sending any more helicopters in because it's too risky; we've lost too many.'

"I looked at Albracht and I said, 'You mean they're not going to help us anymore?'

"Albracht said, 'For all intents and purposes, we're on our own right now.'

"And I said, 'Bullshit! What do you mean these people aren't going to come and protect us? We don't have guns, we have only small arms, and they say that they're not going to do anything? We're on our own now?'"

We *were* kind of on our own. But, as I tried to explain to Hopkins, the Mike Force was putting something together. If we could hold just one more night, they'd be here. I said that I didn't know, just at that moment, exactly what was planned.

Hopkins lost it. He is a very brave man. A good soldier. He had done as much as any man to defend our little corner of hell. The fact is, however, that under prolonged combat, every man can be broken, and there is no shame in it. Hopkins had reached his breaking point and couldn't take any more. He began screaming at me: "I said, this is bullshit! You get me the fuck out of here! This is bullshit. If my country's not willing to protect me, get me the hell out of here!"

Our medic, Doc, had been in a corner watching and listening. He moved over to Hopkins, repeating his name in a soothing voice. He gave him an injection of some kind, something to calm him, and in a few minutes Hopkins was asleep.

I called for a medevac; I still had to get Red Caldwell out as well. But it would be a long time before anything that didn't explode or ricochet could land on Kate.

Not every artilleryman in our small garrison was actively involved in our defense. A couple of the more senior noncoms, I am reliably told, remained under cover during every firefight. One PFC—he should be very glad that I never got his name—was sent to load wounded men on a chopper. When the medevac took off, he was on it.

I pulled my other go-to guys, including Koon and Geromin, and a few other artillerymen who had been active in our defense, into the CP. As I told them what was going on and shared my assessment of our situation, I also explained my very real hope that the Mike Force would get us out. As I spoke, I looked around the dim, crowded room, peering at their dirty, stubbled faces—there was hardly water enough to drink, let alone wash or shave. I told them, as if they didn't already know, that PAVN had hit us with almost every goddamn thing they had for more than three days. We had bled and we had died, but we held our hilltop still.

Like Hopkins, these were all good soldiers, first-rate guys, a little volunteer squad who'd individually and collectively moved around Kate to wherever they were most needed, wherever that day's enemy assault was coming from. Even under the heaviest attack, Koon was out on the perimeter manning an M60 machine gun, meeting the tip of the PAVN assault spear and pouring heavy lead into it. I realize now that he and I were not so different: We were both from small Midwestern towns. Both with tough, unyielding fathers. We'd both enlisted right out of high school, looking for adventure, looking for a good fight—and we had sure as hell found one.

As I spoke, updating our situation, I studied their faces. One man—if I ever knew it, I can no longer recall his name—was hunched over, cradling his jaw, looking very much like the famous Rodin sculpture, almost a living *The Thinker*. I looked into their bloodshot eyes, and I said, "Listen, we're all under some heavy-duty pressure here, boys, and we've got to watch out for each other."

Just then I saw "the Thinker" tremble—a tiny movement. In seconds he was shaking violently. Then he broke down, muttering, "I'm sorry; I just can't take this anymore." He began to weep, and I could see how strongly this affected all of us—how it created an even more intense bond between us. I told him, "Hey, it's all right, man, it's all right." After a little while, Doc came in and sedated him as well.

In 1969 I had yet to start college. I didn't know how much was then known about what we now call post-traumatic stress disorder. In Vietnam we called it combat fatigue or battle fatigue; our fathers' generation called it shell shock. All the same thing. I didn't need a degree in psychology to understand what had happened to these men. Lord have mercy, I knew what we had been through, what we were still going through. I never, ever felt anything but sympathy and brotherhood for these guys.

And even though we were now desperately shorthanded, they had to be evacuated. I'd rather go into battle with five men that I can depend on with my life than with a hundred that I can't be sure of.

So I had no problem sending these men back to BMT, where they would be safe and could get medical attention. They had served their country and their buddies as well as they could, and they simply had no more to give.

It was quite a while before we had a medevac pilot willing to risk flying in and out of Kate. When that brave soul was finally en route, Zollner asked him to take Ross's body as well. The pilot refused, and I got on the horn and, like Zollner, demanded that he take Ross. The pilot was wiser than both of us. He knew that lingering to take someone already beyond help would increase the risk to our wounded. He took the living, but left the dead. Later, when we finally got some of our dead evacuated, I personally carried Ross's body and stowed him on the chopper. Even in the bulky body bag, he seemed as light as a child.

As it got dark, as our ammo dwindled again to only one or two magazines per man, and to only a few boxes of linked 7.62 rounds for all our M60 machine guns, Spooky came on station. The small-arms fire stopped as PAVN infantry pulled back. The incoming mortars and rockets halted. Pierelli should have been in the sack, catching a few z's before spelling me on the radio so I could catch a few of my own. But on Kate he had trouble sleeping, so he went back into the mortar pit, spreading a little 81 mm HE love around the ridges and tree lines.

I, too, couldn't sleep. I was pretty sure that if the neighbors attacked at first light, as they usually did, we wouldn't be able to stop them. We just didn't have enough bullets. Not nearly enough. One big push and they'd be all over us.

MEANWHILE, at Bu Prang, the wheels were turning. Captain Charles Childers was the Pleiku Mike Force adjutant. We would later become good friends, but just then we had yet to meet. He was in on the rescue operation planning.

"We had two Mike Force battalions [near] Camp Bu Prang," Childers recalls, "and by the night of 31 October, both were in active contact with the enemy." Both were commanded by an Australian, Major William J. "Bill" Brydon, a seventeen-year veteran of the Australian Army who had seen combat against guerrillas in Malaya and Borneo.

"Brydon was one of those wonderful, larger-than-life Australian characters who never went anywhere without a very large can of Foster's Lager," says Childers. "He always rode helicopters with his feet on the outside skids. His combat kit was a torn T-shirt, an M16, and a Foster's; that's how he went in, and that's how we brought him out. He was much beloved by everyone—and, boy, he was a mean sonofabitch!

"Brydon had his headquarters at Camp Bu Prang. One battalion was to the south and west, and one just outside the camp. When Kate had deteriorated to the point that Hawk was going to lead them out, Brydon's mission was to set up a corridor on each side of the escape route that Bill would use, so that he wouldn't be overrun en route. Hawk had no idea about this. It was happening at night, and most of the time nobody knew where anybody else was."

Oh! I have slipped the surly bonds of Earth,
And danced the skies on laughter-silvered wings;
Sunward I've climbed, and joined the tumbling mirth
Of sun-split clouds,—and done a hundred things
You have not dreamed of—wheeled and soared and swung
High in the sunlit silence. Hov'ring there,
I've chased the shouting wind along, and flung
My eager craft through footless halls of air . . .

Up, up the long, delirious, burning blue
I've topped the wind-swept heights with easy grace.
Where never lark, or even eagle flew—
And while with silent lifting mind I have trod
The high untrespassed sanctity of space,
Put out my hand, and touched the face of God.

—Pilot Officer John Gillespie Magee, Jr., "High Flight"

FIFTEEN

Ken Donovan is tall and trim. He radiates self-confidence from his heartbreaker's face, he has unusually small hands for a man his size, and he sometimes refers to himself in the third person. "I graduated from high school in '66, when either you had enough money to go to college and keep your student deferment or you went to the Big Green Machine," he says. "I was shoveling sand in a Buick foundry, trying to earn enough money for junior college in Flint, Michigan."

After his first semester, he cut a political science class to visit the Army recruiter. "One of those life-defining points," he says. "One sergeant said, 'How would you like to work on helicopters?' and I said that it sounded pretty cool.

"Then his buddy said, 'What are you doing right now?' and when I explained that I was in junior college, he says, 'Do you wear glasses?' and when I said no, he asked if I'd like to fly. I said, 'Where do I sign on the dotted line?'"

A little over a year after he enlisted, Donovan, age 20, flew his first combat mission for the 155th AHC. After learning to fly helicopters on the flat, dry Texas plains and then the flat, low farmland around Fort Stewart,

Georgia, he had to learn on the job about the joys of mountain aviation in Vietnam's Central Highlands: "Our airfield at BMT was at about 2,000 feet," Donovan explains. "The hotter the air gets and the higher you go, the thinner the air becomes. That impacts the amount of lift that your rotor system can generate. Most of our landings could be best described as controlled crashes. In a Huey, normal-operating-engine RPM was 6,600. Going into an assault landing at around 6,200 engine RPM, the low RPM alarm begins beeping in your ear. The controls start to get a little mushy. Sometimes, when we'd break the trees, the leader would call, 'Pick your spots,' and that meant we had permission to move a little out of formation and pick a spot—some LZs were burned-off bamboo with stumps sticking three or four feet out of the ground. At such a low RPM, we often didn't have enough power to hover. Our own rotor wash caused the bird to run out of what we called 'left pedal'—the nose would start to turn to the right. It would get pretty interesting."

It got even more interesting when flying into and out of Duc Lap; the Special Forces airfield there was more than a mile high.

After a few months of ash-and-trash missions and flying air assaults for the US 4th and the ARVN 23rd, Donovan and his platoon were "volunteered" to fly for the legendary Special Operations Group. These were hush-hush missions, "black" operations that usually involved either inserting small groups of men into Cambodia to run intelligence and assassination operations, or retrieving them.

"If you flew slicks, which Donovan did, you'd fly one week supporting the missions going across into Cambodia, typically carrying two or three Americans and five or six of what we called Sioux Indians—South Vietnamese or Chinese mercenaries," Donovan remembers. "They were all dressed in North Vietnamese Army uniforms and basically wore nothing that would identify them with the US Army. So we'd spend a week flying SOG missions about seventy-five miles on the wrong side of the fence; and then the first platoon would take over that mission from us, and we'd fly regular air assaults, and log missions in-country."

As October 1969 and the end of his yearlong tour approached, Donovan decided to extend his tour. The choice seemed simple: "A bunch of us were scheduled to go home in October, and as crazy as it sounds, we said, 'Do we want to go home, take a leave, report to our new unit, and then come back to duty at Christmastime?'"

Instead, they all agreed to extend their tours for a few months, go home before Christmas, and then either start a new assignment after Christmas or get out of the Army a little earlier than expected.

"I think that contributed to our success during LZ Kate and the larger battle of Bu Prang," Donovan opines. "We had very experienced aircraft commanders. A combat unit is almost a mythical thing. This is hard to explain to civilians, but [most combat unit members believe] it's better to get killed than to look bad in front of your buddies. And I'm not saying this because I was in one, but I think all aviation units are elite units. I've said this on a number of occasions: *Ken Donovan is alive today because of the guys he flew with.* But every Army unit, to a certain extent, is about the luck of the draw. We had an exceptional group of pilots, crew chiefs, and door gunners."

From what I saw of the 155th AHC birds landing on or flying over Kate, it certainly was an elite unit. A few minutes before the end of Halloween, Ken Donovan and Les Davison were among a small group of determined 155th pilots who set out to bring in our desperately needed ammo and supplies.

"I was flying missions all around Kate," Donovan recalls. He had helped evacuate other firebases, but this was to be his first time landing on Kate.

Because of our situation, and to a lesser extent because of what was going on around Bu Prang, Duc Lap, and their remaining firebases, the 155th had been reinforced with slicks and gunships from other helicopter companies. BMT's local VC celebrated the new arrivals by lobbing mortar rounds at the 155th base at BMT's North Field. Donovan and a few other pilots began moving aircraft to East Field to disperse them.

"As I was moving an aircraft, I got a call to report to Operations, ASAP," Donovan recalls. "There were already some very senior aircraft commanders there, to include Les Davison and my roommate, J. C. Cole. The Old Man came out, Major Dean Owen, and he said, 'Okay, guys, we're going to resupply Kate tonight. You guys are the aircraft commanders; I'll have a more detailed brief for you in about an hour or so. You have the pick of the unit on who you want to fly with tonight.'

"Somebody had a really stupid idea to go in with sling loads, from which Dean Owen saved us," Donovan continues. "It was a pretty straightforward deal—we had four slicks to do the resupply, we had a fifth aircraft for command, control, and recovery of aircraft if needed, and we had four gunships, a team on either side, to escort us in."

I was not aware of any of this at the time, of course. But keep in mind that a normal daylight resupply usually involved only one or two slicks, with one or two gunships escorting if they were available. By now, however, everyone flying in the highlands knew that the ground fire around Kate was ferocious. That night, Shadow had the early over-watch mission, so before midnight, when I learned that a resupply was imminent, I got on the radio and kind of double-talked the situation. Shadow fired all around us, keeping our nasty neighbors' noses dirty. Or so I hoped.

While the pilots were being briefed, SP5 Mike Wilcox, Donovan's crew chief and among the unit's most senior crewmen, was drinking beer. "The First and Second platoons' crew chiefs and door gunners were well into a drink-a-thon in the enlisted barracks area," he recalls. "This was not an unusual activity once the aircraft maintenance had been completed and guards posted on the perimeter. We gathered in the Second Platoon hooch, where we had built a bar a few months earlier. Although we had all been very active flying missions around Bu Prang and the firebase areas, we assumed the war was over for the day, and the Schlitz and Falstaff tasted pretty good.

"Missions into the Bu Prang area were guaranteed to pass the day quickly, as there were a very large number of bad guys around. The gunfights in the LZ Kate area were at the level where you could actually see large numbers of dead [PAVN] laying in the open. Being young and bulletproof, I found it was an exciting way to pass the day.

"Well after dark, I was summoned to Operations, which was unusual. As I entered, I could sense a buzz of urgency. Something extraordinary was about to happen," Wilcox continues. He soon learned what was planned.

"Plan A was sling loads. Plan B was to load ammo and supplies in the doorways of the ships; two Special Forces guys would kick them out as we hovered over Kate," he explains. "I was told to ask for volunteers to fly this mission, that things would probably become very ugly, in terms of possible aircraft loss.

"None of the platoon guys in the 155th knew any of the guys on Kate, but upon requesting volunteers, I was amazed to see that every crewman was ready and willing to go—more than enough to fly a second mission if it was needed," Wilcox concludes.

Because the only Falcon gunship pilot senior to him was on R&R in Bangkok, Warrant Officer 1 Les Davison, with less than a year of flying experience, was senior Falcon gunship team leader. "Along with several other Falcon and Stagecoach pilots, I made my way to the Operations hooch in the darkness of the blacked-out airfield," he recalls. "As we entered, the clock showed 0010 hours; the CO and platoon leaders were poring over tactical maps, and the Operations officer was on the field phone. Obviously, all had been busy since the mission alert came down. The eyes of the pilots in the audience were mostly bloodshot—and a little scared. We had an idea what was coming.

"When all were present, Major Owen led the briefing. We had all flown into or near Kate during the fighting, and were familiar with the tactical situation. The firebase was holding out, but the defenders were low on ammunition and weren't sure they could wait until first light for resupply. We were tasked with delivering four slick loads of M16, carbine, and M60 ammo. Mission planning called for five slicks and four guns.

"If we weren't alert before, we certainly were now. I'd never been on a mission where we took an empty rescue ship. GULP! The best, most experienced pilots had been picked to fly this one, with two senior aircraft commanders in each slick. And credit to Major Owen: He knew it was a tough mission, but he didn't just send others out to accomplish it. He would be copilot in the lead ship. As the company commander, he didn't fly enough to be one of our best pilots, so he could not have been as sharp as guys who flew every day. But he knew where he needed to be for that particular mission, and he was there. Not every CO would have flown that mission.

"In a similar vein, Colonel B. R. Wright, commander of the 17th Aviation Group, appointed himself copilot of the fifth slick, the command and control, and chase aircraft.

"Our briefing covered the weather, the enemy situation, radio frequencies, and formations. Then Major Owen looked to me (the gunship lead) and asked, 'Are the Falcons going to go in hot?'

"Pete Cosmos, brand-new as an aircraft commander but never at a loss for words, piped up, 'Damn straight we will!' Major Owen said nothing, but turned his head to look at me.

"I've often wondered whether Pete's outburst affected my response—and I just don't know. I said that I'd rather wait to see if Charlie will let us do it without shooting. 'We'll be on both sides of you, ready to bring smoke—and if they do start up, we can pinpoint the source and be right on it. But you slick guys are the ones hanging out, so we'll do whatever you want.'

"Major Owen didn't hesitate. 'Okay, we'll go in cold unless Chuck starts something. They're still loading the birds. Start time will be 0110, crank on me. Good luck.' "

Donovan picks up the story: "We were to take off after midnight, so I went over to the gunners' hooch, and while they were playing cards, Jim Abbott, who had been flying all day, lay down on a bunk and went to sleep. After a while we walked out to the aircraft revetments. I strapped in, and we started going through the checklist."

Davison goes on: "[After the briefing] everybody got their gear and headed to the ships, to find the crews already there. After making sure everything was set, most of us wandered back to the platoon hooches for coffee, smokes, a few quick hands of poker, and probably to write a letter or two home. Even the pilots who weren't flying joined in, and the Dustoff guys too. As they say, you could have cut the tension with a knife.

"Although it was still too early, the Falcon card game broke up and we headed slowly toward the revetments. The slick pilots were doing the same. There were quite a few flight crewmen and others around, but it was unusually quiet. We all knew this one was different. We rechecked the ships, again—and then waited. There was little of the usual happy-go-lucky banter between and among the crews; instead, lots of nervous chatter and forced laughter. Time dragged.

"Finally it was 0110," Davison continues. "We'd been strapped in for a good five minutes listening for the telltale whine of the CO's ship starting up, but heard only silence. At 0115, more nervous chatter, but still no crank. What's the problem? Nobody knows. I sent the door gunner over to the major's ship to find out. At 0118, still quiet. Then the blare of the public address system covers the compound. 'Will Mr. Abbott please report to his aircraft.' The gunner came back, telling us what we already knew: 'Can't find Mr. Abbott.' Jim is one of the coolest heads around—that's why he's the lead aircraft commander. This is *not* like him."

Donovan: "I heard somebody in flight operations over the PA system: 'Will Mr. Abbott report to his aircraft *immediately*!'

"He's flying with the Old Man, but nobody woke him up! In a couple of minutes he comes running out, still zipping up his flight suit."

The mission began with Donovan and the other slicks flying to the East Field to be loaded with ammunition boxes. "Two Special Forces guys . . . volunteered as kickers," Donovan recalls. "They hopped in, and then we launched. I had my crew chief and door gunner give their helmets to the kickers, and I briefed them about what to expect and what would happen in the event that we were shot up. Or shot down.

"The scariest part of the mission was in the first five minutes. There were some weather issues around BMT; when we were climbing out, we flew into the clouds in formation. J.C. was flying number three and I was chalk four, the last aircraft. He was kind of strobing in and out of the clouds in front of me as we were climbing out. Jim Abbott made a [radio] call, 'Climbing out at 69 knots at 500 feet,' so that we didn't overrun the aircraft in front of us. A good call.

"Maybe fifteen minutes out of BMT, we broke out on top of the clouds, and we had more than a half-moon; it was a fairly bright night. As we approached LZ Kate, we were blacked out at altitude, in trail formation, with two gunships on either side of us. The game plan was that [the men on

Kate] were going to dig a hole in the ground and put a strobe light in it," recalls Donovan.

When I got the word that our ammo was inbound, I had my strikers go to a hundred percent alert and told them to prepare to return fire if the enemy shot at those choppers.

Donovan picks up the resupply sequence: "For some reason there were a bunch of artillery guys on the FM frequency and I think they were shooting or something, and it got so cluttered that I told Jim Hitch, my copilot, to turn off my number one switch; that way I was no longer monitoring the FM."

Davison: "It was nearly 0130 when we finally cranked. The flight out to Kate was uneventful—except for the damn lump in my throat. And that as we approached Kate, Falcon 4—Denny Fenlon—quite clearly told me that he was moving his team to the slicks' right side—but I had to ask him to repeat it three times before I could understand. Even my ears were scared!

"As we neared the LZ, any hope for surprise—as if a flight of nine Hueys at altitude on a quiet, clear night could surprise anybody—was lost when we couldn't pick up Kate's strobe light," Davison continues. "We had to make a 360-degree orbit over the area. The lump in my throat just kept getting bigger and bigger.

"When Stagecoach 6 turned inbound, our two Falcon gun teams were in position to follow him in, one team on each side. High above, Chalk Five, the command aircraft, vectored the lead slick to the strobe. Down into the darkness we went, all eyes on Stagecoach Lead. At 500 meters [from the LZ], Jim began to slow the helicopter. Over the firebase he came to a hover just long enough for the ammo boxes to be pushed out—then we heard, 'Six is coming out.'

"OK! But—were the bad guys just setting up for Chalk Two? Two was in right behind Lead, and he made it OK, and then Three was in," Davison recalls.

Donovan was Chalk Four. "I shot an approach at around 30 knots and 25 feet," he says. "The H-model Huey has a chin bubble on both sides of the aircraft so that the pilot could look down between his feet. When I saw the strobe light between my feet, I gave the order to kick it, and they kicked about 2,000 pounds of ammo out in about ten or fifteen seconds. Crew chief Mike Wilcox said, 'We're up, sir!'

"We lifted out and I was stunned—the bad guys never even shot at us!"

Davison: "The drop went off without a hitch. I'd never admit it to them, but those Stagecoach guys had big [gonads]!"

We finally had our ammo. And a macabre surprise: A very large number of body bags that I had not requested.

As for me, I have a good idea why the neighbors didn't come out for midnight target practice: Shadow and an AC-130H Spectre, the biggest and baddest Air Force gunship of all. He remained in the area, orbiting high above the Falcon and Stagecoach resupply. When Spooky 41 came on to relieve Shadow, Alabama asked for my needs. I told him to fire a little here and there, keep the PAVN heads down, keep them guessing about who would be next.

Because just then, everyone on Kate was busy pulling 20-round cardboard boxes of 5.56 mm ammo out of the wooden shipping crates, ripping the boxes open, and jamming one bullet at a time into one magazine after another. Before dawn we had filled all our magazines, and had several crates of ammo in reserve—almost enough, I reckoned, to stop another major assault. Almost.

SOMETIME that night, an Air Force EC-47 intercepted a radio message from the B3 Front—PAVN headquarters for the Central Highlands—to the commander of the 66th PAVN Regiment. US Army cryptologists at Long Binh decoded it, but it was a long time before I knew anything about it. The message was that our nasty neighbors had been ordered to end all their foolish dithering, all their fruitless mass assaults on our perimeter, and all their subsequent retreats, dragging their dead and wounded. The 66th was told that no more delays were acceptable. They were to take Firebase Kate immediately.

"All quiet along the Potomac," they say,
"Except, now and then, a stray picket
Is shot as he walks on his beat to and fro,
By a rifleman hid in the thicket.
'Tis nothing—a private or two, now and then,
Will not count in the news of the battle;
Not an officer lost—only one of the men
Moaning out, all alone, his death-rattle."

—Ethelinda Beers, "The Picket-Guard"

SIXTEEN

In the dark hours of the early morning of November 1, I received a coded message from A-236: Detachment B-20 of the II Corps Mobile Strike Force (Mike Force), headquartered in Pleiku but then at Bu Prang, would mount the operation to come to our assistance. My drooping spirits soared: My Special Forces brothers were coming to help us in our time of dire need.

Then PAVN dropped the other shoe: A little after daybreak, heavy shelling from Cambodia resumed. Apparently they had more guns than our fast movers had knocked out, or they had managed to repair some of the damaged ones. And there was a new wrinkle: artillery airbursts that drove everyone to cover. Our defenses were fast disintegrating, and I soon understood that we could not survive very long against this kind of shelling. Another day of artillery airbursts would be the end of us.

Hardly had the last echoes of the explosions died when PAVN turned on the rock and roll and came dancing up our hill, firing everything they had at us.

A little after midday, during a brief pause in the mortars and rockets, a minor miracle: A Huey slick flew low and fast through the ground fire, then very slowly hovered across to the generator pit. First Lieutenant Mike

Smith, sporting a bandage on his head but otherwise looking good, leapt out, followed by a big package.

"When I jumped out, not only did I have the six feet or so to jump [to the hilltop], I also had another few feet down into the pit, so it kind of hurt my legs," says Smith.

The chopper flew off, and Smith climbed out of the pit and limped over to the FDC. I was glad to see him—but he was the last man I'd expected to see back on Kate.

Down in the FDC, one of the guys asked Smith, "What's the situation?"

"You guys are in big trouble," replied Smith, for our first good laugh in way too long.

"When I got back to the field hospital at BMT, the doctor took something out of my head, sewed me up, and said that I should stay there for a couple of days and get better," Smith explains. "So I kind of hung out in the Provisional Artillery Group headquarters. Information about the battle began to trickle in. I was hearing that all kinds of forces were building up around Kate. And I'd listen [to radio traffic] and learn what was going on with the 5/22d, because Lieutenant Colonel Delaune had command and control of [Kate] and that whole situation.

"Then I learned that Ross had been killed," Smith recalls. "At that point, it was the sort of deal where, if your unit is in a situation, and you know everybody there, and you kind of know what's happening, it just doesn't make sense to send some brand-new guy in to replace you. They were my guys, and I felt kind of stupid, because I was not there with them, and they sent in some other guy to get killed. It's my outfit and my people, so I should go back. So I went to see Colonel [Francis] Bowers [commander of the Provisional Artillery Group], and said that if he didn't have a problem with it, I wanted to go back out to Kate."

Bowers approved the move.

The package he brought was a Ma Deuce—an M2 .50-caliber machine gun. In that place and at that time, it was a white elephant. "Nobody knew how to set the head space and timing," explains Koon. "So we never used it."

Actually, Pierelli knew how to set head space and timing. "If a .50 came in, and they had also brought a head space and timing device with it, I could've done it; that wouldn't have been a problem."

Every US Army M2 .50-caliber machine gun that I've ever seen had a timing and head space tool attached to it. But such were the conditions on Kate—not much socializing of any kind, and merely visiting the guys on the other end of the hill could cost your life—and the insular culture of the very different units occupying it, that Koon didn't even know Pierelli's name, much less that he was a Special Forces–trained light- and heavy-infantry weapons specialist. In fact, Hopkins didn't know *Koon's* first name until years after he got out of the Army.

I would have loved to have had that gun on Kate even a day earlier, when we could have put it to good use. But on that day, it didn't make a bit of difference: We had no .50-caliber ammo.

Nevertheless, I was very glad that Smith was back. I had begun to plan, in my head, an escape and evasion operation. In the short while that he had been on Kate, Zollner had been a tremendous help to me. But even with the two of us and Pierelli, riding herd on about 145 men, many of them wounded, as we tried to extricate ourselves from a hilltop surrounded by thousands of enemy soldiers would be very chancy. Having along Mike, a hard-charging guy with plenty of courage, an officer that all of Kate's artillerymen knew and respected, would improve our chances of survival.

But at the moment, Smith's arrival was just in time to catch PAVN's daily flying explosives festival and the USAF air show.

"We artillery guys were pretty much in our bunkers, letting the Air Force do their thing. All I remember from that afternoon was lots and lots of fast movers, and whatever big-ass bomb it is that makes one helluva noise when it blows up," he recalls.

IN early evening I got word that the Mike Force rescue would entail a reinforced battalion consisting of three rifle companies from the 1st Battalion and two rifle companies from the 5th Battalion.

I asked Pleiku to actually land the Mike Force companies on Kate if possible. If not, I told them, I wanted them to land close enough to fight their way in to us through the enemy lines, to buttress our defenses. They were to be our reinforcements, our redemption.

I guess I wasn't thinking too clearly at that point.

Word came back that they needed an alternate plan: First, there wasn't enough open space on or close to Kate to land enough helicopters to carry even one rifle company. And there was an overwhelming number of NVA troops entrenched around the base of our hill and on nearby heights.

A third message clarified the earlier one: A primary force of two companies would air-assault into our immediate area and secure a position within a few hundred meters of Kate's perimeter to cover the withdrawal of everyone on Kate. Three more companies would then be inserted with orders to block the enemy and provide direct security once our withdrawal began.

We waited. Twice an hour or so, the incoming mortar and rocket fire resumed, punctuated from time to time by still more artillery. And more ground attacks.

In late afternoon, I saw the swarm of dots that represented a dozen or more Huey slicks, escorted by several gunships, approaching from the northwest. Enough lift ships, I judged, to carry *one* Mike Force company. They dipped down out of sight at a distance that I judged to be maybe two kilometers or so. The choppers rose, empty, and hurried away. A little later, they returned to insert a second company. But before the last of those choppers were down, the wind brought the faint rattle and chatter of small-arms fire, along with the louder echo and crash of mortar impacts and the sharp crack of RPGs. I tuned my PRC-25 radio to the Mike Force frequency and heard their advisers—Australian Special Air Service, by their accents—talking to Mike Force headquarters. I understood from this that two rifle companies were boots on the ground, but they had been surrounded almost immediately by PAVN infantry and were taking mortar fire.

Worse, the intensity of ground fire was such that, with darkness approaching, the remaining three companies of the rescue force were forced to abort their landing. Opposed by elements of the PAVN 66th and 28th

Regiments, the two Mike Force companies were heavily outnumbered and terrifically outgunned.

Wisely, they broke contact and withdrew a few kilometers away from Kate, where they dug in and assumed defensive positions.

It became painfully clear that Kate was cut off, surrounded, and dependent for survival on whatever decisions I made next. There would be neither rescue nor reinforcements anytime soon.

For the first time since I arrived on Kate, I began to consider abandoning the hill. Do not misunderstand me: I had come here to fight. My Montagnard strikers had come to fight and had done so, individually and collectively, with great distinction. Some of the artillerymen had joined them, and had acquitted themselves well, inspiring one another with their valor no less than they inspired the strikers. No matter how tough things got, I had never considered anything except finding a way to hang on. With each attack, I had concentrated on what we needed to survive it, and did the same for the next one. We regrouped, redistributed our ammo, moved our machine guns, shifted a squad here and there, and schemed to get more supplies and ammo. Once we had learned the rules of PAVN's game, after we had hunkered in and dug deeper, our casualties were fewer, mostly flesh wounds that were not life-threatening; my wounded strikers stayed and fought on until we could get a medevac in. More often, we'd get them out on a chopper that dropped in to bring ammunition. Even so, I now had more than a dozen dead strikers in body bags.

I would never surrender. I never even considered it.

But now our artillery pieces had taken so many direct hits that they were little more than scrap metal. We were defending an impact area, and nothing more. Again, ammo was dangerously low. The Buffalo had been emptied; our water supply had dwindled to what remained in our canteens. Any chopper pilot bold enough to try resupplying us stood a better-than-even chance of being blown out of the sky. I had to begin thinking about if and how we could safely abandon Kate.

Right on cue, the leaders of the CIDG force came to tell me that they were leaving. They had discussed this among themselves, and agreed that Kate could no longer be defended. And that we would very soon be overrun.

"Captain Albracht came [into the FDC] and said, 'We've got a really serious problem,'" recalls Bob Johnson. "I was there, along with Lieutenants Smith and Zollner. Albracht said, 'The Yards have told us that they're leaving . . . They're going to boogie out. They said that there are too many NVA out there, and they'll have much better odds leaving on their own terms and fighting their way out than staying here and getting overrun.' I knew that once they've cracked your defensive line, everyone gets slaughtered; the Yards wanted no part of that. Albracht said that he would ask the Yard commander not to leave until nightfall, and as soon as it was dark enough, we would all leave together.

"I knew then that our ass was grass," Johnson continues. "It was very peculiar. When I learned that I was going to Vietnam, I realized that my life was fated to be what it was going to be. Before I left for Vietnam, I decided not to worry about it, not to deal with it. I'll do my job. Whatever happens, happens; if I come back, I come back and resume my life. Going into that ordeal with that mind-set made it much easier for me to get through whatever happened. I felt almost like I was an observer of my own life during that period of time. But I was also very well aware of how untenable our situation was if we stayed there."

After talking to Smith and Zollner, I went to see the Montagnard leaders. Through an interpreter, fighting though the language barrier, I told them that they were right. That it *was* time to leave. But we should leave with air cover. We should wait until full darkness. We should all leave together.

They discussed this, right in front of me but in their own language, and after a few minutes their spokesman replied: They would wait. We would all leave together.

Through Bu Prang, I communicated with Major Brydon, and he agreed that his force would send a small element, perhaps a platoon, to infiltrate the area near the north end of the base of Ambush Hill. They would guide us back to the main force, dug in several kilometers away.

Even then, I didn't want to leave Kate. But I had to consider the facts: Our howitzers were useless. The enemy was zeroed in on every one of our bunkers; many had taken multiple hits. Some had collapsed or were partly so—our physical defenses were crumbling. Fifteen of the original twenty-seven artillerymen on Kate had been wounded, and one of their replacements, Ross, was dead. About a third of my original 156 CIDG strikers, which included the platoon of reinforcements, had been killed or wounded. We had ceased to be a fire support base. A few more artillery shells, and our cratered hilltop would look like the surface of the moon, with about the same population.

I saw no choice but to send an encrypted message to Special Forces Command declaring the situation untenable and requesting permission to abandon Kate.

Their reply was swift and directly to the point:

"Permission to abandon denied."

PART THREE

Shoe the steed with silver
That bore him to the fray,
When he heard the guns at dawning—
Miles away;
When he heard them calling, calling—
Mount! nor stay:
Quick, or all is lost;
They've surprised and stormed the post,
They push your routed host—
Gallop! retrieve the day!

—Herman Melville, "Sheridan at Cedar Creek"

SEVENTEEN

The message was a shocker. What the hell? For a moment I felt more alone than I had ever been.

But we couldn't stay on Kate. I grew up idolizing men like Davy Crockett, Jim Bowie, and William Travis. They stood their ground at the Alamo, sacrificed their lives, because they knew it would buy Sam Houston time to raise the army that eventually won Texas its independence. If holding Kate had meant saving others' lives or advancing America's cause, I would have died there. But Kate no longer served any purpose. So it came down to a simple choice: Do we stay and die in place, or do we attempt to escape and evade the enemy? It was clear to me that it was better to leave, better for my men, better for their families and loved ones, and better for my country if at least some of us lived to fight another day.

I took a few deep breaths and composed a somewhat longer message. Choosing my words for maximum impact, I explained in greater detail the condition of our hilltop impact area, our lack of resources with which to mount an active defense, the inoperative condition of our howitzers and therefore the loss of our raison d'être, and finally an educated guess at how many thousands of enemy troops were in the surrounding hills and valleys.

But this second message was *not* a request. I concluded by saying that we *were* leaving. I didn't ask permission, but I added that a little air support on our way out the door would be very helpful. Then I encoded what I'd written with a CAC code—a group of randomly generated letters and numbers substituting for each character in my message. I read the encrypted message over the radio to Rocco DeNote at Bu Prang.

With his radio operator, SP4 Billy Weaver, to spell him only long enough to take a leak, for five days DeNote had faithfully relayed our support, ammo, and supply requests to B-23 at BMT. He had done everything but hold my hand over the radio since the shooting started. He had secure voice and secure teletype circuits to B-23; after decoding my message, he sent it to the "B" Team commander, who passed it up the line. While I waited for an answer, I began making preparations for leaving.

"ACCORDING to the plan, we would march through triple-canopy jungle in the dark until we linked up with a relief force at least a couple of miles away," recalls Bob Johnson. "Captain Albracht had the grid coordinates for the linkup. The relief force was [composed of] Special Forces leading Montagnard troops. Until that time—all through the siege—I had assumed that the US Army would come to the rescue of Americans who were stranded, as we were. I thought the relief force was at least a couple of US Army companies. I did not know that there were no American troops involved in any way in relieving the siege of Kate," adds Johnson.

I, of course, was by then well aware that no American unit was coming. What I didn't know until many years later was that while I awaited a response to my last message, high above Kate, at an altitude beyond the range of even PAVN's spiffy new 37 mm ack-ack guns, the three-star commander of I Field Force Vietnam and his aide were circling in a Huey fitted out as a command and control bird. Lieutenant General Charles A. Corcoran, who answered only to General Creighton Abrams, boss of all US forces in Vietnam and its waters, had received my classified message.

Like virtually every senior officer in Vietnam, he had chosen his own call sign, a reflection of his self-image. A call sign so different and unique that anyone who might hear it on the air would know at once that they were talking to the boss.

For all I knew, Corcoran was a warrior genius, Alexander the Great reincarnated. Even if he was merely a run-of-the-mill American three-star general, however, he should have known that as ego-gratifying as that might have felt, his choice of call sign was dangerously stupid. Just a year earlier, Major General Keith Ware, a World War II Medal of Honor recipient and the first OCS graduate to pin on the silver stars of a general officer, had been lured into a Viet Cong ambush by a bogus radio call. And this was Ware's own fault: As commander of the First Infantry Division, nicknamed "the Big Red One," Ware chose the call sign "Firefly One." Ignoring advice from his own division signal officer on the advisability of keeping *any* call sign longer than a month, much less for his entire tour of duty, he had "Firefly 1" painted on the underside of his command Huey's fuselage.

By 1966, US intelligence was well aware that the Viet Cong had an active and effective signals intelligence organization, roughly the equivalent of the US Army Security Agency. The Viet Cong systematically monitored and decoded US, ARVN, and Allied forces radio transmissions on hundreds of frequencies, including those used by aircraft and ground forces. They maintained what we would now call a database of call signs and frequencies, from which they had identified the commanders of virtually every Army, Marines, and Air Force unit of battalion size or larger in South Vietnam. From repeated sightings of Ware's aircraft, they had matched it to his call sign. When some of his troops were operating near the Cambodian border, the VC set up an ambush on what was meant to look like an active landing zone; when Firefly 1 was spotted in the area, a Viet Cong impersonating an American soldier called on a captured radio to ask Ware for help in evacuating a critically wounded GI. When Ware landed, his aircraft was riddled with machine-gun fire and everyone on it was killed.

Within weeks, this incident became part of the "Lessons Learned" curriculum in several Army officer schools, including the Command and General Staff School, the Army War College, and the Signal Officer Advanced Course, at which my coauthor learned this lesson in 1969.

Ignoring the fate of Major General Ware, General Corcoran, who as a boy had roamed the streets of Laredo, Texas, decreed that he would be known on the air as "Pawnee Bill," a reference to Gordon W. Lillie, a Wild West show performer and contemporary of "Buffalo Bill" Cody.

"Pawnee Bill *Alpha* was Corcoran's squeaky-voiced aide," recalls De-Note. "Pawnee Bill Alpha called Bill Albracht—Hawk—from way high over Kate. We used several different frequencies at Bu Prang Camp, but for whatever reason, Pawnee Bill couldn't communicate directly with Hawk," DeNote continues. "Two or three times, Pawnee Bill came back on the air with the same fucking request—to verify the size of the force surrounding Firebase Kate.

"So I got on the frequency, identified myself by call sign, and said, 'Pawnee Bill Alpha, if you don't believe them, drop your fucking helicopter 10,000 feet and take a look for yourself. OUT!'

"And the voice that came back—a voice that sounded like God—said: 'This is Pawnee Bill. Roger, copy; OUT!'

"Somebody in [the Camp Bu Prang] radio bunker said, 'You fucked up!'

"I said, 'What are they gonna do, relieve me and send me to Nha Trang so that I can surf and eat at the Dairy Queen?'"

Shortly after that exchange, the order was given for Firebase Kate to execute an escape and evasion. That could only have come from Corcoran, or from Lu Lan, the ARVN two-star general commanding II Corps (who was directly under I Field Force). Thanks, Rocco, for having my back when I needed it most.

When permission to withdraw came, it was accompanied by the recommendation that we leave under cover of darkness and use an Air Force gunship as covering fire. Apparently, Pawnee Bill and his Flying Wild West Show believed that my troops and I might have held off a small army for five days, but that we were also stupid enough to attempt an escape and evasion operation in daylight.

On the other hand, we were definitely foolish enough to attempt escape and evasion as an intact unit. After 1953, when the lessons of the Korean War had sunk in, every US Army basic trainee has been taught that men in a unit trapped behind enemy lines stand the best chance to evade capture by breaking into small groups of three to five men, each group leaving separately at different times and from different places on the perimeter, and taking different routes in attempting to evade the enemy while returning to the safety of their own lines. Then and now, I believed that my Montagnard strikers, left to their own devices, would have done just that, and that probably most would have survived. They had lived in this region for their entire lives. They were at home in the highland jungles, and they were superb hunters and stalkers.

If Dan and I had attempted escape together, just the two of us, I would have given us a better-than-even chance for survival: We were Special Forces, trained and comfortable in jungles and in rough terrain. Comfortable moving around at night. Not so Kate's artillerymen. I doubted that more than a few would have any idea what to do in the jungle, and most of them already showed symptoms of battle shock.

But if there was even the slightest chance for their survival in a group, I couldn't abandon them. We would all leave together. We would take our chances together.

As the sun set around 1720 hours on the night of November 1, the fast movers broke off their bombing runs and returned to base: They were not equipped to operate at low altitude in the dark.

They were replaced by a pair of A1H Skyraiders from the USAF's 6th Special Operations Squadron at Pleiku Air Base. Affectionately dubbed "Spads," after the French-built biplane famously flown by World War I ace Captain Eddie Rickenbacker (and by *Peanuts* cartoonist Charles Schulz's Snoopy), the Skyraider was an enormous, single-engine fighter-bomber. Designed for service in World War II, it could carry four tons of ordnance—more than its own weight—in bombs, rockets, and ammo for four 20 mm cannon or a minigun pod. Heavily armored, it could absorb a lot of ground fire without endangering the pilot or a vital aircraft system. Best of all, the Skyraider could fly at night and remain in the air as long as seven hours.

About 1900 hours, with Kate in total darkness, one of the Skyraiders, its ordnance expended and low on fuel, returned to base. The other, call sign Spad Zero Two, with Major Gerald R. Helmich at the controls, orbited overhead; it was supposed to remain until a Shadow gunship arrived to take its place.

Shadow was going to walk us out, firing its lethal miniguns ahead of us to sanitize a path for us to meet up with the Mike Force.

I gathered everyone—strikers and artillerymen—in the vicinity of Kate's north end, the only slope that could easily be traversed, and the one from which we had taken the least amount of enemy fire. It was dark and the sky was clear; slightly more than a half-moon would rise about 2300 hours. By then I wanted to be long gone. We got busy with preparations to move through our own wire and then through enemy lines.

In my heart of hearts, however, I believed that we were merely dead men walking: I didn't see how it would be possible to evade the thousands of PAVN troops roaming the hills and valleys surrounding Kate. I kept such thoughts to myself as I circulated among the artillerymen, telling them how we would join up with the Mike Force near the bottom of Ambush Hill, that everything was under control, that if we stuck together and didn't panic, we would all be fine. Many of these guys had lain up in their bunkers for days, suffering from the effects of battle shock and hopelessness from days of almost continuous shelling and the knowledge that they were surrounded by a vastly larger enemy force known for its cruelty to prisoners. I did all that I could to instill hope in these men, and to boost their morale. It seemed, at least to my untrained eyes, that they did perk up a little.

After I'd explained our situation, I told everyone what to do to prepare to escape Kate and then evade the enemy.

"We were ordered to destroy all equipment, especially the FDC radios, destroy all papers, to leave all personal effects behind except for dog tags, so that when [*sic*] we were captured there would be less that they could use against us in interrogation," Bob Johnson recalls. "We were to carry as much ammo as we could, and of course take our helmets and flak gear and weapons. We fully expected to fight our way through the slot at the bottom of the hill and across Ambush Hill. We expected that we would take heavy casualties in the exit from the firebase. We were to move at a fast walk or a slow trot, definitely not to run, which would expend our energy before we actually got into battle. But we wanted to move quickly through the area. We were in a very vulnerable situation."

"There was another guy named Johnson, a gun bunny—we called him Peewee—and he was kind of a weird dude," recalls Koon. "He piled up a bunch of his stuff and took some old powder bags and set it on fire—he must have had a flame twelve feet high! It lit up the whole place, and we started getting mortars and rockets. That was on Peewee."

I had Pierelli send some of the artillery guys to finish the howitzers with thermite grenades, devices that burn white-hot, generating enough concentrated heat to melt a barrel's hardened steel. Cannoneers call this "spiking a tube." Apparently, this was a rarely used procedure.

"I was involved with going around to the howitzers with Sergeant McFarland," recalls Koon. "He was so excited about getting to throw thermite grenades down the tubes of these guns that he couldn't wait to do it!"

We also used thermite on the artillery unit's heavy communications equipment, the useless .50-cal machine gun, the FADAC computer, the generators, and all official documents.

I had decided that it would be hard enough to get everybody off Kate in one piece, and then survive a night march of several miles, at least, through trackless, triple-canopy jungle. It would become impossible with the added burden of carrying our dead. It was unfortunate, but I decided that the needs of the living outweighed the respect and courtesies due our departed comrades: We would have to leave the dozen or so dead strikers stacked on Kate's helipad.

I worried over how the artillerymen would handle themselves if we had to fight our way out. Would they panic and run? Stand frozen, waiting for someone to shoot them? I hoped that a few would put up a fight, at least fire their rifles at the enemy. My strikers had shown that they could fight, and fight very well, from foxholes and other protected firing positions. Would they know what to do in an ambush? Would they assault their ambushers or take off into the jungle? It was too much to worry about, I realized, when I wouldn't be able to do much about it.

Except for the faint buzz of the Skyraider orbiting overhead, it was eerily quiet. For the first time in five days, I was not actively involved in defending Kate, and I had a few minutes to reflect. I ran through our E&E plan again in my mind. I couldn't see how it could possibly work—but I also couldn't think of anything better.

A Shadow gunship had been promised for an hour after dark, and I listened to my PRC/25 radio for his call. I wanted to start the E&E now—*right* now. Waiting was brutal.

Thinking ahead, Pierelli had positioned his infrared strobe light in the center of Kate. Once we departed, this light would become a beacon that would serve as Shadow's reference point.

For the first time since arriving on Kate, I was in a situation that I could not control in any way. The enemy had attacked us almost without pause for days—and I expected them to renew their assault at any moment. What was going on in the darkness beneath our summit? What was PAVN waiting for? What were they up to?

Then came word from Main Tripod—Bu Prang Camp's new call sign. The Shadow we expected at about 1900 hours had experienced mechanical problems and returned to base. We would have to wait a little longer, until a second bird could be scrambled.

"I'd seen a Spooky in action the night before I got hit," says Mike Smith. "Spooky 41 was the number I remembered. [That night] a Spooky was supposed to be on-site; we all watched the sun go down, then it got darker and darker and there's no Spooky. It was like something in a movie, where at the last minute the cavalry comes riding over the hill to save the good guys. But now it's *really* dark, we're ready to go—and Jesus, where the hell is the guy? My heart sank. *Maybe,* I thought, *the cavalry can't make it. Maybe there's* not *going to be a Spooky.*"

Koon: "There was a rumor about the Montagnard leader that if any of his men were badly wounded, and had to be carried or something, he'd shoot them. He wouldn't let that slow us down. If they couldn't make it on their own two feet, too bad."

About 1930 hours, with everyone nervous and antsy, Main Tripod called again: The second Shadow had also experienced a mechanical problem and had to abort the mission. We would have to wait for a Spooky to be scrambled in its place.

I got back on the radio with Spad Zero Two; Major Helmich told me that he was low on fuel. To return the hundred miles to Pleiku Air Base, he could cruise at 200 miles per hour, burning comparatively little gas. Or he could land at BMT or Nha Trang to refuel. But a strafing run meant cranking his giant Wright Duplex-Cyclone engine to turn out every one of its 2,700 horses. He'd dive at 335 miles per hour, followed by a high-speed climb back to altitude—and all that sucks up a lot of the high-octane stuff. Helmich said that he could stick around a little longer, but that he had fuel enough for only one more strafing pass.

So now it's nut-cutting time: Do we stay and wait for Spooky, or take our chances with just the Spad and a single strafing pass? I decided to save the Spad for our walk-out, in case we were attacked.

But we couldn't wait much longer to leave.

He brings his regiment home—
Not as they filed two years before,
But a remnant half-tattered, and battered, and worn,
Like castaway sailors, who—stunned
By the surf's loud roar,
Their mates dragged back and seen no more—
Again and again breast the surge,
And at last crawl, spent, to shore.

—Herman Melville, "The College Colonel"

EIGHTEEN

By 1940 hours, I decided that if a Spooky gunship was coming, it ought to be within radio range. Big Tex Rogers had volunteered to carry my radio and serve as my RTO. As the artillerymen crowded around in the darkness, I took the handset and called Spooky.

No answer.

I waited an eternity—maybe two minutes—and called again.

No answer.

I tried a third time.

No answer.

Frustrated and angry, I turned to Tex. "This damn radio isn't working!" I hissed into the gloom. Tex swallowed a smile. In his calm, amused Southern drawl, he whispered, "Sir, you need to release the push-to-talk switch."

Those tactical radios operate on a single frequency. When I squeezed the handset "talk" button, it disabled the receiver and turned on the transmitter. I looked down at my hand: I held the push-to-talk in a death grip. My transmitter was *on*, my receiver *off*. I relaxed my hand, releasing the switch.

"All of a sudden the radio goes, 'This is Spooky 4-1; we're coming in,'" says Lieutenant Mike Smith. "Everybody got excited—the cavalry was riding to our rescue."

Embarrassed, I managed to mumble thanks to Tex. Again I understood that I was just as frightened as everyone else. Panic is more contagious than the common cold. If we were to have any chance to get out alive, I needed to remain calm and focused.

Silently, cloaked by the night, I now made my peace with the Almighty. I resigned myself to the realization that I would not see another sunrise: I could not envision a scenario where this would end well. Not only did I *know* that I would die, I knew *where* it would be: as I entered the gap in the jungle leading to Ambush Hill.

So I prayed not for my own life but for the lives of those who had been entrusted to me. And then, unbidden and unexpected, I was filled with a sense of calmness and well-being. It felt like a good night to die.

"Alabama" Dykes was again Spooky's mission commander. It would be a little while before he would be in position to fire for us.

I didn't want to leave anyone behind, so I told the men that I was going to run back to the south end and make sure. Turning to leave, I heard gunfire—small arms—coming from that direction.

"The captain said that he was going to run back to the other end," recalls Nelson Koon. "He said if he's not back in five minutes, to leave without him. We all said, 'If you don't come back, we ain't going anywhere,' because we didn't know the lay of the land like he did. So everybody was shaking hands and whispering, 'Well, if I don't make it out and you do, get ahold of my parents and let them know what happened here.'"

It took only seconds to reach the south end. The shooting had stopped. All our foxholes and fighting positions were empty. As I squatted on my haunches in the darkness, listening, I heard, faint but clear, the unmistakable sound of barbed wire being snipped. And the muffled clatter of sandals moving up the hillside. They were no more than fifty meters down the hill and coming! The hair on my back and neck stood up; I started back for the north end. Then I heard the soft, evil cough of a nearby mortar firing, and went prone just as the first round exploded a few meters away. Then another blast, a little farther north. A few seconds later, another—the enemy was walking fire south to north along the length of the firebase toward where everyone was massed for evacuation. When the barrage ended, I ran to the north end to find that one man had been killed. Then came a popping sound from high above—a mortar illumination flare. Then another pop, and then another.

Kate was naked to any observer on the eastern ridge. Everybody flattened on the hard ground. My heart was a kettledrum, threatening to explode from my chest—I was certain that hundreds of enemy infantry were about to spill over the south crest and come at us, firing.

There was no time to lose. When the last flare burned out, I jumped to my feet and announced that we were leaving. But before we took more than a few steps, our point man, in the act of clearing our wire for the main body to pass through, accidentally set off a trip flare. Again, everyone hit the ground. As the shifting, unearthly orange light of the flare floated down on us, we waited for the mortars. None came. That flare seemed to burn forever before it sputtered out.

Everyone got back on their feet. For a moment, it was utterly still. Then I heard the welcome sound of the Skyraider diving low toward our hilltop, hoping to make the neighborhood bullies think that he was on a strafing run. But as he barreled over, low and fast, he didn't fire; I knew that he was low on fuel and almost out of ammo.

I expected a Mike Force element to be waiting at the foot of Ambush Hill. I had been told that they would lead us to their main body, a few miles away. To make it easier to enter their perimeter, I put everyone into a single file.

I gave the order and we moved out—but after forty or fifty meters, the line stopped. I worked my way to the front and found the point man twenty meters from the gap leading to Ambush Hill. Frozen with fear, he was unable to move forward. Spooky was still too far to fire and clear our path. The enemy was on our heels; I must act immediately.

I moved up and took the point.

I understood that I was about to die. But it had to be done, and there was no one else. My carbine was slung beneath my right arm and held waist-high on full automatic, my finger resting on the trigger. I gripped the radio handset in my left hand.

"Follow me," I said, and stepped into the night.

At a rapid walk, I led the column into and then through the gap, well aware that it was a textbook example of a perfect ambush choke point.

As the troops moved past me and into the open, Tex and I remained at the mouth of the gap until Pierelli, who I had stationed near the middle of the column, relieved me. His job was to ensure that the troops stayed together and kept moving. Because I was all but certain that the enemy would come up behind us, I instructed Dan to form a small rear guard to cover our withdrawal. He was the one man that I was comfortable entrusting with this vital task.

In earlier clear radio traffic with Spooky and Shadow about our planned escape, I tried to make sure that they knew our precise route. This was critical, because we expected one or the other to fire its miniguns ahead of us. My plan was to bring our column across the open space toward Ambush Hill, and then descend to the west, or left, of the hilltop, thereby avoiding what I believed was the heaviest enemy concentration, then link up with the waiting Mike Force.

Now, unexpectedly, I found myself near the gap and out of position to direct the point man. I had briefed him on the importance of turning leftward out of the gap, and then to pass to the left of Ambush Hill's wooded summit. In the darkness, however, I couldn't tell if the man who had minutes earlier frozen was still on point, or if someone had taken his place. Guided by the hand of God, he led the column to the *east*, or right, of Ambush Hill. I was annoyed and worried, until I realized that without Spooky overhead to clear the way, the exact route was less important than avoiding contact.

And by this time, the main body of the column was committed and moving rightward. In a few minutes, we passed close to the top of Ambush Hill; had an enemy force been concealed in the trees and brush near the summit, it was so dark that we could not have seen them.

But there was neither sign nor sound of the enemy as we started down the slope toward the wood line near where, three days earlier, my patrol had been ambushed and the point man mortally wounded. The head of the column entered thick, pitch-black jungle, dimpled here and there with deep bomb craters, many fringed by the battered remnants of trees—King Kong's obstacle course, with giant toothpicks haphazardly studded across it. In minutes, the troops were dangerously disorganized and scattered everywhere. Pierelli and I began grabbing men, pushing or pulling them back into the column, trying to restore order and discipline. By remaining at the jungle's edge, we got the men headed away from Kate in a northerly, downhill direction, making sure that each followed the boots in front of him.

I got on the radio and called the Mike Force element waiting below us to advise them that I was about to enter their perimeter.

No answer.

A moment later, SAS Major Brydon, the commander of both Mike Force battalions in the vicinity, replied from Bu Prang.

No Mike Force troops awaited us below Ambush Hill, he said.

They were miles away, to the northwest, and we would have to find them.

I was pissed, but before I could react to this shocker, great green balls of fire came hurtling down the slope, just over our heads, and the stuttering roar of a heavy machine gun broke the silence. I thought that Spooky was firing on us.

I yelled, "Cease fire!" into the radio. The Skyraider pilot came back that Spooky was not firing and wasn't yet on station. Then, through the foliage, I saw that the fire was coming from the top of Ambush Hill.

Warren Geromin: "We were trying to avoid a North Vietnamese .51-caliber [12.7 mm] machine gun, and when that opened up, oh man, it was like a flaming thing with green tracer rounds like strobe lights that just lit up! We were close enough to see the muzzle flashes—I could almost see the crew members on the gun—something dark, moving around. We stopped and somebody poked me and said, 'Geromin, open fire,' and I thought, *Wait a minute; something's not right.* Then the gun opened up again and I could see through that green light that our guys were between me and the gun—we were going downhill. If I had fired, I'd have gotten them first. Then the Yards who were near the gun started throwing hand grenades at it. Someone yelled that the enemy was shelling us, and we tried to run but couldn't get far because there were so many bomb craters there at the bottom of the hill and it was pitch-dark.

"So I did something that we'd been told never to do—if we got lost, we weren't supposed to light anything, but because everything was so messed up, I lit a cigarette lighter real quick, because nobody was expecting to see a North Vietnamese soldier who was speaking English. Someone recognized me. He said, 'Okay, put out the lights; we'll have to figure this one out.'"

"There were a couple of areas where the ground was mush," recalls Pierelli. "When a bomb hits, it really breaks up the ground, so there were times when we would walk into and out of a crater. About a half hour into this, once we scattered in there, I heard somebody yell, 'Sarge, Sarge!' When we were on the hill, we knew where our people were, who was with whom, so they knew where I was. I said, 'What's the matter?' [An unidentified American soldier] said, 'We're lost! I can't find the people up front—I lost them!'

"I gathered everybody around and said, 'Look, be quiet, here's what we're going to do: I'm going to go first; the man behind me is going to grab my web gear. Everybody hold on to the person in front of you, and we're going to do that until everybody's hooked up. Under no conditions do you let go.' I also told them that we had to be completely quiet so that we could hear the enemy; you learn that in basic, that sound travels farther at night. I listened, and off in the distance I heard somebody walking, breaking brush. So I started going, and about every thirty or forty steps I'd stop, I'd listen; we were getting a little closer. I did that about five or six times and found the guys up front, but I wanted to make sure that I was following the right people," Pierelli continues.

"I could hear English being spoken, so I went up to whoever it was, an artillery guy, but by that time we were walking away from that machine gun, we were moving about ninety degrees away from him, we were distancing ourselves from the enemy. We started this E&E about 2000 hours, full darkness, but fortunately it wasn't pitch-black; otherwise it could've been a real disaster."

About then, Mike Smith, very near to Pierelli in the darkness, was having second thoughts about being in the dark jungle. "The night belongs to Charlie," he says. "We'd learned that. And I'm an artillery guy. I've never walked around in a jungle in a combat situation. We were all afraid, but we're not stupid; we knew that we had to do something, that we had to keep going."

Koon: "Before we left, Captain Albracht told us, 'If we take fire, don't shoot back. They might be trying to recon by fire. They may not know where we are, but if we shoot back, then they'll know.' Some of the guys had left their M16 and everything else. They walked off with nothing. Once the flare went out, we started down the hill and we're out [where Ambush Hill descends into the jungle] and a machine gun opens up on us.

"Some of the Montagnards were afraid to go into the jungle. They didn't know what was in there, but they knew we were surrounded. But once that machine gun opened up, those Montagnards beat feet for the tree line.

"Albracht had to try to stop them and all of us. We ran into the tree line and guys were yelling, 'US!' to let them know that we were Americans and which ones were Montagnards. Then we're down in the jungle and the tracers are going over our heads because they couldn't get their barrel down low enough to hit us. We hit the dirt, and then this guy, a staff sergeant, laid his M16 across my arm and opens up, trying to hit that damned machine gun. Somebody said cease fire to him, and he stopped."

I believe that Koon is correct: After I realized that it wasn't Spooky, I recognized the gun firing at us as a PAVN 12.7 mm, a crew-served machine gun. But why was this tripod-mounted weapon firing over our heads? It had to be because, like the GI version that it was modeled on, that big, heavy gun was attached to a traversing and elevating mechanism. That supported the heavier end, and allowed the gunner to sight and zero in on distant targets, and return to them later. This T&E device has a limited amount of vertical travel, both up and down, and the steep angle at which our hillside declined exceeded the limits of the mechanism. In simple terms, the PAVN gunner couldn't lower the weapon's muzzle far enough to hit us. Had the crew known in advance that it was going to be firing that low, of course, they could have dug out the hillside and sited their gun properly. That makes me think that they had hastily moved the gun from where they had set up, on the other flank of Ambush Hill.

I still shudder to think what would have happened if the point man had followed my original plan. Had we gone to the west side of Ambush Hill, our column would have presented itself head-on to that gun. The gunners could have fired down the length or our line, which then would have been stretched almost back to the gap. A single bullet from a 12.7 mm can tear a man's arm from his body. It can punch through the torsos of four or five adults standing one behind the next. With the PAVN assault force coming down behind us from the south, we would have been caught in a crossfire. I doubt that any of us would have survived.

But that was not to be our fate.

Despite the ineffectiveness of their fire, those frightening green tracers caused the men in our column to panic. Men began crashing pell-mell through the brush. I raced ahead to take the lead of the main body, yelling for them to continue northward along the tree line. As I had a little earlier, I grabbed every trooper I could find and pushed him in the direction of the column. Behind me, Pierelli was doing the same.

I had supposed that his security squad was covering our back side, but at that point in our hegira, it was all that he could do to round up our guys and get them moving in the right direction. For those few minutes of half-panicked confusion as we came off Ambush Hill, we had no rear guard.

"We withdrew from the edge of the grassy slope about 20 meters or so into the jungle and got ourselves organized," recalls Bob Johnson. "The captain said that we wouldn't be able to see each other in the darkness, but it was very important that we stay together, be soundless, no whispering or talking. We had to walk as quietly as we could possibly walk. He told us to check our gear to make sure that nothing was rattling. Then he said that we should keep one hand on the shoulder of the man in front of us. But first, he told us to get down on your knees and brush aside the litter on the jungle floor. 'Dig deep down into the rotted leaves. They're phosphorescent. Put some of them on the back of the person in front of you so that if your hand slips off, you'll be able to see them.'

"And that worked like a charm," Johnson added.

Koon was having his own problems in the dark, repeatedly stumbling over unexploded mortar rounds and rockets, well aware that stepping on one in the wrong place might cause it to explode. "Once we hit the tree line, I think the B-52s must have been along in here because we were falling into bomb craters. You couldn't see very well because it was pitch-dark and then we looked at the ground and a lot of the tree leaves were glowing, and I thought, my God, what if it was some kind of chemical from the bombs? We put it on the back of our helmets and then the guy behind us could see where we were. It was pretty good for that."

ONCE I found the head of the column, I moved forward as quickly as the darkness and terrain would allow. After several minutes, I stopped to regroup and reassess the situation. Smith and Zollner took a head count of their artillerymen; two were missing. My striker leaders said that when the automatic fire began, several of their troops had separated from the main body. There was no way to look for them in the thick jungle blackness without endangering everyone else. I could only hope that the missing GIs had joined company with the missing strikers and that they would all find their way back to Bu Prang safely. Frankly, that was an awful lot to hope for.

I still expected to link up with Mike Force, but I was no longer sure where *we* were or even where they were. Spooky was finally on station, however, so I told Alabama where the PAVN heavy machine gun was sited, a location he knew well from previous missions, and that there were no more friendlies on Kate. Almost immediately, Spooky's miniguns began ripping up the terrain on Ambush Hill and then on Kate itself. I received word by radio that more aircraft were en route to pound Kate.

We took advantage of the noise from Spooky's engines and miniguns to mask the sounds of our passage through thick jungle as we put space between us and Ambush Hill. When I thought that we were far enough north—more a feeling than any sense of the actual distance—I turned, and we began moving westward. I had a vague sense of where the rescue force was dug in—little more than a hunch, my guess of about where I saw the helicopters touch down, and a look at my map—but based on what I was told before leaving Kate, I still expected to find a Mike Force element in the immediate vicinity of our abandoned hilltop.

I know that the enemy was all around us; when I could no longer hear Spooky, I halted the column to listen. After several seconds, an almost infinitesimal change in air pressure, the suggestion of a phantom breeze, brushed my face. The tiniest of vibrations nudged the soles of my feet. Then came the faint, softly rhythmic scrape of feet treading hard earth.

I signaled DOWN! and we all fell forward, a row of dominos collapsing front to back. The sound grew louder. As I pressed my body into the earth, the vibration was more intense, but still barely discernible.

To our left, through the foliage, was a darker darkness, movement where there should be none.

Men rushed by in the jungle only about ten meters away, moving eastward in a closely bunched column stretching several hundred yards and parallel to our column, following some hidden path cut, tunnellike, through the foliage.

The Mike Force?

Whispering, I radioed and said that if they are on the move, we were now on their immediate left.

The Mike Force replied: "We are dug in." Definitely *not* moving.

Then the men marching past us, close enough that we could smell the sour odor of their unwashed bodies, must be PAVN.

All we could do was lie prone on the jungle floor, listening to the sound of our own breathing and feeling the drum beating in our chest as we waited for all those troops—hundreds, I believe—to pass—a long and very scary time.

When they had disappeared into the night, I waited a few minutes more, against the surprise of a rear guard trailing the main body.

Finally, I signaled everyone to get to their feet. That simple act generated enough noise to make me wait another few minutes, to wait until it was completely quiet except for the normal sounds of a jungle at night: insects engaging in six-legged social networking, the high-pitched twitters and haunting calls of night birds, the faint croak of tree frogs. In the distance, some creature—perhaps a wild pig, or maybe even a tiger or a leopard—made an odd sound, something between a grunt and a cough.

Humans, of course, both grunt and cough.

I waited another few minutes, then called Mike Force again. This time they sent coded grid coordinates of their position.

I could only hope that they were as good at map reading as I thought I was.

At my signal, the column resumed its slow, stealthy trek through the jungle. I navigated by compass, stopping from time to time to check the azimuth, and keeping a rough count of my paces to give me some idea of how much ground we had covered. Except for an occasional glimpse of the starry sky, we were in almost total darkness. Each step I took was slow and deliberate. My boot-shod toes felt for the ground, trying to avoid a root that I might trip over, or making noise by crushing a twig.

I also hoped that I wouldn't step on a cobra, a tree viper, a krait—any of the thirty poisonous snake species living in this jungle. Or that some twenty-foot-long Burmese python wouldn't drop from a tree to wrap itself around my chest and crush the life out of me.

"There was no sign or sound of any humans as we continued up and over hills, and through streams," recalls Bob Johnson. "We climbed a hilltop and there was an open field with an old, French colonial–style house. Even though we were in triple-canopied jungle, we could look past the trees and see the plantation buildings."

Moving even a small group with stealth in such terrain is agonizingly slow and difficult—and, as I now learned with a large group, virtually impossible. Nevertheless, we continued our slow progress, each step made with purpose, at all times knowing that we risked not only our own fate but the lives of our buddies.

Forty miles away, at Camp Coryell, the northern of BMT's airfields, Les Davison was in the 155th AHC operations center. "I'd just returned from flying some mission," he recalls. "Somebody told me that Kate had been evacuated and the guys were walking out, through the jungle. My first thought was that we'd be lucky if we saw any of those guys alive."

There's a Legion that never was 'listed,
That carries no colours or crest,
But, split in a thousand detachments,
Is breaking the road for the rest.
Our fathers they left us their blessing—
They taught us, and groomed us, and crammed;
But we've shaken the Clubs and the Messes
To go and find out and be damned
(Dear boys!),
To go and get shot and be damned.

—Rudyard Kipling, "The Lost Legion"

NINETEEN

After walking for what felt like an hour or so, I called a pause to our march. I had not seen or heard further sign of friend or foe. Nor was I very sure where we were. I called for Smith, Zollner, and Pierelli to make their way to the head of the column, and in whispers told them that I wanted to go out ahead of the group, alone. I wanted to try to pinpoint our exact location on my map by using terrain features as reference points. I had to do this myself because, from all the information I had, the only other man with us who I could trust to read a map and match it to the surrounding terrain was Pierelli. I had to believe that I knew more about maps than he did. So it would be me.

When I returned, I told the others, I would probably make just enough noise to be challenged. My reply to this challenge would be two short flashes from the red-filtered flashlight I carried.

White light can be seen for miles in the darkness. Red light won't carry as far.

We had to assume that the enemy was still combing the jungle for us; that presented the distinct possibility that I could be captured. My final instruction to Dan, Maurice, and Mike was that if I approached and did not flash red twice, they were to assume that I had been compromised and start shooting.

I went out about a hundred meters, moving quietly, but looking around as I moved. I came to the edge of a jungle clearing, hoping to find a height or some other landmark that would help me get a fix on our position. But even in the clearing, only starlight battled the darkness.

Scanning for terrain features, I didn't watch where I put my feet. I tripped over a tree root and fell flat on my face, brushing against tree limbs and underbrush as I toppled.

Slowly, I climbed back to my feet, then systematically checked myself over.

My red-filtered flashlight had been clipped to my suspenders. It was gone. I dropped to my knees and searched the ground all around with my hands.

No flashlight.

Still on my knees, I crawled in gradually expanding circles from the base of the tree.

Still no flashlight.

By my own order, I would not be allowed to return to the column without that flashlight. There was no fail-safe. No backup plan.

Fighting the stirrings of panic, I returned to the base of the tree, and then slowly felt my way up to its limbs. Then outward until my hands touched . . . plastic. My fingers found a ribbed cylinder. Snagged on a small branch by its carry clip was my precious light.

I had failed to locate us on the map, but it was apparent that I had exceeded my nightly quotient for solo reconnaissance.

I eased back the way I came, used the flashlight to signal as promised, and got my troops moving again. As before, we proceeded by dead reckoning: I knew where we had started from, and now I knew the coordinates of the Mike Force's position. But without the ability to locate ourselves on a map, I couldn't do more than move toward what I hoped was their approximate location.

The bug in my beer bottle: The enemy was also looking for the Mike Force. The good guys might have been forced to move.

• • •

ABOUT three hours after leaving Kate, a gibbous moon rose, pouring cold, bright light on the jungle clearings, enough to allow me to view terrain features and get a better feeling for our approximate location. We seemed to be close to where I had supposed we were; I altered course slightly and we moved out again, still exercising the greatest caution: Bright as the occasional clearing and small openings in the jungle canopy were, beneath the thick rain forest vegetation it was like wearing sunglasses in a coal mine.

About 0230, or more than six hours after leaving Kate, we reached a point on my map that I judged to be close to the Mike Force perimeter. We were in thick jungle at the edge of a large open field; I put several of my men in concealed positions along the tree line. Across the field, fifty to sixty meters away, a large clump of tall trees rose above thick underbrush.

Concealed beneath those trees, a man could see anyone approaching across the open field in the moonlight. It was exactly the kind of location where a small infantry unit could dig in and defend against a larger force.

And that, I believed, was where the two Mike Force rifle companies sent to rescue us were waiting. While I was deciding how best to approach their position, I heard a soft but unmistakably metallic clank coming from that distant wood line.

Somebody was there. It might be our rescuers. It might as easily be a PAVN unit.

I just couldn't know.

I got back on the radio and asked the Mike Force to send a man into the clearing so we could confirm that we were in the right place.

The Mike Force replied that *we* would have to send a man forward into the field.

I could have sent Pierelli, of course, or even Smith or Zollner. Any one of them would have gone if I'd asked them. As would almost any of my strikers. But this was my job, I decided. I couldn't risk another man's life if I wouldn't risk my own. I told Pierelli, Smith, and Zollner to remain with Tex and our radio while I attempted to make physical contact.

Before I left the tree line, I radioed the Mike Force, whispering into the microphone that in a few minutes I would attempt to make contact. They rogered their understanding. I was nevertheless reluctant to step into the field, because I was still not certain that we were in the right spot. Many terrain features look similar in moonlight; we might be miles from where I thought we were. And even if my navigation was spot-on, I couldn't be sure that the Mike Force was across that field.

We could be right in the middle of a PAVN bivouac: If that grove was a good location for a couple of hundred Mike Force strikers to dig in and hole up at night, it was an equally good place for a PAVN unit.

My final words to Pierelli, Smith, and Zollner were that if I walked into a PAVN position instead of the Mike Force, the enemy might not realize that I had others with me. If I was killed or captured, they were to forget about me, melt back into the jungle, and, as soon as it was safe, lead the troops quietly and quickly northwest to Bu Prang.

Feeling naked in the moonlight, my weapon slung over my shoulder, I stepped into the field, realizing as I did so that even if I was walking straight toward the Mike Force, there could also be a thousand guns pointing at me from the jungle on either flank. I took a step forward, then another, calling as I went, in a parade-ground voice, "I am an American; are you the Mike Force?" I repeated this several times as I moved across the field.

There was no answer.

I kept calling and I kept walking. Finally I reached the tree line and there, to my left, a Mike Force striker stared back at me from a foxhole.

Sergeant First Class Lowell Stevens, the Mike Force ground commander, appeared from nowhere to grab my arm.

"Go back and get the rest of your men," he whispered. "And keep your voice down. There's all kinds of fucking pith helmets and AKs around here. Get your guys, and then let's get the hell out of here."

Feeling more naked than ever, I ran back across the open field. I got my troops moving across the field, and I'm pretty sure that at first they didn't understand that we had found the Mike Force.

Koon: "We were halted for a while. Then we started forward, but nobody ever told me we were linking up, and all of a sudden I slipped and fell into a hole. First thing I thought was that I'd fallen into a *punji* pit. It's pretty dark, so I looked and there's a gook on my left and a gook on my right and I was sitting there with my M16 and I said, 'Are you guys friendly?' And they smiled at me, and then somebody said that we'd linked up with the friendlies.

"When I told Albracht this story, he wanted to know what I would've done if they said, 'No, not friendly.' I guess we would've had a shoot-out right there in that hole."

Bob Johnson: "We waited until the captain came back and told us that it was safe to move forward. We crossed a field and into a tree line. Then somebody grabbed my boot, pushed it back, and said, 'Don't step on me.' And that's when I knew that we had linked up with the relief force."

Warren Geromin: "All of a sudden somebody's hand came up and grabbed my foot. They said, 'Don't shoot! Don't shoot!' They were the good guys; the Mike Force, down in their foxholes."

As soon as I had everyone inside the new perimeter, SFC Stevens told me that he had ordered his men not to acknowledge me when I approached them, because he couldn't tell if I had been captured and compromised. And, he explained, there was a vastly superior enemy force in the area, in at least two groups. Earlier that night, he and his men had heard them moving outside their hidden perimeter. He believed—I don't know why—that the enemy was primarily looking for my group.

We were not yet safe. It would be daylight in a few hours; we must leave the area before we were discovered. Even our combined force would not match that of our pursuers. We realigned our formation, with a Mike Force company at either end of our column and my Kate evacuees between them.

We assumed that the PAVN commander would know that we wanted to reach Bu Prang. It followed that they would try to intercept and ambush us. We therefore took evasive action, swinging miles out of our way, sticking to the jungle and moving at a slow and cautious pace.

After daylight, during a break, mail was distributed to some of the Kate artillerymen.

"Somebody had brought some mail off Kate that had come in with the last chopper," says Koon. "I got one letter, from my sister, and in it there were three pieces of Wrigley's Spearmint gum. I was dying of thirst, but we didn't have any water. That chewing gum quenched my thirst until we got to Bu Prang; to this day, I still thank my sister."

Once we resumed our march, my exhausted mind slid into autopilot. I left everything to the Special Forces noncoms that led each Mike Force company: Sergeant First Class Stevens and Sergeant First Class Don Simmons, both ten-year Army veterans. Most of the remainder of the march is a blur in memory; the only thing I recall from after the linkup and our subsequent departure was that we came out of the jungle and took a dirt road for a short distance to Camp Bu Prang, arriving there about 1130 hours on November 2.

When the camp came into sight, I was jolted into full consciousness and then infused with a fleeting moment of pride.

One of the artillery sergeants—one that I had seen very little of during the fight—called out, "Hold your heads high, men; be proud. We just walked off Firebase Kate!"

We had moved through enemy territory for over sixteen hours to evade a powerful and determined enemy force. Considering all that we had been forced to overcome on this journey, it must be marked as a minor miracle.

I am confident that Kate could not have survived, nor could our escape have been successful, without Dan Pierelli as my right hand, calm, focused, and a consummate professional. I knew that he would handle whatever came up. He thus enabled me to concentrate on whatever was in front of me at the moment, without needlessly worrying about anything else.

Lieutenants Smith, Kerr, and Zollner, artillery officers completely out of their element when forced to serve as infantry, were individually and collectively magnificent during the siege no less than during our escape and evasion.

Koon, Hopkins, Tiranti, and Geromin—a generator operator!—and a few other artillerymen who overcame their understandable fear of flying explosives to leave shelter and fight alongside our CIDG strikers were critical to the defense of Kate. I don't know that any of us would have survived without their efforts as a roving infantry reserve force.

Sergeant Tex Rogers, who volunteered to serve as my RTO during our escape, never faltered, never wavered, never lost his cool—was simply magnificent. Through our entire ordeal we were separated only twice, each time by necessity. Afterward, Tex confessed that he suffered from night blindness!

Nor would any of us have lived to tell Kate's tale without the pilots and crews in Spooky and Shadow, with Al Dykes, the Alabama boy, foremost among them. Likewise, their Air Force brethren flying the fast movers that had broken up one assault after another. All of us are eternally indebted to Army Captain John Strange and Air Force Major George Lattin, forward air controllers and pilots extraordinaire.

The courage and skill displayed by countless Army aviators and crew were all that barred the door to our deaths. I commend in that particularly Major Dean Owens and his entire 155th AHC, and especially pilots John Ahearn, Les Davison, and Ken Donovan. Also, Ben Gay of the 48th AHC and Jim Matlock of the 189th AHC.

Nolan Black, Maury Hearne, Clyde Canada, and Douglas Lott, the pilots and crew of Joker 85, gave their lives that we might live. We never met, but I will never forget you.

INSIDE the camp, I learned that one of the two missing artillerymen had indeed joined with a few Montagnard strikers who were separated from the group. It was so dark, he said, that at first he couldn't tell whether he'd found a group of North Vietnamese or the CIDG! They had all hiked straight back to Bu Prang, avoided enemy contact, and arrived safely about the same time that my group was linking up with the Mike Force.

That left only one man unaccounted for: PFC Michael R. Norton, a gunner from the 105 section from Charlie Battery, 5/27 Artillery. He was said to have departed Kate with us, but had disappeared before the linkup. An aerial search was launched around Kate and the route that we followed to the linkup.

A chopper pilot that I met several days after we walked out told me that another chopper pilot told him that search pilots made passes over the area between Kate and Bu Prang for three days in an attempt to locate Norton.

On one of these forays, the pilot said, a hunter-killer team saw a man waving his hands frantically in an open field. He wore green Army jungle fatigues with a boonie hat pulled low on his head. The pilot made a cautious landing approach, but as they were about to hover in for a landing, the door gunner yelled, "Gook!" As the pilot pulled up hard and fast, the surrounding jungle erupted with small-arms fire. As the chopper flew off, the man in the field ran toward the place where the fire came from.

The man in the field, set there to bait a trap—was that Norton? Unlikely. Probably, it was an enemy soldier dressed in one of our uniforms. It's possible that PAVN captured Norton and took his clothes, but the fatigues might just as easily have been abandoned on Kate when we left. Or were from some other source entirely.

In addition, my coauthor has heard variations of this story from at least half a dozen people, not all of them Vietnam veterans, over the last forty years. None who told the story claimed to have firsthand knowledge. It was always something they had heard from someone else.

As we researched this book, two of the artillerymen who served with me on Kate said that they'd been told by others that, as we were leaving, Norton went back to get something he'd forgotten. Others said that he came off the hill with the unit, but got separated in the confusion during the PAVN machine-gun attack. I have no idea if either account is true; again, no one claims firsthand knowledge. By my own observations, Norton might easily have fallen into a bomb crater or a shell hole and hit his head or broken his neck. For his family's sake, I hope that someday, somehow, his whereabouts are accounted for.

FROM October 28 through our escape on the evening of November 1, my world had been a tiny hilltop in Hades where fire and steel rained from the sky, a cordite-reeking cosmos of unending perdition. As time's river meanders onward, I have often reflected upon those days, and as I do so, my memory becomes clearer, my senses keener. At times, uninvited, I can almost hear the crash of mortars and the fiery screech of flying rockets. My nostrils are assaulted by the metallic smell of blood and the stench of violent death. I have never felt more needed than I was on Kate, nor have I ever felt more fear. I had come to the firebase for what amounted to a mundane purpose, but a new and far more important need arose. I was called upon to lead a hundred and fifty fighting men, many suffering from wounds or battle shock, through a gauntlet of fire—lead them to safety. I did not volunteer for this; the task was thrust upon me. Once I could comprehend exactly what I must do, I had resolved that no power on earth would prevent me from delivering these men from harm's way—or I would die trying.

I truly do not understand how we escaped that night; it could only have been the hand of God that guided us. Although I do not dwell on it, it comes to mind more often than I care to admit. A smell, a sound, a flash of light, even a conversational turn of phrase, and I am back on Firebase Kate, fighting for my life. The experience has battered and burned an everlasting wound on my soul.

THE AFTERMATH

For six days I had hardly slept, fueled by not much more than adrenaline and Army-issued uppers. Now I needed nothing more than sleep. After a quick debriefing, I tumbled into my bunk and immediately lapsed into unconsciousness.

I was awakened about ten hours later by the sudden rude noise of incoming mortars and the ear-shattering *crack!* of a large-caliber recoilless rifle.

The mighty PAVN force that had been distracted and diverted by Kate for nearly a week now fell on Bu Prang itself. Everyone on Special Forces Team A-236 had an assigned battle station; mine was behind the .50-caliber mounted on top of an elevated bunker at the apex of the camp's defenses. Scrubbing sleep from my eyes, I took up my post and almost immediately spotted PAVN's recoilless on a hillside more than half a mile away, barely within range of Ma Deuce, my venerable .50-caliber Browning M2. Firing short bursts, I walked my tracers toward the reckless rifle's signature firing flash.

That woke the gunner up. He responded with an HE round to the base of my position, blowing me backward off the bunker roof.

I climbed back up and returned fire, a long burst.

He fired again, almost immediately; I saw the flash, noted that the projectile's fiery tail appeared to be headed directly at me.

I jumped to the ground first; the explosion was a near miss.

A very near miss.

Shaken but not injured, I remounted the bunker, righted my overturned .50, and poured a stream of fire directly onto the gun position. This PAVN gunner and his loader had guts—they stood their ground and managed to get off two more rounds in rapid succession. Both exploded harmlessly, several meters short. I raked the entire position until it went silent.

My gun was overheated. The barrel needed to cool, but PAVN had moved into RPG range, and his B-40 rockets were added to the incoming deluge.

Spooky and Shadow gunships appeared overhead. After a brief radio reunion with my friends in the sky, I directed their fire on the rocket positions. To get a better look, I left my bunker and moved to an exposed location. From there I pinpointed the RPG nest, and vectored the gunships' fire on them. Spooky and Shadow unleashed their particular versions of fire and brimstone onto these positions, and in minutes all incoming ceased.

Months later, I would be awarded the Silver Star for this action.

But that night, once the threat had passed, all I wanted was a bed.

I awoke on Monday, November 3, and was greeted by a public information officer from Fifth Special Forces Group Headquarters in Nha Trang. He said that a horde of media was waiting to interview me about Kate.

To tell the truth, I wasn't really in the mood.

Smooth and self-assured, the PIO told me that Fifth Special Forces Group Commander Colonel "Iron Mike" Healey had insisted on it.

So I girded my loins, and all that. Before I was permitted to meet the press, however, the PIO went over a list of dos and don'ts to remember when speaking about our "gallant Vietnamese allies."

I had to ask him: Which particular gallant Vietnamese allies is he talking about? And where the hell were they when we needed them?

He had no answers to those questions.

I showered, shaved, put on clean jungle fatigues, and faced the media circus that had gathered from every corner of South Vietnam.

Apparently I got through it all right—it's all just a blur now.

A little later that day, "Iron Mike" himself, a living legend in the flesh, flew in to personally make known his pleasure with my performance on Kate. With my entire "A" Team standing at attention, Healey extolled my accomplishments, described how proud he was of me, how I exemplified the best traditions of the Special Forces, and so on and so forth, at distressing length.

I was more than a little embarrassed. Then Iron Mike asked where I wanted to go next—to include becoming his aide. As I opened my mouth to speak, a gremlin—no doubt merely passing by on some errand of greater mischief—leapt into it. From deep within me, the gremlin summoned the spirit who had been Alleman High's "most fun to be with" of the Class of 1966. This spirit turned off my brain and seized control of my voice. "I'd like to be the officer in charge of the Nha Trang Dairy Queen," said this imp of Satan through my mouth.

The team loved this response. Iron Mike—not so much. His friendly smile drooped into a half snarl.

"That position is filled," he growled.

The gremlin departed to complete his original shenanigan. The spirit within me vanished; as I regained control of my wits, I assumed that I had ruled out any chance of becoming Iron Mike's aide. As if that was a job that I'd ever want.

"How about the II Corps Mike Force?" I said.

"You've got it," he replied. Not willing to waste even one more minute on a clown, Colonel Healey performed a smart about-face, mounted his chopper, and flew off.

TWO days later, on the morning of November 5, Bu Prang received a priority message from Lieutenant General Corcoran ordering me to a ceremony at Ban Me Thuot to recognize the American defenders of Fire Support Base Kate. Alas, near-hurricane-force winds lashed the Central Highlands that day. All birds—especially those with rotor blades instead of feathers—were grounded. General Corcoran nevertheless dispatched a slick to pick me up. Apparently Pawnee Bill believed that his three stars outranked Mother Nature's breezes.

The chopper's arrival was, of course, delayed by weather. As it finally came into sight, I was approached by one of the Mike Force commanders. Several of his strikers had been seriously wounded in the previous night's attack. Their wounds were much more than Bu Prang's medics were equipped or trained to handle, and they would probably die without surgery in a well-equipped hospital. He'd been trying to get them out, but even the wonderful lunatics who flew medevac birds were grounded.

Only my special slick was flying. The Mike Force commander asked if I would get his wounded to the BMT field hospital.

I asked the pilot if he could do the medevac, and he replied that he'd fly me wherever I wanted to go. We loaded the wounded and took off. At the hospital I helped get them to the emergency room before heading for the general's ceremony a few miles away.

We landed and I started for the building where I had been told to report to General Corcoran. On the way, I ran into Mike Smith and several of the troops from Kate.

A Silver Star was pinned to Smith's fatigue jacket.

"Where the hell were you?" he asked.

"Unavoidably detained."

Smith said that Corcoran had waited for a few minutes, and then became irritated at my tardiness. Time waits for no man. Nor do lieutenant generals. Corcoran conducted the awards ceremony without me, and left.

In truth, this was my first indication that I had been invited to an awards ceremony. Or to accept a medal. According to the men from Kate, I was slated to receive a Silver Star as an "impact award"—a medal given shortly after an action and before the paperwork goes in. In my case, I would learn, once statements could be taken from witnesses, the Silver Star would probably be upgraded.

I had missed the ceremony, but I was back in the rear with a bunch of guys that I had shared a lot with. We discussed it among ourselves, and agreed that we were all due an in-country R&R.

So we took one, then and there.

And while I was in BMT, I made it a point to go to B-23 headquarters and find Captain Richard Whiteside. I laid into him for cutting my ammo request in half, and I got a little carried away. Okay, it was more than a little. When I tried to get my hands on him, he ran, calling for help. I chased him around his desk a few times before two senior noncoms grabbed me. (They later told me that they were hoping that I'd catch him before they had to step in.)

I later heard, thirdhand, that the awards guy at Fifth Special Forces understood that IFFV Artillery would write me up for a decoration. His opposite number in IFFV Artillery, however, probably believed that my write up was a Fifth Special Forces responsibility. I seem to recall that Fifth Special Forces was then and for some time to come ramrodded by my friend and admirer Colonel Iron Mike Healey.

Neither full colonels nor lieutenant generals trouble themselves with the minutiae of paperwork. They have rooms full of aides and staff officers for that purpose, allowing them to stay focused on the big picture.

If there was ever any paperwork for a medal with my name on it, it disappeared.

If I had a do-over, would I have let wounded strikers die so that I could get a medal? Of course not. No medal could compare with the lessons that we learned about ourselves on Kate. The experiences that we shared, and the unbreakable bonds forged in the heat of battle—these will live within us till our last breath.

VIEWS FROM HIGHER UP

On November 6, 1969, B. Drummond Ayres, Jr., the highly regarded correspondent of the *New York Times*, filed a seven-hundred-word cable on the fighting in and around Bu Prang and Duc Lap. Datelined "BANMETHOUT, South Vietnam," the opening paragraph summed up what must have been stunning news to New Yorkers:

"United States military officials said today that they had decided not to commit any ground troops to the fighting taking place southwest of here between South Vietnamese and enemy forces."

A little later in his dispatch, Drummond quoted "a headquarters officer" as saying that "our intent is to force the South Vietnamese to fight a big one on their own. The name of the game these days is 'Vietnamization.'"

Had Mr. Drummond cared to interview me for his report, I would have been delighted to describe some of the exciting, crowd-pleasing moments in this "game." But I was not "a headquarters officer."

ABOUT the time that Drummond filed his report, Ken Donovan, the pilot who had brought in our last big load of small-arms ammo, was coming out of the 155th AHC mess hall after a long day of flying.

"At the time, I was the unit's senior aircraft commander, and as I came out of the mess hall, Major Owen grabbed me and said, 'Donovan, how's it going out there?'

"I said, 'Sir, this thing's probably going to drag on for a while longer, but I want you to remember what a 21-year-old warrant officer told you in November of 1969: The war is over.'

"And that was because we had been putting South Vietnamese infantry battalions into LZs and a few days later we'd pull out what was left, a company or two at the most. They just didn't have the small-unit leadership necessary to conduct warfare at a platoon level," explains Donovan. "I had a lot of respect for the North Vietnamese, who were some hard-core dudes. We killed them at every available opportunity, because they'd stand there and fight.

"I could never understand why the South Vietnamese weren't willing to do the same thing."

GENERAL Corcoran completed his Vietnam service on February 23, 1970. As was customary and proper, he submitted a lengthy, classified end-of-tour report. The narrative portion ran to 21 pages, single-spaced, and discussed in considerable detail every aspect of combat operations, logistics, pacification, and Vietnamization efforts that had been on Corcoran's plate for his year as IFFV commander. It was well written, concise despite its length, and described a far-flung organization that was imperfect but nevertheless effective and steadily improving.

The report was widely disseminated throughout the US Army, including all major commands and training organizations; it has since been declassified.

Two sections stand out in my mind:

> **Artillery:** ". . . Limited resources result in split battery configuration being the norm rather than the exception. While efforts are made to maintain unit integrity, demands have at times required a 105 mm battery to be split four ways. While Vietnam has long been

considered as a battery commander's war, all too often we find the brunt of conducting operations resting on the shoulders of the junior officers."

Vietnamization: ". . . The two most significant battles fought in South Vietnam in 1969 were fought in II Corps as a test of Vietnamization in the Highlands. The battle of Ben Het convinced II Corps that they could do the job. The battle of Bu Prang and Duc Lap convinced Saigon. The final test will be the conviction of the people."

FINIS

A few days after we walked out, I was in B-23's club in BMT putting away a few beers, and I saw Danny Pierelli. I went over and sat down, and we caught up for the first time since we got back to Bu Prang. Then I told him that I was going to the Mike Force in Pleiku. I was very happy about it, and it showed.

Dan didn't get it. He sort of blinked. "What?" he said.

"I'm going to the Mike Force. I couldn't get in it when I first arrived in-country, because I had no combat experience. Now I do, and the group commander says he'll approve my transfer."

Dan kind of blinked again.

I plowed ahead. "I'm sure that I can get *you* in too."

Now I had his full attention. Dan stared at me as if my face were green with purple polka dots.

"You're absolutely insane," he said—and that caught me off guard.

"What? We're Special Forces! This is what we *do*!"

"What are you talking about?"

"Why wouldn't you want to be in the most elite unit of an elite force?"

I asked, and he shook his head as though I were a child without a brain in my tiny noggin.

"No," replied Dan. "*I* am going to get a job back here at the 'B' Team. *I* am going to send radio transmissions. From *here*, in Ban Me Thuot. And when my tour is up, I'm going to go home."

It was my turn to stare. He shook his head yet again.

"Bill. I'm done," he said. "And you! The Mike Force? You're absolutely insane."

Maybe so.

We few, we happy few, we band of brothers;
For he today that sheds his blood with me
Shall be my brother; be he ne'er so vile,
This day shall gentle his condition;
And gentlemen in England now abed
Shall think themselves accursed they were not here,
And hold their manhoods cheap whiles any speaks
That fought with us upon Saint Crispin's day.

—William Shakespeare, *Henry V*

EPILOGUE

I have stayed in touch with some of the men with whom I served on Kate. Among these, a few maintained contact with still other Kate alumni. When we began to assemble research for this book, we were able to find a few others. Nevertheless, we were able to speak with less than half of the Americans who actually served on Firebase Kate. What follows is a brief description of what became of those with whom I could reconnect, and a few of those with whom I could not. I greatly regret that we were not able to speak with every single American soldier who served under enemy fire on Kate.

Klaus Adam

Klaus flew back to Kate a few days after we escaped; by then it was a smoking ruin. He stayed just long enough to do a bomb damage assessment so that he could submit paperwork supporting combat loss reports for the howitzers and other Charlie Battery equipment that he was responsible for as commanding officer. While acknowledging that Kate had borne the brunt of the fighting, Adam also wanted to be sure that we knew that "the guys at Annie and Susan all busted their nut to support Kate. Unfortunately, we were too far in range, and that was where the tactical error was made."

Adam rotated home in early 1970, transitioned from the Army Reserve to the Regular Army, transferred to the Signal Corps, and served twenty-seven years before retiring as a major. He lives near Killeen, Texas, where he is highly respected for his community and church work.

John Ahearn

After bringing Lieutenant Maurice Zollner to Kate, Ahearn flew back to his base at BMT. It was dark when he landed; he parked his Huey, then reported in to operations. "The next morning I'm having breakfast," Ahearn recalls, "and our assistant maintenance officer gets me out of the mess hall and chews my ass up one side and down the other. There were holes in my aircraft tail boom. The gunship pilots thought it could have been shrapnel from rockets because they were putting them right under me as I approached. Shrapnel or bullet holes, who knew? It was bad form on my part not to have found the holes, but it was dark and we weren't going to stand out there with a flashlight—there were always North Vietnamese lurking around the perimeter."

Less than a month later, Ahearn flew a resupply mission to a microwave radio relay station on the lip of a dormant volcano south of Dak Lak. This was hands down the most dangerous spot in all South Vietnam for a helicopter. "The site was very actively under attack," he recalls. "North Vietnamese were outside and inside the volcano. I did a fast approach and dropped off supplies, picked up wounded, and on the way out I got hit in the legs with a couple of AK-47 rounds."

His copilot, Larry Pluhar, flew him and the other wounded to safety.

"Forty years later, I found out that the mission was actually a check ride to qualify me to become the province adviser's aircraft commander," he says with a sigh.

Ahearn left Vietnam in an Air Force ambulance plane on December 8, his 24th birthday. "I went to Camp Zama in Tokyo," he recalls. "I was very fortunate that they saved my left leg—it was touch-and-go about losing it."

Ahearn was then evacuated to St. Albans Naval Hospital, near his home in New York City. A few months later, while recovering from one in a series of reconstructive surgeries, he received word that his friend Marlin Johnson, copilot on his only mission to Kate, was killed in action on April 20, 1970.

Ahearn remained at St. Albans until the following August. "The Navy orthopedic surgeon told me very directly that I wouldn't pass a flight physical again and I should start thinking about a new career," he recalls. "I had a wife and an infant son, and a lot of time to sit in a hospital bed thinking about how I was going to make a living. I realized that if I couldn't fly, I didn't want to be an engineer."

Before he was wounded, Ahearn had been assigned the additional duty of unit property book officer—essentially a bookkeeper charged with maintaining records of all accountable property in the company, from helicopters and spare parts to machine guns and the mess hall coffeemaker. "I was successful at that job, and that led me to go back to school and get a degree in accounting. Then I got an MBA in finance, and became a CPA. I joined an accounting firm and had a very successful corporate career."

Now retired, Ahearn lives in Scottsdale, Arizona.

Lucian "Luke" Barham

Barham's recollections of his time on Kate are, by his own description, hazy and incomplete. He recalls relieving another Special Forces officer soon after Kate was established, but cannot recall his name or rank. He also recalls having *two* Special Forces noncoms with him during his weeks on Kate, but cannot recall their names. He does, however, insist that he went on daily recon patrols and saw no sign of the enemy. He was replaced on Kate by an officer whom he recalls only as a "Lieutenant Silver," in order that he could take command of Team A-234 at An Lac.

"Maybe that wasn't his name—I heard that he got a Silver Star, so maybe that's why I remember him as Lieutenant Silver," Barham says.

Barham returned to Vietnam in 1972 for about three months on a classified mission called Project Friday Gap. This was a Military Intelligence operation to instruct men from Cambodia's short-lived Khmer Republic in Special Forces staff procedures. (Recall that Barham speaks Cambodian.) These students returned to Cambodia to become the staff for Khmer Special Forces. The Khmer Republic was swept away by the genocidal Khmer Rouge in 1975.

Barham left the Army in 1973 as a captain. In 1975 he was hired as a civilian contractor to train Saudi Arabia's National Guard, an elite palace guard. In 1980 he switched employers to work on the Saudi Naval Expansion Program. When he returned to the States in 1985, Barham went into construction; he owned a construction company in Utah. In 2005 he was employed as a contractor in support of FEMA for the Hurricane Katrina recovery effort. In 2012 he went to New York for FEMA in support of the Hurricane Sandy recovery effort. His home is in Summerdale, Alabama.

Francis "Butch" Barnes

Butch, who served on Firebase Susan and whose gun was taken out of service just when Kate needed it the most, now lives in Antioch, California, and is an engine maintenance supervisor for Delta Airlines.

Nolan Black

Shortly after Kate was abandoned, the remains of Nolan Black and his crew were recovered by elements of the 7/17th Cavalry. The stunning Washington, DC, memorial wall listing the names of America's fallen in the Vietnam War has spawned several adjuncts, including a searchable database of the names on the wall. Comments are allowed, and what follows here was taken from the public comments on Black's page. They are in many ways typical of comments for all who were lost in this war.

From Black's Widow, Carol:

Nolan, I miss you as though you left us yesterday, and here it is 30-plus years later . . . I feel your presence at times, as if you've never left. Laura is a beau-

tiful woman, you would be so proud of her. She is kind, loving and strong. She was married a month ago. Dad gave her away and it was beautiful! I felt as if you and Mom were there, looking down on her. Others have written about knowing you while in Vietnam . . . While it is painful, it is also beautiful to know that you are being remembered and held close to their hearts, too. I love you, miss you and am proud of you.

Carol, Later:

Happy 60th Birthday. I have been thinking of you a lot lately. Wondering what you would look like as a 60-year-old. Somehow, all I can picture is the way you were the last time I saw you. Laura and I were talking about you last evening. We played a little "I wonder, what would have happened, if you came back." I pictured you having retired from the Army as a jet pilot [sic] and now working for UPS, doing their flights. We would have been able to take some of those trips we talked about. Maybe even bought the house on the ocean we dreamed of. I saw a happy family, with you enjoying Laura's daughters, your granddaughters Sarah and Ashley. I know you would have been every bit the loving grandpa, as you were the loving daddy. You would have been the strong dad for Laura as she went through her painful divorce. We would have continued to grow in our love for one another, and in our faith in God. Happy birthday, keep flying high and wait for me. Someday, we will fly together, forever.

From His Daughter, Laura:

I was born in 8/68, so I never really got to know my father "in person," but through my mother, Carol, and my grandparents, I have come to know him. I know he loved to fly and was proud to serve his country, so I know that his death was not in vain. I was brought up to be proud of him and all others who have fought. A Purple Heart Chapter in Wisconsin bears his name. He lives on, through us and all others. I am very proud, of him and all the other heroes, alive, or gone, but not forgotten.

I wanted to thank all the guys who have written me letters about my dad. They mean more to me than you could ever know. Please continue.

From Steven Parker, a Roommate in Vietnam

I think of you often. I remember the late-night conversations about your family, your dreams, fears, your dedication. I also remember the day you died, in support of Firebase Kate. It still wakes me at night. From all the Blue Stars and Jokers. God Speed, Nolan, keep watch for us, we're right there on your wing. Catch the wind.

After Nolan's death Carol remarried. She believes that her Nolan is *"with the Lord in heaven, living the rest of eternity at peace surrounded by the love he so well deserves,"* she wrote. Their daughter, Laura *"is a wonderful, devoted mother and grandmother who . . . exemplifies the love of a mother for her children."* Laura has connected with two other children of her birth mother.

Carol says that she now lives a life *"filled with sorrow, joy, peace, struggles and the bittersweet memories of the first love of my life, Nolan Eugene Black. A part of my heart was torn from me when he died, and it remains gone to this day. The raw edges have scarred over with time, but the missing piece is with him."*

Reg Brockwell

Brockwell left Vietnam in March 1970 and spent the remainder of his two-year service at Fort Sill as an assistant operations officer. "I was offered the general's aide position if I'd extend for six months in Vietnam," he explains. "By that time, I'd decided I wouldn't stay there six more minutes."

After release from active duty, Brockwell returned to Houston and resumed his former job at Shell Oil. "About forty of us had gotten out of the military at roughly the same time," he recalls. "Shell told us that we had a year, because that's what [a federal law said] they had to give us, but we'd better find another job. Sure enough, at the end of the year they called us all into an auditorium and told us we were gone. I looked for another chemical engineering job, but couldn't find one that I liked or that I felt was suitable. Trading stocks was my hobby, and one day my Merrill Lynch stockbroker asked me if I'd ever thought about doing that for a living. I tried it, and I loved it, and 35 years later I retired and converted it back into a hobby."

This book would never have been written without a big push from Brockwell: "Initially I was going through a lot of documents trying to find out what had happened to a Bronze Star that I'd been told that I'd been awarded—I *had* been awarded one in an impact ceremony, but the paperwork had never come through," he explains. "In Vietnam it was *Go here and do this*, and *Go there and do that*. I had no idea what the big picture was. After I came home, I started looking at the big picture. I had a recurring nightmare at the time where I was walking into this village and it said, 'Welcome to Bon Sar Pa.' I had no idea where it was. I don't know if it was suppression or what, but in my nightmare I was always in a situation where I was totally overwhelmed. Then, in the mid-seventies, I saw a movie starring Burt Lancaster called *Go Tell the Spartans*, which was based on a book called *Incident at Muc Wa*. A small firebase was surrounded, and the people had to walk off. [In Vietnamese, *muc wa* means "too much."] All were killed except one. I went back and started looking at some maps and I saw that Bon Sar Pa was on the road between Duc Lap and Bu Prang, and close to a volcano near [firebases] Martha and Helen."

He continues. "Things started coming back to me. I read a booklet written by an SF soldier, *Special Forces at War*, and he mentioned . . . Kate, Annie, and Susan. I remembered still more and started doing some research through the archives in 1992. Later I went out to Texas Tech and used their archives of the Vietnam War.

"I began to realize that I was selfishly looking for a potential Bronze Star, and some of the people on this firebase, namely Bill Albracht, had received nothing for what I considered to be a very heroic deed. So I interviewed Major Lattin and several other people along the way, and I was finally able to get in touch with Albracht and [confirmed] that he didn't receive any recognition for [his role as Kate's commander]. Then I talked to Sergeant Pierelli and, beginning in 2005, I wrote *The Battle for LZ Kate*, copyrighted it in 2007 [and then posted on the Internet] for the sole purpose of [revealing] what, at that time, was probably the better-known, but least publicized, battle of the war.

"As I did the research, things kept coming back. I was going through my pictures one day and looked at those that I'd taken of the 105 crew from Kate who had lost Norton. The 5th of the 27th artillery ended up naming a firebase for Norton, but when you think about what had happened to Ron Ross and Michael Norton, it was really depressing. Nobody seemed to have a handle on what was going on. It almost seemed like the US military had said, 'We just have to write this bad deal off.' It almost came down to the point that they said, 'There's nothing that we can do.'

"I have a couple of *Stars and Stripes* articles that basically talked about how the Vietnamese, who were nowhere in sight, were pounding the NVA at Bu Prang and these firebases," he says, throwing up his hands, as if to say he can't believe it.

Brockwell and his wife still live in Houston.

William J. Brydon

For his role in our escape and evasion, Australian Army Major Brydon was "mentioned in dispatches," which entitled him to use the initials M.I.D. after his name forever thereafter. His citation read, in part: "During this operation, Major Brydon controlled his companies with outstanding ability. When a fire support base in the area was threatened by the enemy and the decision had been made to vacate it, he planned and controlled the successful withdrawal of the Allied garrison using his own companies as a screen. The calm and professional manner in which Major Brydon executed this withdrawal averted a potentially serious situation, Major Brydon's professional ability and his untiring efforts to improve the effectiveness of those under his command have set a fine example to United States, Vietnamese and Australian Commanders involved in the Special Forces program and reflect great credit on himself, the Australian Army Training Team and the Australian Army."

Brydon retired as a lieutenant colonel and died of a heart attack at age 74 at his home in Beenleigh, Queensland, Australia, in 2006.

Mike Caldwell

Mike recovered fully from his shrapnel wounds. Following his discharge from active duty, he returned to his home in West Sacramento, California, and for several years worked at McClellan Air Force Base. After qualifying for a small business loan program for wounded veterans, he started a trucking business. Today his six trucks haul industrial waste to a variety of disposal sites.

Les Davison

John "Les" Davison left the Army in October 1970 and returned to Illinois to earn a BA and an MA. When his GI Bill benefits ran out, he pushed paper for several US government agencies. While working, he attended law school night classes and became an attorney in 1987. Davison took early retirement in 2001 and works summers in various national parks. He is also a substitute teacher in Arlington, Virginia.

Les provided the table below, listing the names of all the aviators who participated in resupplying us on the night of October 31.

Tail #		Crew (pilot/copilot/crew chief/gunner)
	Slicks	**Gunships**
152	CW2 James C. Cole WO1 Jerry Watson Sp4 Peter Barthman Sp4 David E. Kadel	WO1 John "Les" Davison 1Lt Norman Simpson Sp5 Craig W. Mosher PFC Thomas M. Moore
254	CW2 Kenneth Donovan 1Lt James A. Hitch Sp5 Mike Wilcox Sp4 Larry Gillikin	WO1 Dennis Fenlon CW2 Robert Collins Sp4 Thomas W. Love Sp4 Calvin Serain

continued . . .

Tail #		Crew (pilot/copilot/crew chief/gunner)
620	WO1 Frank G. Uhring WO1 David J. De Sio Sp4 Ernest C. Plummer Sp4 Edward J. Close	WO1 John "Jack" Coonce WO1 Kenneth Shriver Sp4 Ronnie Wiles Sp4 Robert E. Blake
073	CW2 James L. Abbott MAJ Dean M. Owen Sp4 Jesse Craig Sp4 Richard Farlow	WO1 Charles "Pete" Cosmos 1Lt Walter Foster Sp5 Gregory Bundros Sp4 Rafael Alvarez, Jr.
765	WO1 Larry D. Ingram Colonel B. R. Wright Sp4 Richard D. Matson Sp4 Johnny D. Bledshaw	

According to Davison, each of the eighteen pilots who flew that mission, including Colonel Wright, the 17th Aviation Group commander, was awarded the Distinguished Flying Cross. The eighteen enlisted crew chiefs and door gunners were each awarded the Air Medal, with "V" device, indicating the award was for valor.

This strikes me as unfair to the enlisted crewmen, who were exposed to the same dangers as their pilots. It should also be noted that pilots flew in armored seats with a front flak vest. Crewmen had only flak vests.

Elton J. Delaune

Every officer learns early in his career that he is responsible for everything that his men do, and for everything that they fail to do. Because Lieutenant Colonel Delaune had operational control of Firebase Kate, our successful E&E accrued to his credit. Soon after leaving Vietnam, he was promoted to full colonel. The Army paid his full salary and allowances, as well as tuition and books, to enroll in an MBA program at Syracuse University.

Later he attended the Army War College. Promoted twice more, he became the very model of a modern major general. Delaune served as deputy chief of staff for resource management for US Army Europe in 1977 and 1978, and retired soon afterward. He died in 2006.

Rocco DeNote

Rocco was *always* there when I called from Kate. He slept on the floor, took his meals there, and left only for brief toilet breaks. He knew everything that was happening and was absolutely invaluable. I put him in for a Bronze Star for Meritorious Service, and he told me that it meant more to him than anything else he received in Vietnam.

After returning to civilian life, Rocco went to college on the GI Bill, then settled in the Cape May area at the southern tip of New Jersey, married, and started a family. He found work with the local police force. In his tenth year as a cop, Rocco was shot in the head by an elderly man wielding a shotgun. His road back to fully functional was long and slow; eventually he made an almost complete recovery. Parts of his memory are gone, especially those relating to playing musical instruments. He became a grandfather in 2013 and now works as a substitute schoolteacher.

Ken Donovan

"Being older now, my attitude has changed from when I was younger," he says. "I think this applies to all the guys who were there: The meaning of our Vietnam experience lies within *us.* Not with the politicians. Not with the commanders. We were willing to step forward to serve our country when that wasn't necessarily the fashionable thing to do. I kept faith with my fellow soldiers, and I was courageous when I had to be, and I think that applied to all of us. I lost about twenty-six friends—flight school classmates and guys in my unit. Forty-some years after the fact, I feel bad because we lost their capability. These men were courageous, intelligent, aggressive, all the good things that we want in our citizens, and we lost that. If we look at most of the guys [that I knew] who survived, we had some doctors, a lot of attorneys, many successful businessmen. Contributing members of society. We lost all that. My overriding emotion is a sense of loss.

"Dick Pugh, one of my flight school classmates, was killed the day after Christmas, 1968. So every Christmas, when I sit down with my family, I toast Dick. I think as long as you're alive in somebody's memory, you're still alive."

About 40,000 American helicopter pilots served in Vietnam. Of those men, 2,002, along with 2,704 crewmen, were killed in Vietnam.

Donovan left active duty in 1971 and earned a degree from Michigan State University. He also joined the Michigan Army National Guard. In 1979, he was offered the opportunity to join the Active Guard Reserve Program, and served as an instructor pilot. Soon after, he accepted a direct commission to second lieutenant.

He flew for twenty-five years. "I did everything that Ken Donovan can do in a Huey," he says. "I had a great time in Vietnam; we lived in the aircraft. During the LZ Kate/Bu Prang deal, on Thanksgiving Day I flew from 0300 hours until dusk the next day, my longest day in a slick."

Donovan's last five years in the Michigan Guard were in a non-aviation assignment as a battalion and then brigade operations and training officer. Donovan retired as a lieutenant colonel in 1985 after twenty-eight years of service. Following that, he worked in the defense industry and retired as VP of sales and marketing for an engineering firm in 2008. Still tall and trim, he lives in retirement near Tampa, Florida.

Al Dykes

Dykes spent his entire Air Force career as a navigator. After Vietnam he served on several different classified programs until he retired from active duty with more than twenty years of service. He then continued to work for the Air Force as an adviser and consultant on a variety of classified programs. Dykes continued to enjoy life with his wife in Fort Walton Beach, Florida. In the course of preparing this book, I was privileged to reconnect with Al; we and our wives became very good friends. He died after a long illness on November 7, 2014.

Ben Gay

Gay completed a second Vietnam tour; after four years active duty, he returned to Virginia, where he enrolled in college and joined a Virginia Army National Guard aviation unit. He graduated in 1974, and then served as a Naval Criminal Investigative Service special agent for eight years before transferring to the Treasury Department, where he served seventeen years as a Customs Service criminal investigator. He retired from federal service in 2000. Meanwhile, he remained with the Virginia Guard until 1996, logging more than 5,000 hours of flight time, including more than 1,500 hours of combat flying. His twenty-five years in the air included a Desert Storm tour in Saudi Arabia and Iraq as a Dustoff pilot with the 986th Medical Detachment.

In 2000, he began a new career with the New Kent County (Virginia) Sheriff's Office. He currently serves as a patrol deputy, commercial motor vehicle enforcement officer, and deputy in charge of the Marine Patrol Unit.

"I give full credit to my Lord for all that I have accomplished in this life," he says.

Warren Geromin

Geromin completed his military service in Vietnam, then returned to his hometown, Middletown, Connecticut. He lives there to this day, employed by the US Postal Service as a maintenance supervisor for a local post office.

Gerald R. Helmich

I knew Major Helmich as "Spad 02," piloting the A1H Skyraider that kept the enemy at bay as we departed Kate on the night of November 1, 1969. Ten days later, a two-seater Army helicopter was downed about sixty miles west of Dong Hoi, North Vietnam, near the border with Laos. An Air Force Jolly Green Giant CH-53 helicopter was sent to rescue the Army pilots. While the first was rescued, one of two escorting F-4 Phantoms was shot down by 37 mm anti-aircraft fire. Due to bad weather and poor visibility, the search-and-rescue mission was suspended until the next day. On November 12, the CH-53 returned to the area to find the crew of the Phantom and to rescue the other Army pilot. Helmich and his wingman flew cover for them. While the second Army aviator was rescued, Helmich was shot down during a low-altitude strafing pass. The crash site was never identified and Helmich remains missing in action and presumed dead. He was 38 years old and his home of record was Manchester, New Hampshire.

Kenn Hopkins

Hopkins was sedated for medevac, but it was several hours before we could get him out. "Next thing I remember," he says, "I'm outside and a medevac is coming. We're going over [Ambush Hill] and I say, 'Don't go over on this side because they have a .50-caliber over there.'"

When he got to Ban Me Thuot, a doctor examined him. "He asked me if I was okay, and I said, 'Sure, I'm fine.' Then some officers came in and debriefed me. I told them what I knew, what we were up against, and why I was there. Then the guilt started, because I left those guys out there," Hopkins says.

The next day he heard that Kate had been evacuated at night. He was returned to Charlie Battery's temporary home in BMT. "When the LZ Kate crew came in, I was deathly afraid that these guys were going to whale on me for leaving them," Hopkins says. "But not at all. They said, 'Where'd you go, Kenn? What happened? You wouldn't believe what we went through.'

"And then they talked about Norton. One of the guys told me that as they were leaving the LZ, somebody hit a trip flare [and] everybody froze. Once the flare died down they started up and Norton said something like, 'God, I left something. I have to go up and get it!'"

Hopkins does not recall who told him that.

His reentry to civilian life was rough. "When I came home, the reaction I received at the airport and the looks that I received from my friends were not supportive. I felt that I had changed, and I was a more complete person. Therefore, I changed my name to Kenn. I liked that four-letter word over the other four-letter words my 'friends' and other people called me. I stayed home for only a few months; then I ran away to Europe for four months to settle down somewhat and unwind. I just could not relate to anyone here, and by the time I returned from Europe, I no longer associated with my 'friends' but made new ones. The old friends wanted Ken back but Ken no longer existed. Kenn was now in charge."

Hopkins earned a university degree in math, worked for a time as a gardener, and now works as a software engineer for a defense contractor. After a lapse of several years, he returned to surfing. He lives in Chula Vista, California, where he grew up.

Bob Johnson

"Christmas, 1969, was a very long day for me," Johnson recalls. "I awakened at a transit camp in Vietnam, was bused to the airport and flew across the International Dateline en route to McChord Air Force Base, Washington. At Fort Lewis, right next door, I was discharged from active duty and took yet another bus to the Seattle-Tacoma Airport. I flew military standby to New York; Christmas ended somewhere over the Midwest. I took a shuttle from JFK Airport to Grand Central Station, where I boarded an Amtrak train to Providence, Rhode Island. My mother picked me up at the train station."

Three days later he returned to his job at the Equitable Life Assurance Society in midtown Manhattan. The following summer he began dating a girl in his office. They married the next summer. In 1971, he took a new job at North American Reassurance Company's Manhattan headquarters. The following year he became a Fellow of the Society of Actuaries and worked in reinsurance operations until taking early retirement in 1993. He now serves as a consultant for reinsurance companies.

While raising his family in Connecticut, Bob was active in the Boy Scouts and enjoyed tennis, golf, and competitive road running. He completed the Philadelphia Marathon in under three hours at age 50. In 2002, he and his wife moved to a golf course community in North Myrtle Beach, South Carolina.

John Kerr

Kerr was flown from Kate to the 71st Evacuation Hospital in Pleiku, where surgeons treated his leg wound. "I was there for six or seven days," he recalls. At the time, Army policy was for evacuees to remain in such hospitals for no more than a week. Those unable to return to duty were transferred to a convalescent hospital. "I went to the Sixth Convalescent Hospital on Cam Ranh Bay," says Kerr, who spent the remainder of the regulation thirty-day post-wounding period there. Soldiers unable to return to duty at the end of that period were then evacuated to Japan for as long as it took them to recover, then sent Stateside for a return to duty or discharge from service.

"After thirty days, my leg was not healed," Kerr relates. "It was still oozing [pus] and the dressing had to be changed twice a day. My doctors said that it would take another couple of weeks to heal, so I would be sent to Japan." Once he was fit for duty, Kerr expected to be sent to Fort Hood, Texas.

"I didn't want to go to Japan. And I didn't want to go back to Fort Hood," he recalls. "I wanted to go back to Charlie Battery, back with my men, to complete my tour of combat duty."

He had watched nurses change his wound dressing twice a day for a month, so he knew how to do that. "I asked them to give me a big bag of swabs and Q-tips, and promised to keep my wound clean for the next two weeks until it healed—if they'd let me return to duty."

Released from the hospital, he hitched a ride out of Cam Ranh Bay and contacted 1/92 Artillery Battalion HQ. "They told me to go down to Firebase Dorrie, near BMT, and replace Captain Adam, my battery commander, who had completed his tour of duty and was due to go home."

Kerr became Firebase Dorrie commander. "We had two 155 howitzers and a 175 gun," he recalls. He was on Dorrie for about a month, including Christmas, then served on several other firebases until his year of combat ended.

Kerr was then promoted to captain and assigned to Fort Sill, where he served as an instructor in the Artillery Officer Basic Course and for Officer Candidate School.

"That was wonderful," he says now. "I just loved that duty." After returning to civilian life, Kerr spent eight years in Minnesota and Wisconsin as a process and quality-control supervisor for Hormel Food Company. Then he returned to Iowa to work for Lyon Energy, the state's only nuclear power plant, as an engineer. "This was state-of-the art, high technology—very interesting, and I learned an awful lot over more than twenty years."

Kerr took early retirement at age 55 "because I wanted to do something else, before I can't do anything." He has taught mathematics at a Cedar Rapids community college ever since.

For his service on Kate, Kerr was awarded the Bronze Star with "V" device (for valor) as well as a Purple Heart for his wound. Because of the tangled chain of command over Kate, he isn't sure who wrote up the medal recommondation and if they had a true picture of what he endured or the professionalism of his conduct. He won't say it in so many words, but Kerr believes that his performance under fire should have earned him more than a Bronze Star. I agree, and I have submitted my recommendation that it be upgraded to the Silver Star.

Nelson Koon

"We were only in Bu Prang a couple of hours and then we were airlifted to someplace out in the middle of nowhere," Koon recalls. "Some bird colonel came in. And he lit my cigarette for me! Then they picked us up again with a Chinook and took us to Ban Me Thuot; we were there a couple of days.

"Lieutenant Smith was awarded the Silver Star there, and Albracht came and he had his green beret on and I asked him what he got for a decoration.

"He said, 'I didn't get anything.'

"I said, 'What?!'

"He said, 'Special Forces is an everyday job.'

"Then we went to Pleiku, and they had an awards ceremony for us there. I don't have much use for the military caste system. Officers got a Silver Star or something, all the NCOs got Bronze Stars, E-4 and below got the Army Commendation Medal. We said, 'What a bunch of shit—we got a Green Weenie with a 'V' cluster.'

"Then [Sergeant First Class] Jimmy Gooch, the Chief of Smoke, came back from R&R. He wasn't on Kate. We were supposed to fly to Ban Me Thuot and then out to LZ Mike Smith. They put us on a C-130, and when we landed and the ramp came down, we were in Cam Ranh Bay! We thought, *This is cool!*

"Gooch thought we needed a little R&R, so for three days, while we were waiting for our guns, we were at the clubs. Then we were at the Cam Ranh Bay replacement station and all these new guys came in wearing brand-new jungle fatigues.

"They said, 'What unit are you guys with?'

"We said, 'We're the artillery.'

" 'Where are your guns?'

" 'The enemy got 'em. We got nothing except our damn packs and our M16s.'

"Then a sergeant major came out and said, 'Hey, guys, I know you've been through a lot of shit, but don't scare these guys before I get them out in the field.' "

When their R&R was over, Koon and the rest of Charlie Battery went back to Ban Me Thuot, picked up new howitzers, and went to Firebase Mike Smith. "When we got there they told us, 'You guys get to rest for a while and relax,' " recalls Koon. "Soon as a Chinook landed and that ramp dropped, we got incoming, 122 mm rockets. We were there for sixty-two days, and we got hit for fifty-two.

"Even though everyone [on Kate] went through basic training and had basic marksmanship training, most of the guys were artillery trained; after their guns were destroyed, they stayed hunkered down. Being infantry trained, it just seemed natural to me to use the M60 and M16. I think Hopkins and Tiranti felt the same. There may have been other individuals or small groups moving around and engaging the enemy; I don't know. All I can vouch for is Hopkins, Tiranti, and myself and the brave gun crew on the 105 howitzer. As for me, it had a lot to do with self-preservation and the will to live. I didn't want to die hiding in a bunker."

Koon completed his tour in October 1970. He left active duty in 1972 and the following year joined the Washington State Army National Guard. Later he returned to active duty as a career counselor. For personal reasons, he elected to leave the Army two years before he would have been eligible for retirement.

Koon then took a job for a firm that bought specialty cars for overseas clients. Later, he worked in automotive shops and in construction. He suffered a stroke in 2003 and is now retired on Social Security disability and a Veterans Disability Pension for hearing loss, PTSD, and type 2 diabetes resulting from Agent Orange exposure.

He lives in rural Moriarty, New Mexico, with his wife, and enjoys traveling.

George Lattin

George Lattin came from Huntington, West Virginia, and enlisted in the Air Force in 1948 at age 17. I knew him as Walt 20, his forward air controller call sign. Lattin's legend began while aloft in his Bird Dog; he observed a flight of VNAF A-37 jets dropping bombs on their own troops. To stop them, he flew in front of the descending A-37s. More than twenty ARVN soldiers were killed; without Lattin, it would doubtless have been much worse.

In late November 1969, during the Battle of Bu Prang, Lattin's Bird Dog was hit repeatedly by small-arms fire that smashed his instrument panel and severed most of the cables connecting the cockpit to control surfaces; he could move only his rudder, and that not much. I talked him back to Bu Prang. To land on the strip there, he flew through a rain of mortar and artillery fire while fighting a crosswind, narrowly missing a barrier across the dirt airstrip to make a spectacular crash landing. He and his backseat observer came away with only a few scratches.

On December 1, a month after he'd kept everyone alive on Kate by bringing in the fast movers to drop bombs and napalm all around our hilltop, a Boxer Phantom crashed near Bu Prang, killing its pilot and weapons officer. A CIDG patrol recovered the bodies. Upon learning that an Army

Huey was coming to bring the remains to an Army morgue in Pleiku, Lattin realized that the identification process and then notification of next of kin would be delayed for several days until paperwork made its way through Army channels to the Air Force. Not willing to keep several families twisting in the wind for days, not knowing what had happened to their loved ones, he flew to Bu Prang, where the Army chopper was headed to refuel. There he approached its warrant officer pilots and asked them to take the remains to the Air Force mortuary at Cam Ranh Bay. The pilots replied politely that they were under strict orders to take them to Pleiku.

Lattin then politely threatened them with court-martial on the bogus premise that they were in combat and could not refuse the direct order of a superior officer. The pilots flew the remains to Cam Ranh Bay, then flew to Pleiku as originally ordered.

There were plenty of Air Force majors who would have faced disciplinary action for what Lattin did, but not him. Lattin retired from active duty as a major in 1970, after twenty-two years of service and logging more than 10,000 hours in the air. Along the way he earned a Silver Star, two Distinguished Flying Crosses, the Bronze Star, a Purple Heart, a dozen Air Medals, and many other decorations.

Terry Malvestuto

Like all noncoms on Kate, Terry Malvestuto was awarded the Bronze Star. He was discharged the following year and returned to his home in Steger, a Chicago suburb. There he joined the community's civil defense organization and rose to become its coordinator. He died at age 60 in 2008 from the complications of type 2 diabetes associated with his exposure to Agent Orange.

Jim Matlock

On the day that Joker 85 went down, Jim was a Ghost Rider pilot flying a slick on ash-and-trash missions out of BMT. He volunteered to bring our ammo and take out some of our wounded. A few days after we walked out, I ran into Jim at Bu Prang and admired his wrist compass. I told him how I'd wished that I'd had one like it when we bailed out of Kate. He took the compass off his wrist and gave it to me. I have it still. Jim lives in Somerville, Tennessee, a fine man and a great pilot.

Dan Pierelli

When his hitch was up, Dan returned to his home in Connecticut and married his fiancée. They now have two sons. Dan returned to school, earned a bachelor's degree and two master's degrees, and worked in the defense industry for forty years. Like much of America, Dan's community suffered greatly from the catastrophic economic recession of 2008. And like many older workers, he was personally afflicted: In 2010 he was laid off by Sikorsky, the manufacturers of Black Hawk helicopters. Dan now does yard work and serves as an on-call substitute schoolteacher, honorable but uncertain employment in tough times. He lives in Southbury, Connecticut.

The passage of time, and possibly the trauma of being under constant bombardment with almost no sleep for five days, have taken their toll on his recall of events on Kate. Many specifics vanished; others faded into fuzzy, generalized memories. I think that this is a good thing. Nobody on Kate, myself included, put more of himself into that battle than did Dan.

William E. Platt

Will was Mike 82, one of the coolest of the cool Air Force FACs that saved our skins on Kate. The son of a glider pilot and an aeronautical engineer, he graduated from Eastern Michigan University, then enlisted for the Air Force pilot program. After earning his wings, he chose to become FAC as a shortcut to the war.

Will retired as a lieutenant colonel in 1988, and lives in Fort Walton Beach, Florida. With more than 11,000 hours as a commercial aviator, he sometimes flies as a fish spotter. His wartime memoir is *Fly and Fight, Low and Slow.*

Gerald "Tex" Rogers

Except for his two years in the Army, Tex lived his entire life in Crane, Texas. He was awarded the Bronze Star, and was honorably discharged in 1970. Returning to Crane, he married Sharron Westfall, and became stepfather to her baby daughter. Their daughter, Misty Renee, was born in 1972. The couple divorced in 1976, and Tex married Margaret Rogers in 1980. Her sons, LaWayne and Shane, took his last name and regarded him as their father. Soon after returning home, Tex started Rogers Dirt Construction to build dirt pads for oil rigs, and other earthworks for the West Texas oil fields. He was also a steer wrestler and a member of the Professional Rodeo Cowboys Association. He loved to hunt and fish and collected arrowheads and other Indian artifacts.

When he reached his thirties, Tex was diagnosed with type 1 diabetes. I'm not a doctor, but my guess is that was the cause of his night blindness. Tex passed away from complications of the disease in October 1995. He was 47 years old.

Ron Ross

All these decades later, I had another thought about why Ron was sent to Kate: Of all the artillery lieutenants who served on Kate, only he had any experience crawling around a jungle. Ross was a graduate of the challenging and highly regarded US Army Jungle Warfare School in Panama, where he had been trained by Special Forces officers and noncoms. Could that be why he was sent to Kate? Had LTC Delaune, or someone on his staff, anticipated that, after what had happened at Firebase Helen, Kate's artillerymen might have to walk out?

I'll never know.

As a final indignity, Ross's death was reported, unofficially, as that of "XO from Charlie Battery, 1/92 Artillery." He was in that capacity for about twenty-four hours, as long as he was on Kate, but the man carried in that slot on the battery personnel roster was Mike Smith. Following custom, the

1/92d's next firebase was established to honor a fallen officer. It was called Firebase Mike Smith.

Ross was posthumously promoted to captain, which had the effect of increasing, slightly, the death benefit paid to his survivors. More than forty years later, I learned that he had also been awarded the Silver Star.

This is the text of the narrative accompanying the award:

> **Award of the Silver Star**
> **(POSTHUMOUS)**
> First Lieutenant Ross distinguished himself by extraordinary heroism in action on 29, 30, and 31 October, while serving as the officer-in-charge of a firing platoon with Battery C, 1/92d Field Artillery. Though assigned to Service Battery, 2nd Battalion, 22d Artillery, he volunteered to command a firing platoon when its platoon leader was wounded in action at Landing Zone Kate. The area came under a severe mortar and rocket attack. Lieutenant Ross, with complete disregard for his own safety, exposed himself to enemy fire in order to direct return fire on the enemy positions. On numerous occasions, he moved throughout the besieged firebase offering words of encouragement to the embattled troops manning the bunkers and artillery. In the early morning hours of 31 October, 1969, the firebase came under intense enemy fire. During this attack, Lieutenant Ross spotted a wounded member of the Vietnamese Security Force near the fire direction center. Ignoring a withering hail of hostile fire, he attempted to carry the man to the safety of a nearby bunker. Lieutenant Ross had nearly reached safety with the wounded soldier, when an exploding rocket mortally wounded him. Lieutenant Ross's exceptional gallantry was in keeping with the highest traditions of the military service and reflects great credit upon himself, his unit, and the United States Army.

Reg Brockwell, who knew and liked Ross, was astonished by this award. "I talked to Tom Klein, who was the battery executive officer at Duc

Lap, and a friend of Ross. Everybody had the same impression: that Ron was being punished [by Delaune], and when he was killed, [Delaune] felt guilty and posthumously promoted him to captain and awarded him one of two Silver Stars in the battalion. I don't want to take anything away from Ron, but he didn't do anything to merit a Silver Star."

That medal was sent to his family. In 2012, as part of the research for this book, I learned that all of Ross's medals, his military mementos, and his burial flag were lost in a house fire. Through the efforts of my good friend Ken Moffett, then serving as Congressman Bobby Schilling's Veterans Affairs officer, a replacement medal was presented to Ron's widow, Trisha, and son, John, along with a flag that had been flown over the Capitol in Washington.

Mike Smith

To this day, Smith regrets leaving Kate after being wounded. "It wasn't like I was dying. I could've stayed. And that's why I went back: I knew every guy there; I knew the firebase; I knew all sorts of things. But that's hindsight.

"I've always considered writing to Ross's folks, but I think that I'd just remind them of how stupid the whole thing was, how useless the war turned out to be."

After escaping from Kate and enjoying a few days' rest, Smith took charge of Firebase Mike Smith (see above), where a few weeks later he was reunited with John Kerr. He served on several other firebases before completing his combat tour. After promotion to captain, Smith was assigned to Fort Sill, Oklahoma, to teach artillery skills.

"I left the service in 1975, after eight years' service," he says. Returning to Colorado, he built a log cabin high in the Rockies. Then he went back to school, earning bachelor's and master's of science degrees in veterinary medicine, followed by a doctorate in education. He became a professor of anatomy and histology. Histology is the study of the microscopic anatomy of plant and animal cells and tissues.

"I taught in the veterinary school at Fort Collins for fourteen years," he says. At age 43 he had heart surgery, and then retired. "In 1994, I found part-time professor work in the Caribbean, and have been teaching histology or anatomy in a veterinary or medical school ever since."

The Smiths lived on St. Kitts for twelve years, Dominica for one, and at this writing are in Grenada for their third year. In 1994, Mike and Elizabeth lost their twenty-two-year-old son, Justin, in a car accident. Since 2000, they have been living on *Justin's Odyssey 3*, a 47-foot sailboat. The Smiths spend their summers traveling and hanging out with their family in their small but comfortable Colorado cabin.

Bernie Tiranti

Following his honorable discharge, Tiranti returned to his home in Chicago. He died after a long struggle against cancer in May 1974, at age 25.

His story does not end there: Five years later, Bernie's mother, Elvira Schmidt, filed suit in federal court on behalf of Bernie's estate, joining with several other cancer-stricken Vietnam veterans and the estates of two others who had died from certain rare or unusual cancers. Named as defendants in what became a gigantic class-action suit were Dow Chemical, Inc., Hercules, Inc., Diamond Shamrock, Inc., Northwest Industries, Inc., Monsanto Co., and North American Phillips. All were associated with manufacturing or dispersing dioxin, the herbicide in Agent Orange.

This was America's first successful environmental class-action suit, and resulted in a multibillion-dollar settlement that included a small sum for each of thousands of plaintiffs, plus reimbursement to the Veterans Administration and the Social Security Fund for costs incurred in treating Agent Orange victims, and funding for education and treatment. The settlement led Congress to pass a law that extended Veterans Administration medical and disability benefits to any service members who served in Vietnam if they suffered from any of a long list of medical conditions associated with Agent Orange.

Maurice Zollner

Zollner was awarded the Purple Heart for the facial wound he suffered on Kate, and the Bronze Star with "V" device for his service on the firebase and during our escape and evasion. I learned this only recently, and subsequently requested that this decoration be upgraded to the Silver Star. Zollner lives in a small Illinois city near St. Louis, Missouri.

AS for me, merely serving in the Mike Force was validation of all the training I had and the sacrifices that I had made since enlisting. Understand: Mobile Strike Force units, along with such special projects such as Special Operations Group, Delta Force, and so on, were the chosen few of America's elite. It would require another book to fully explain the depth, scope, and missions of the II Corps Mike Force, or, as it was affectionately known, the Death Brigade.

I was wounded a second time in April 1970 while clearing bunkers during the Battle of Dak Seang. As it was getting dark, we arrived at our last bunker. I asked one of my Yards to do a low crawl and flank the bunker, get in close, and toss a grenade through the firing aperture. I still remember the look he gave me! I'll never ask a man to do something I hadn't done or wouldn't do—so off I went. I approached the bunker from its east side and eased up to the firing port. At this point Charlie and I played blindman's bluff. I threw a grenade inside, and he threw it back, but not close enough to hurt me. Then a ChiCom stick grenade came flying out. I was prone and too close to the grenade for comfort, but too far to throw it back. I had just started to roll away when it exploded. For a second or two I was Superman, flying through the air. It knocked the wind out of me, but the shrapnel wounds were not serious.

I remained with Mike Force until May, when I was hit again, this time by mortar shrapnel. There was then a theater-wide policy to the effect that anyone awarded a third Purple Heart could request immediate transfer to a Stateside duty assignment. I seem to remember that this was how a young naval type—a tall, skinny swift boat commander with a lot of hair and a Massachusetts accent—cut his combat tour to four months.

I was not ready to come out of the field. I was not ready to stop fighting. I was not ready to leave my men . . . but I would obey orders. When I was told to report to Nha Trang for a staff job, I was reminded, not for the first time, that soldiers are sometimes ordered to perform tasks they find distasteful.

To my mind, I served with the finest combat unit that America ever fielded. They were the best of the best, heroes every one. I tried to be the top soldier in every unit that I served in, but I never thought for a minute that I was the best of *that* bunch. Nevertheless, I completed every mission to the best of my ability. I was unhappy about coming out of the field, but after a period of reflection I decided that maybe it was time to cash in my chips and leave the casino with all my body parts. I thought it might be a good idea to take a little time to decompress before returning to the world of clean water, clean sheets, hot showers, and food eaten from plates. I believe in fate, but I also believe in the chain of command; I saw that they had conspired to take me out of harm's way. I was 22, healthy, brimming with self-confidence, and there was a big, wide world waiting to be explored in the Land of the Big PX.

So I reported to my desk in Nha Trang. My war was over. Two months later, I flew home with a second Silver Star, five Bronze Stars (three for valor), two Air Medals (one for valor), the Vietnamese Cross of Gallantry with the rarely awarded silver star, a Green Weenie for valor, a Presidential Unit Citation, a bunch of campaign medals, and, of course, the three Purple Hearts.

From the day I enlisted, the only award that I truly coveted was the Combat Infantryman Badge, the instantly recognizable mark of a fighting soldier. The Army awards the CIB to infantrymen and Special Forces soldiers in the rank of colonel and below who personally fought in active ground combat while assigned to either an infantry, Ranger, or Special Forces unit of brigade size or smaller. I am grateful for my other decorations, but anything past my CIB was just gravy.

AFTER I left active duty, I returned to the Quad Cities and enrolled in Augustana College. I also took command of an Army Reserve company. In 1975, after earning a BA in business and sociology, I became a special agent of the US Secret Service. In a career spanning more than twenty-five years, I protected six presidents, their families, and a parade of visiting foreign heads of state. I also worked undercover on counterfeiting details and investigated criminal violations of Treasury laws.

Meanwhile, I married and started a family. That marriage ended in 1989, when my children, Nick, Clint, and Jenny were seven, eleven, and sixteen. I was awarded full custody, and we returned to the Quad City area, where I became resident agent in the Secret Service office there. Of all the things that I have accomplished, raising three children as a single parent to become healthy, morally upright, and productive citizens ranks at the top. In 1996, I met the lovely and talented Mary Moran in church; she has completed my life. We were married in 1999; together we have five children and seven grandchildren.

When my youngest child graduated from high school in 1999, Mary and I returned to the nation's capital, where I served as assistant special-agent-in-charge of the Secret Service's Washington, DC, office. Upon retiring from government service, I moved to Michigan to become manager of Ford Motor Company's executive security operations.

We returned to the Quad Cities in 2005, and I launched my own security firm, which allows me to work as much and as often as I choose.

I soon became active in community and veterans organizations, as well as helping to found Veterans for the Constitution with Ken Moffett, a good friend, Vietnam veteran, and former law-enforcement officer. When Bobby Schilling, a local businessman, ran for Congress in 2010, our organization worked hard to raise money and support his ultimately successful campaign. Bobby then offered me the position of veterans affairs officer in his Quad Cities office. I declined and suggested Ken, who was in any case next on Bobby's list. Then Bobby asked if there was anything that he could do for me.

There was: A couple of years earlier, I had been contacted by Reg Brockwell, who was researching the events that occurred on Firebase Kate so many years earlier. Brockwell encouraged me to write an account of my recollections. Seeking closure to the ordeal of Kate and the military decoration that had been promised but never received, I gave that incomplete but factual account to the man whom Bobby two years later would defeat at the polls, Congressman Phil Hare. Hare accomplished very little on my behalf.

So I told Bobby about Kate, and asked him to research the missing award and help me find closure. He gave that task to Ken, who took the ball and ran with it. Ran right out of the stadium: Over several months, he accumulated hundreds of documents, tracked down more than a dozen men who had served on Kate with me or in the skies above us, and asked them to provide statements regarding my actions. Presented with this package of information, Bobby decided to recommend me for the Medal of Honor.

Instead, in November 2012, the Department of the Army awarded me a Silver Star, my third, for my actions on Kate. This is the text of the award narrative:

> **Captain William L. Albracht**
> **Fifth Special Forces Group (Airborne)**
> For Gallantry: In action from 28 October 1969 to 1 November 1969, during combat operations against an armed enemy of the United States, as Executive Officer of Detachment A-236, Company B, 5th Special Forces Group (Airborne), 1st Special Forces, while in the Republic of Vietnam. Captain Albracht's calm and reassuring leadership as the Officer In Charge of Fire Support Base Kate enabled his forces to successfully withstand the initial waves of enemy attacks. The following day, with complete disregard for his own safety, Captain Albracht moved under intense enemy fire carrying a wounded Soldier to safety and directing incoming medevac helicopters. Despite his shrapnel wounds, Captain Albracht refused evacuation and continued to lead his Soldiers in fighting enemy forces and ultimately withdrawing from the base. Over the period of six hours, Captain Albracht and his Soldiers successfully evaded enemy forces while moving through the jungle under cover of darkness to meet United States forces at the rescue

position. Captain Albracht's bravery, self-sacrifice, and exceptional tactical skill enabled the defenders of Fire Support Base Kate to not only defend their position until the last possible moment, but also successfully escape prior to being overrun. Captain Albracht's achievements are in keeping with the finest traditions of military service and reflect great credit upon himself, the 5th Special Forces Group (Airborne), and the United States Army.

This terse summary of five days of almost constant combat against overwhelming numbers of well-armed, courageous, and determined enemy troops, followed by a seemingly impossible escape through their lines, may seem to fall short of describing the scope and hazards described by the firsthand accounts of this book.

The men on Firebase Kate were thrust by circumstance into a life-or-death struggle. Volunteer or draftee, American or Montagnard, each man rose to confront every challenge, to overcome every obstacle before him, and did so in a selfless and courageous manner. The opportunity to lead such men under our nation's flag was far more of an honor than any that this citizen soldier can imagine.

APPENDIX

The Spooky Chronicles

Spooky aircraft were equipped with a tape recorder to record air-to-air and air-to-ground radio transmissions sent or received during a mission, as well as internal crew communications via intercom. The following transcript of recordings over and near Firebase Kate was provided by Major Al Dykes, USAF (Ret.), who served as Spooky 41's navigator and mission commander. The original transcription was made by US Army Special Forces Lieutenant Colonel Hugh Pries (Ret.). For clarity and brevity, it has been severely redacted.

Dates of tapes: 31 Oct 69, 1 Nov 69, 2 Nov 69, and 30 Nov 69.
Location: FSB Kate (YU581548), Republic of Vietnam.
Transcriber's Notes:

- No effort was made to correlate time of transmissions with elapsed time on the recordings, nor to account for pauses between transmissions.
- Although stations identified themselves phonetically in the audio, phonetic pronunciations were deleted.
- Ellipses denote pauses or portions of the tape that were unintelligible.

- When multiple stations transmitted simultaneously, only the first intelligible transmission was transcribed in its entirety.
- Due to atmospheric conditions, individual personnel speech patterns, multiple simultaneous transmissions on the same frequency, or recording issues, some portions were unintelligible. This transcription was made from tapes recorded more than forty years earlier; portions have deteriorated into unintelligibility.
- Conversations between the mission commander with other Spooky crew are indicated as *PILOT* or *GUNNER* or *LOADER*.

Station	Individual/Unit	Location/Notes
Chicken Hawk (Hawk)	CPT William Albracht	Firebase Kate Bu Prang
Spooky 41 Victor Crew 1—Vin Crew 2	CPT Al Dykes CPT Wells	Phan Rang Spooky 41 navigator/ mission commander Follow-on navigator of Spooky 41
Unjust Chaser	SSG DeNote, Commo Chief A-236	Bu Prang Special Forces Camp
Juliet	Division Control	BMT
Peeper 38	Artillery SMAJ?	Firing clearance for Hawk
Carbon Outlaw 25	USAF air traffic control	Gives Peeper 38, 60 and Chowder 60 authorization to fire at ground targets

continued...

Station	Individual/Unit	Location/Notes
Peeper 60, 62, Delta	USAF Gunships	
Grand Palette Juliet		
Shadow 48	Replaced Spooky 41 on 31 Oct 69	
Ragged Scooper		Control element for Spookies and Shadows
Chicken Hawk's Buddy, Beak	Lt. Maurice Zollner	Changed his call sign to Beak due to shrapnel thru the nose
Spad Zero Two	USAF Major Gerald Helmich	A1H Skyraider air support for Kate
Kangaroo Control		No flares until clearance due to 4 different elements; any Viking call sign
Lima Salines	Mike Force	
Cab Zero Seven		
Mike Eight Zero		
Roadrunner	Oscar 3	
Main Tripod	SSG Denote, Commo Chief	Bu Prang, Special Forces Team A-236
prybar	USAF aircraft run by Main Tripod	
Papa 43	Team on ground in Tape 3	

Night of 31 October—1 November

MAKING CONTACT

Chicken Hawk: Spooky 41 this is Chicken Hawk.

Spooky 41: Roger Chicken Hawk, this is Spooky 41, go.

Spooky 41: Chicken Hawk are you on Victor [VHF radio], over?

Chicken Hawk: Spooky 41 this is Chicken Hawk.

Shadow 61: Spooky 41, Shadow 61, Chicken Hawk is on Fox Mike (FM radio).

Spooky 41: Roger.

Chicken Hawk: OK buddy, is he in our area?

Spooky 41: We heard him talk to you once, called him back, couldn't get an answer.

Spooky 41: Chicken Hawk, Chicken Hawk Fox Mike

Chicken Hawk: Aww, roger, Spooky 41, are you picking me up?

Spooky 41: Roger, loud and clear.

Chicken Hawk: . . . how far are you from my location?

Spooky 41: Stand by one.

Spooky 41: About 15 minutes out, over.

Shadow 61: *(Unintelligible)* . . . I don't know if they advised you but we left a Lulu for you to help mark the camp. It's about 200 meters 080 bearing from his camp.

Spooky 41: Roger, sir, appreciate that much.

Spooky 41: Sir, do you have contact with Chicken Hawk at this time?

Shadow 61: Roger, we do.

Spooky 41: OK he's talking to me and he comes in sometimes, sometimes he don't. Uhh, can you ask him if he reads me please?

Shadow 61: Chicken Hawk you reading Spooky aren't you?

Chicken Hawk: This is the Hawk, I can read him loud and clear, loud and clear.

Shadow 61: Roger . . . reading you loud and clear Spooky 41.

Spooky 41: Roger, I read you that time Chicken Hawk. How do you read me now, over?

Chicken Hawk: Lo . . .

Spooky 41: Chicken Hawk you were broken, I'll give you a call back in a few minutes.

Shadow 61: Can you flash a landing light?

Spooky 41: Roger we just flashed landing light.

Shadow 61: Roger we're almost due west of your position.

Spooky 41: Roger we have you in sight.

Chicken Hawk: I'll be putting out a strobe for you, right on our firebase here. We've only got one, ahh, and its low on batteries, so I'm going to put it in and let's get a real good adjustment and then I gotta turn it off. Is this OK with you?

Spooky 41: Roger that, and Chicken Hawk, Outlaw 25 said that he'd kind of like us to just fly around a little bit before we start expending or dropping too many flares so we can, ahh, so we can extend our time with you, over.

Chicken Hawk: That's a roger roger roger on that buddy. Like I was telling the 61, I've worked him before, real good people there, and ahh, as long as they hear you up there, you put out a little bit here and a little bit there, they're not going to try a hell of a lot because . . . they know you can shoot up every time they move with you people up there.

Spooky 41: Roger that and by the way, Happy Halloween, the Spookies are out.

Chicken Hawk: *(Laughing)* Roger that. Listen, have I ever worked you before?

Spooky 41: I was over here the other night buddy.

Chicken Hawk: OK, real fine, real fine, I'm glad you're familiar with the area. Give you a little update, this has been heaviest yet, we took all kinds of shit today. I ain't kidding you, every time we turned around we were getting it. So that's why when I'm directing you all around the perimeter, believe me it's all there.

Spooky 41: Roger buddy, and I got a question to ask you. Is your position on top of a scraped-off hill with about 50 meters from your position a tree line starts and just north of your position another bald hill with a clump of trees right in the center of it?

Chicken Hawk: That's us baby, you been here before.

Spooky 41: Roger, I know where you're at.

SHOP TALK

Spooky 41: Ahh, roger on that and ahh, I hope it stays cool down there for you.

Chicken Hawk: Hey buddy, another day like today and ahh, I tell you, I don't know.

Spooky 41: What all did they hit you with today, over.

Chicken Hawk: Everything from 57 recoilless to 82 mortars to small arms and ahh, what the hell did I leave out, oh yeah, how the hell could I forget the good old B-40 rockets.

Pilot: . . . he left out the kitchen sink.

Spooky 41: Go ahead, Hawk.

Chicken Hawk: You're up in world news a little bit, who's ahh, who's in the limelight here in country, who's catching the most shit right about now?

Spooky 41: You boys are catching it, believe me.

Chicken Hawk: Is that right, ahh, we're the ones that are catching the most right now in country?

Spooky 41: That's a roger on that old buddy.

Chicken Hawk: I don't know if that makes me feel good or not.

Spooky 41: Yeah, I just hope this doesn't turn into another Duc Lap like last year.

Chicken Hawk: Old buddy, I'm with you on that.

Spooky 41: Roger, they, ahh, had a big rice cache down here on the border of II and III Corps on one of the in route things, I forgot, it was something like 9 tons of rice that they had brought in there.

Chicken Hawk: Roger that, roger that, ahh, I know that area. Ahh, I'm from Unjust Chaser's location which is not too far from here, ahh, I think you boys know it by a different name or something but this, ahh *(unintelligible)* . . . I'm in now. And it's been quiet and all of a sudden, my God, overnight it just turned into, ahh, well what it is now.

Spooky 41: Roger that, we were talking about before we got over here that it kind of reminded us of Duc Lap last year when we had 4 Spookies overhead all the time.

Chicken Hawk: Roger that, hey listen, I heard Duc Lap caught a little bit the other day.

Spooky 41: Yeah, they took a little bit, seems like, ahh, from our intel reports they were kinda coming in between you there down here and they're kinda spreading out. Its hard to tell what they're gonna do.

Chicken Hawk: Yeah, it sure is, it sure is. I don't know what it is they want with this firebase but, ahh, we'd better get some stuff in here tomorrow or they just might get it.

Spooky 41: Roger, it, ahh, suits all the Spooky boys if we could get to stay over here in the day time too, but they just won't let us.

Chicken Hawk: Roger, I understand that, ahh, I do understand that. But I tell you one thing, the most important thing we got going for us at night is you guys upstairs. Let me tell you. . . . and they know you're up there like I said and they're going to stay down and they're not going to mess with us too much, well it's good to get some sleep now and again and have some peaceful time. We got a lot of wear and tear here on the boys, ahh, they all holding up pretty good but, ahh, I don't know, ahh, that battle fatigue gonna get to a lot of people here pretty soon if, ahh, this shit don't slack off.

Spooky 41: Roger that, I know what you mean and you tell all those guys down there we're pulling for you and we're going do what we can from up here.

Chicken Hawk: I don't have to tell them, they already know it. Ahh, oh shit ever since the first night and it really didn't take no building up because you've been living here with me like I said and more.

Spooky 41: We're gonna try. We were just talking saying we wish we had everything in the book that we could stay here and drop on those guys, but all we got is beaucoup miniguns, so we're gonna use what we got.

Chicken Hawk: Roger that buddy, as long as you got those, we'll keep their heads down and we'll keep this area safe tonight.

Spooky 41 Internal: Man those guys got it rough down there.

Spooky 41: Carbon Outlaw 25, this is Spooky 41 Victor.

Pilot: . . . Gotta take a leak real quick before we start here.

Carbon Outlaw 25: This is Carbon Outlaw 25, go ahead.

Spooky 41: Roger, Carbon, you gonna have a replacement for us when we start to pull out of target? We'd like to keep something over these boys maybe all night if we can.

Carbon Outlaw 25: Roger, we've got you scheduled for a 15-minute overlap.

Spooky 41: Sounds good, these guys been taking it, as soon as we pull off target and get home we'll be ready to go again.

Carbon Outlaw 25: Roger, roger, thank you very much.

Spooky 41: Roger that.

Spooky 41 Internal: OK then we got about an hour and 40 minutes before the time I gave him at 30 so you wanna start now?

Pilot: Moon's coming up.

Spooky 41 Internal: Roger that.

Spooky 41: Chicken Hawk, Spooky 41.

Chicken Hawk: Spooky 41, this the Hawk.

Spooky 41: Roger buddy, old lady up here is ready to clear us to do a little talking for you.

Chicken Hawk: OK real fine. Tell you what, let's put it to the Echo, the Echo of our location. . . . Sierra Echo and work it on up to the November Echo. How's that sound?

Spooky 41: Roger that sounds good, we're gonna come in right now and drop a flare and, ahh, we'll start working on the Echo, the Sierra Echo and bring it up to the November Echo.

Chicken Hawk: Roger, roger on that, OK, ahh, walk it right into the wood line there, right in the wood line if you can.

Spooky 41: OK now, all your friendlies are inside your perimeter there, except the ones to the November Whisky, is that Charlie?

Chicken Hawk: That is a definite affirmative.

Spooky 41: OK and how far to the edge of the wood line, how close to the edge of the wood line do you want us to bring it, over?

Chicken Hawk: I tell you what you bring it in as close as your little heart desires right in there because we get probes during the night and they kinda sneak up there when nobody's watching and I'd like to surprise them.

Spooky 41: Roger. We've also found out that if we shoot out a couple of hundred meters, it drives them into the perimeter, also, so we'll try to drive them out a little bit.

Chicken Hawk: That's fine buddy, that's fine. Use every trick you got.

WORK BEGINS

Spooky 41: Roger, stand by.

Spooky 41 Internal: OK, they're ready to go babe.

Gunner: . . . ready to drop the flare . . .

Pilot: . . . from north to south . . .

Spooky 41 Internal: Roger that.

Gunner: OK. OK, flare will be lighting just a second, we'll take a look at . . .

Pilot: The flare should be . . . position . . . fairly strong wind from the east.

Spooky 41 Internal: OK, there's his position right there, brother, by the pipper . . .

OK, now see that bald spot to the east side over by that little bitty knob?

Pilot: OK, where the, ahh, ground marker is?

Spooky 41 Internal: Yeah, OK, let's start up close to his perimeter where those tree lines [are] on the southern edge of it and work north.

Pilot: Close to his perimeter?

Spooky 41 Internal: Right, let's start right along the tree lines and work out.

Pilot: . . . right in this valley.

Spooky 41 Internal: OK.

Spooky 41: Hawk, we're coming in hot.

Pilot: OK, guns on the line . . .

Pilot: What about this valley, right in here?

Spooky 41 Internal: Looks good.

Spooky 41: Hawk, this is Spooky 41.

Chicken Hawk: OK Spooky 41, this the Hawk, go buddy.

Spooky 41: OK, we're coming in hot.

Chicken Hawk: OK, I'm going out and observe.

Spooky 41 Internal: Looks good, OK bring it in a little closer.

Gunner: Miniguns on line, sir.

Spooky 41 Internal: You got his position well marked, that right?

Pilot: Roger, got it.

Spooky 41: Just keep to the tree line out.

Pilot: How's that?

Spooky 41: OK, let's . . . shoot over their head.

Pilot: OK.

Spooky 41: OK, you can shoot right in there.

Pilot: OK, bring it up closer to him?

Spooky 41: Yeah.

Pilot: That OK?

Pilot: How's that?

Spooky 41 Internal: That looks good.

Spooky 41 Internal: OK . . . You're still looking good . . . OK, you can come a little closer right on to this side here in front of the pipper now . . . OK now bring it up the east side here.

Pilot: OK.

Spooky 41 Internal: All along that tree line . . . OK, I'll let you bring it a little closer to him next time on that pass . . . We got plenty of time. . . . I'll just fire on the, ahh . . . south thru the north on the east side there firing over their heads. . . . You can put fire on southern perimeter of them.

Pilot: Right there where the pipper is?

Spooky 41 Internal: Yeah right back by the edge. There you go.

Spooky 41: Hey Hawk, how we looking baby?

Chicken Hawk: Hey, this the Hawk, this the Hawk. Hey buddy you're looking real fine. I was out there watching you and you're putting it dead in on them. I'd like you to put a few rounds in on the other side of the slopes as you, ahh, OK, ahh, I'll explain myself here. As our camp sits here on this hill, all right, then you [go] down to the east side, you go down the hill past the wires and you hit the, ahh, bottom of the hill, then you hit the dense vegetation and then you start going on up the other side up the other slopes. OK, during the daytime they're rocketing us from all points around the camp, so at night time they might just figure its safe to pull back to the other side of the hill, you know, so, ahh, put a few rounds on the other side of the ridge lines here and maybe we can shake them up a little bit.

Spooky 41: Ahh, roger that, we'll do it.

Pilot: . . . mean this ridge line up to the east?

Spooky 41 Internal: Roger, you got it good, right in there.

Pilot: . . . how's that look?

Spooky 41 Internal: Looks good. Just kinda work all the way around them, Vin.

Chicken Hawk: Hey Spooky 41, this is the Hawk. Are you talking to one of your people? Over.

Spooky 41: Ahh, sorry about that, I was talking to him, I'm giving him good clearance here.

Chicken Hawk: OK, go ahead buddy, ahh, that's OK, ahh, thought somebody else [was] down here directing you and if somebody else was directing you I was gonna say who.

Spooky 41: Ahh, just forgot to switch back, just get too excited sometimes.

Chicken Hawk: OK, roger that good buddy, go ahead.

Spooky 41: Okeydoke, we're gonna drop another flare.

Spooky 41 Internal: Oh shoot . . .

Pilot: Roger, we'll get another flare out here

Spooky 41 Internal: Just on the other side of first little valley is where they been taking it . . . and we can just move on around the southern edge around to the western edge of him there within about 200 meters of the camp.

Pilot: Roger.

Pilot: That last flare was a little too far out.

Spooky 41 Internal: Roger that.

Pilot: *(Unintelligible.)*

Spooky 41 Internal: All right, go ahead.

Spooky 41 Internal: OK, now you mark on this side too, see the hill out there above the pipper? Right pretty close to him?

Pilot: *(Unintelligible.)*

Spooky 41 Internal: OK, you mark from there right on around to the south and right up that other ridge line up there.

Pilot: OK.

Spooky 41 Internal: That little valley of green trees between us and that little patch and the bald spot is, ahh, they were taking some probes in there too. We can work all that area.

Pilot: OK.

Spooky 41 Internal: Go past that other bald spot to the northwest, that little tiny one.

Pilot: *(Unintelligible.)* OK, I'll get out here and rolling.

Spooky 41 Internal: Roger.

Spooky 41: Hawk, this is Spooky 41. We're gonna start working all around you, babe.

Chicken Hawk: OK buddy that sounds real good, real good. Go ahead.

Spooky 41 Internal: Looks good . . . Looks good. . . . Should come over to this side, you see this other clump of trees you can hit, ahh . . .

Pilot: *(Unintelligible.)*

Spooky 41 Internal: Yeah on this side and the other side.

Pilot: OK.

Spooky 41 Internal: You're looking good on both places.

Pilot: OK.

Spooky 41 Internal: You see above the pipper? There's another ridge line over there.

Pilot: Roger that. Look good?

Spooky 41 Internal: Yeah and work that one too.

Pilot: OK . . . Still looking fairly well? . . . OK, I'll work this ridge line up here.

Spooky 41 Internal: Yeah, why don't you fly right over them to work it then shoot back at it.

Pilot: OK, over their heads?

Spooky 41 Internal: Yeah, if you go right over top of them it's not going to hurt.

Pilot: OK, we fire to this side too?

Spooky 41 Internal: Yeah, fine.

Pilot: How's that look?

Spooky 41 Internal: Good . . . OK, right up there where this light is, that's the part of the ridge, work north and south . . .

Pilot: OK, and, ahh, gunner, let me know when half our ammo is gone.

Gunner: Roger, sir.

Spooky 41: Carbon Outlaw 25, this is Spooky 41, we're expending at this time.

Carbon Outlaw 25: Roger, Spooky 41, this is 25, we copy.

Spooky 41: Roger, 25, we'll give you a call when we're half expended.

Carbon Outlaw 25: That's a roger, thank you sir.

Spooky 41 Internal: *(Unintelligible)* . . . another flare out. . . . No I don't see it.

WORKPLACE BONDING

Chicken Hawk: Hey Spook, this the Hawk.

Spooky 41: Go ahead Hawk.

Chicken Hawk: Hey, that's real good, that's real good. You're gonna get some long hours in aren't you?

Spooky 41: Ahh, we don't mind as long as it's helping you boys out.

Chicken Hawk: That's really good. OK, buddy that's real fine.

Spooky 41: Roger.

Chicken Hawk: *(Unintelligible)* . . . all you boys that fly the big birds up here, your Spookies and your Shadows and everything, what do you guys get together someplace and have a drink together now and again?

Spooky 41: Ahh, occasionally we do, occasionally, some of us drink, some of us don't drink but we usually get together and shoot over the bull.

Chicken Hawk: OK, listen when you guys get together I want it to be known that Chicken Wolf, as I was known then or the Chicken Hawk or the Hawk or whatever and everybody here just, ahh, man, without you guys . . . I tell you we would just admire it if you guys came down here for autographs.

Spooky 41: I'll tell you something old buddy if you ever get over to Phan Rang area, you better come in to see the Spooks and the Shadows cause we'll, ahh, the drinks are on us.

Chicken Hawk: Oh, ahh, understand. Ahh, I, ahh, I think I've worked a bunch of you now. I've worked 61s and of course the 41s and the 21s and a couple of others off and on and, ahh, a lot of other people here have.

Spooky 41: Ahh, roger that, ahh most of the Shadow 6 numbers are, ahh, out of Phan Rang and, ahh, all of the Spooky 4 numbers are out of Phan Rang.

Chicken Hawk: Ahh, OK, buddy, hey, ahh, listen, when I get out of this stuff I got a little vacation coming to me anyway and if I get that way I'll definitely stop in and see you boys.

Spooky 41: Roger that and if you miss us, stop in Alabama and I'll still buy you a drink.

Chicken Hawk: *(Laughing)* OK there, buddy, roger that and if you get up north, Illinois way, you gotta stop in my place too.

Spooky 41: OK.

Spooky 41 Internal: Hey Vin, let's go on over the west side and hit that hill over there a little bit too.

Pilot: To the west?

Spooky 41 Internal: Roger.

Pilot: OK.

Spooky 41 Internal: It's the first hill over yonder there's two *(unintelligible)* looks like a pussy, right in the middle of them.

Pilot: OK. Let me work this one on this side, then we'll work them over there.

Spooky 41 Internal: Roger.

Pilot: How we looking?

Spooky 41 Internal: That's the side, that's the side, there you go.

Chicken Hawk: You're chewing up some stuff out there, you really are

Carbon Outlaw 25: Spooky 41 this is Carbon Outlaw 25.

Spooky 41: Carbon Outlaw 25, are you calling Spooky 41.

Carbon Outlaw 25: That's a roger, sir. How much moonlight do you have down in the area, where you are? Over.

Spooky 41: Ahh, we have a fair amount of moonlight, but not enough yet to really see the ground yet. We're still having to use flares.

Carbon Outlaw 25: OK, sir, thank you very much.

Spooky 41 Internal: OK, it's above the pipper now. It's about due north of that light there on the ground.

Spooky 41 Internal: Bring it up a little bit, bring it up a little bit, there you go.

Spooky 41 Internal: Do you see what I'm talking about Vin?

Pilot: Roger. It's in front of the pipper right now.

Pilot: Roger that, just between him and the cup of the brassiere?

Spooky 41 Internal: That's right. Work it all along those tree lines there.

Carbon Outlaw 25: Carbon Outlaw 25, Victor.

Spooky 41: You calling, ahh, Spooky 41, 25.

Carbon Outlaw 25: That's a roger, sir. What've you got, you got a quarter moon, ahh, or half moon, ahh, or a full moon?

Spooky 41: Ahh, roger, stand by just a second . . . We got about a half-moon.

Carbon Outlaw 25: Roger, thank you sir.

Spooky 41: And be advised, that the ground, ahh, you can start to see some mountains, but not real well yet.

Carbon Outlaw 25: OK, sir, thank you.

Spooky 41: Hawk, this is Spooky 41.

Chicken Hawk: Spooky 41, this the Hawk, go.

Spooky 41: Roger, old buddy, you know how the trees come up to the north and then kinda cut off these two little bald mountains, just north of your position?

Chicken Hawk: Spooky 41, this the Hawk, go ahead.

Spooky 41: Roger, Hawk. You know how the trees come up behind your position to the north [and] kinda cut off those two little bald hills, the one you're on and the one just north of you?

Chicken Hawk: Roger, roger, only too well.

Spooky 41: OK, we're gonna work that over a little bit if that's all right with you.

Chicken Hawk: Fine, fine, go ahead.

Spooky 41: OK, and where else would you like for us to move? We're trying to work over all the little peaks and ridgelines around you.

Chicken Hawk: Listen, if you hit the peaks and ridgelines around here that'll be fine.

Spooky 41: OK and, ahh, we're going to try to stay out about 200 or 300 meters from your November Whisky, we're not going to get much past that.

Chicken Hawk: Roger, roger, roger.

Spooky 41 Internal: Looking good. You can work all that tree line then.

Spooky 41: Hey Hawk, this is Spooky 41.

Chicken Hawk: Spooky 41, this the Hawk, go buddy.

Spooky 41: Roger, can you tell me if my bullets are hitting the ground?

Chicken Hawk: Roger, roger, wait one.

Spooky 41: Hey Hawk, I'm just kidding you.

Chicken Hawk: Goddammit buddy, you had me going on that one, I'll say that.

ON TO OTHER BUSINESS

Grand Palette Juliet: Spooky 41, Grand Palette Juliet over.

Spooky 41: Roger, Juliet, this is Spooky 41. Go ahead, over.

Grand Palette Juliet: I understand you're very busy, sorry to bother you, ahh, higher request to know if Kate is in contact with Mike Strike Force element northwest of location, over.

Spooky 41:	Roger, stand by.
Spooky 41:	Kate, Kate, Spooky 41.
Chicken Hawk:	Spooky 41, Spooky 41, this the Hawk. I'm taking stuff, what do you need?
Spooky 41:	OK, ahh, Juliet wants to know if you're in contact with Mike Strike Force to the north, over.
Chicken Hawk:	Roger.
Spooky 41:	OK, break, break, Juliet, that's a roger.
Juliet:	This is Juliet, roger, thank you much. No further. Out.
Chicken Hawk:	Spooky 41, this is the Hawk.
Spooky 41:	Go ahead Hawk, Spooky 41 over.
Chicken Hawk:	Hey, ahh, are you hearing those explosions, explosions? They sound like they're coming from the Whisky, the Sierra Whisky, over?
Spooky 41:	Negative, I haven't heard a thing. What's it sound like, ahh, ahh, gunfire?
Chicken Hawk:	No buddy, it sounds like an Arc Light, like a distant Arc Light.
Spooky 41:	Ahh, OK roger, you got one down here about 10 miles from you.
Chicken Hawk:	Roger, that's probably what it was then.
Spooky 41:	Roger, if they get to firing on us, we'll shoot at them.
Chicken Hawk:	*(Laughing.)* OK.
Spooky 41 Internal:	Vin let's see how much ammo we got left.
Gunner:	Approximately 9,000 left sir, half a load.

Spooky 41 Internal: OK, we got about an hour and ten. Why don't we hold off a while.

Pilot: Roger . . . We can hold off until about 0100 [hours] and then fire out 30 minutes and, ahh, hope to stay with them another 15 to 20 minutes.

Loader: . . . 14 flares . . .

Spooky 41 Internal: OK.

Spooky 41: Hawk, this is Spooky 41.

Chicken Hawk: Spooky 41, this the Hawk, go buddy.

Spooky 41: Roger, ahh, we're down to about half a load right now. What we're gonna do is . . . stay up here for about, ahh, 40 minutes and just orbit the area and then we'll come back in and work off the other half of our load and stay with you up to about, ahh, pretty close to one o'clock, ahh, pretty close to 2 o'clock.

Chicken Hawk: Ahh, roger, roger that buddy, OK, when you come back in to work off that other half, ahh, don't work it *all* off, in case they, ahh, something happens.

Spooky 41: Ahh, you know it, we're gonna save some.

Chicken Hawk: Roger, roger, on that buddy, ahh, sounds real fine. I'll let you know if something happens here, we get a target here and I'll bring you right back down.

Spooky 41: Ahh, OK, and if you want to rest a little bit, we're watching for any muzzle flashes or anything else, so we'll keep you posted if we see anything.

Chicken Hawk: OK, certainly appreciate that.

Spooky 41: Roger, and I'll leave you alone for about 20 or 30 minutes and then I'll have a little commo check with you.

Chicken Hawk: Roger, roger, if you don't get me the first time, give me a couple of calls, OK.

Spooky 41: Roger, and if I don't get you then, I know what your coordinates are, we'll wake you up.

Chicken Hawk: *(Laughing.)* Ahh, I'll tell you what, I think I better stay awake for this.

Spooky 41: That's OK.

Chicken Hawk: OK, buddy, ahh, I'll be waiting to hear from you.

Spooky 41: Roger.

Carbon Outlaw 25: Be advised Shadow 48 will be, ahh, relieving you and, ahh, he should be up here around Zero Zero Four Zero, they are launching him at 15 past, over.

SHIFT CHANGE

Chicken Hawk: Ahh, this is Chicken Hawk's buddy.

Spooky 41: OK, ahh, Chicken Hawk's buddy, we're ready to shoot.

Chicken Hawk: Pour it on there buddy.

Spooky 41: OK, we're gonna work the general areas we were working a while ago, if you wanna move us, let us know.

Chicken Hawk: We'll give you a skinny as soon as we get any over.

Spooky 41: Roger. OK, buddy let's go.

Chicken Hawk: Spooky 41, Spooky 41, this the Hawk, over.

Spooky 41: Hey, Hawk, welcome back.

Chicken Hawk: Hey buddy, I'll be back only for a little while, I gotta get some shut-eye here. Hey listen, ahh, I'll talk you in. And when you come back, I hope you do, with this new guy coming in, will you brief him on what you been doing and shooting, because you're doing an outstanding job there on your own putting it in where you think its good and that's exactly where we need it, ahh, could you brief the new guy coming in too? Over.

Spooky 41: Roger, I've already given him, ahh, a small rundown, but we're gonna wait and show him the area and brief him real good and, ahh, we've put in a request to turn us around as soon as we get back and we hope our highers will let us come back and spend the night with you.

Chicken Hawk: Well I do too buddy, I do too. OK, buddy, listen, I'll be on the floor here and if you got anything for me, ahh, feel free to ask for me, OK, buddy?

Spooky 41: OK, and, ahh, I'll just call you Chicken Hawk, buddy, huh?

Chicken Hawk: Roger, roger, that's affirmative.

Spooky 41: OK.

Spooky 41 Internal: Might not hurt to put a little fire around those fires burning down there, they might be cooking up fish heads and rice with them.

Pilot: OK.

Spooky 41:	Chicken Hawk buddy, Chicken Hawk buddy, hey, how's things going?
Chicken Hawk:	Ahh, Spooky 41, this is Hawk's buddy, ahh, really going fine there, really doing an outstanding job, just keep moving it around, ahh, that's all we can ask of you.
Spooky 41:	OK, ahh, if you have no special area, we're gonna work up and down the east side and, ahh, the Sierra side and the Whisky side a little bit.
Chicken Hawk:	That sounds real fine, ahh, that whole, all the way around us we get shit all day long, over.
Spooky 41:	Roger, ahh, we're also working over these little fires, I guess, out here, we figure they might be cooking up rice and fish heads and we wanna cut a little of that out.
Chicken Hawk:	That's it, we'll starve them so and so's out.
Spooky 41:	I'm with you buddy. Break, break, Shadow 48, this is Spooky 41, you copy on my Fox Mike?
Shadow 48:	Roger, Spooky 41, Shadow 48 here. Break, break, Chicken Hawk, Shadow 48.
Spooky 41:	Shadow 48, you'll be working Chicken Hawk's buddy, B-U-D-D-Y, Chicken Hawk's laying on the floor getting some sleep so we just call him Hawk Buddy.
Shadow 48:	Roger that, Chicken Hawk's buddy, Shadow 48.
Chicken Hawk:	Spooky 41, this the Hawk's Buddy, over.
Spooky 41:	Go ahead, Hawk Buddy.
Chicken Hawk:	This the Hawk's buddy, we decided to change my

call sign, here, to, ahh, we, ahh, call me the Beak, I took a piece of shrapnel through the nose, ahh, we thought you'd get a kick out of that, over.

Spooky 41: You took a piece of shrapnel through the nose?

Chicken Hawk: That's affirmative, ahh, so from now on, you can just call me the Beak.

Spooky 41: OK, Beak, we'll be calling you that then and, ahh, how bad was it?

Chicken Hawk: Oh, it just made a nice little neat hole clean through, over.

Pilot: Hey, I got a flash!

Spooky 41: Well, maybe the boys can fix you up. Hey and be advised, we just got a flash on the ground.

Beak: Pour it on, pour it on. Get that son of a bitch!

Spooky 41: Roger, he's to your echo on the ridgeline, over there, we're pouring it in on him now.

Beak: Roger, roger, OK, that's a point, where you're putting on there is where we've been receiving a lot of the stuff from today. All over the echo side is where we're getting the bulk of it.

Spooky 41: Roger that, we're fixing to put it on him.

Beak: Go ahead, bring some smoke on his young ass.

Spooky 41 Internal: Flare on the *(unintelligible)* spot here. That looked like a mortar tube flash to me.

Copilot: Yes sir, that's what it looked like to me.

Spooky 41: Hey, Beak, did you all take any incoming coming in?

Chicken Hawk: Hey, Spooky 41, this the Hawk, listen, ahh, negative on that, we didn't take anything incoming, so I think you got a secondary.

Spooky 41: Might have, 'cause it sure looked like a mortar splash.

Chicken Hawk: That's real fine, I hope so, buddy, I hope so, that's one more crew served we won't have to contend with tomorrow.

Spooky 41: Roger that and, ahh, old Shadow's coming along with some equipment on board that he might be able to pick out some of this stuff a little better than we can.

Chicken Hawk: Well, he'll have to show me.

Spooky 41: He's got, ahh, he's a second-generation Spooky.

Chicken Hawk: OK, buddy, OK, I'd say he's got some real fine sophisticated stuff and, ahh, the country boys are going to have to take a backseat sometimes, but I don't know, I'm from Missouri, Show Me, right?

Spooky 41: OK, he's going to do you a fine job, so no sweat.

Pilot: We got a flare.

Chicken Hawk: Ahh, I've no doubt of it, no doubt whatsoever.

Spooky 41: We're all trying to do the same thing.

Chicken Hawk: Roger that. OK, I'm going to turn you back over to Beak.

Spooky 41: Roger that.

Shadow 48: Spook, this is 48, how about you being our PR man for a while?

Spooky 41:	Hey, ahh, I don't know if I can handle that or not, you know I'm getting short.
Shadow 48:	Doing a pretty good job, babe.
Spooky 41:	Well, I hope you can use that equipment you got, these boys need some help.
Shadow 48:	We'll do our best.
Spooky 41:	Ahh, Beak, this is Spooky 41.
Beak:	Spooky 41, this is Beak, over.
Spooky 41:	OK, we're fixing to drop a flare, we got one out right now, ahh, we're going to go ahead and expend our ammo, we're getting pretty short and, ahh, we're going to try to get Shadow to come up here in just a minute real quick and show you this and then we're going to have to pull out of the area for just a few minutes, over.
Chicken Hawk:	Ahh, roger that, Spooky 41, ahh, hey, if those guys are going the other way, let them go, over.
Spooky 41:	OK, ahh, they're not going to be able to stay where they're going very long.
Shadow 48:	Ahh, Spooky 41, 48, we're going to hold here north and we will, ahh, we seen the base down there, so we'll be working with you after this other activity is over.
Spooky 41:	OK, we're going to have to be pulling out as soon as we expend because of, ahh, fuel. Ahh, you say you see the base under our flare?
Shadow 48:	Roger that we got a good copy on the base.
Spooky 41:	OK, this thing looks like a big brassiere down here

is, ahh, bald area to the north of their camp and we be getting most of the activity of the eastern slope over here and Beak down there can work you after we leave, over.

Shadow 48: Roger that, is this a complete perimeter here on top of the hill?

Spooky 41: That's a Charlie, and they got about a 50- to 75-meter radius from their perimeter down through the tree line on all sides.

Shadow 48: Roger that.

Night of 1 November: The Escape

Unknown Station: Tell them we're circling right 8,500 right above them . . .

Unknown Station: That's a lot of shit out . . .

Unknown Station: . . . understand we'll be cleared to drop flames right above . . .

Chicken Hawk: *(Unintelligible)* . . . we're going out buddy, we're going out.

Spad Zero Two: OK, Hawk, this is Spad, you're going to have to talk slower if you want these people to talk to you.

Spooky 41: Hey Spad, Spooky 41, stand by just one second.

Spooky 41: Listen *(unintelligible)* . . . circling at 8,500 right above them . . . you can see it out your window they're taking incoming and the *(unintelligible)* is on the other side. Tell them to move out and we'll go down.

Spooky 41: Spad Zero Two, Spooky 41 is in orbit above you now, and if you move out, we'll go down and get the situation under control if we can, over.

Spad 02: OK, Spooky, do you have that flare at this time?

Chicken Hawk: OK, Spooky good buddy.

Spooky 41: Hey there, Chicken Hawk, take it easy there, my friend. We're right here, we're coming in right now. What's your sitch, Hawk?

Chicken Hawk: *(Unintelligible)* . . . the tree line, coming down the valley.

Spooky 41: Roger, roger, you're down in the tree lines in the valley in the north west of the figure eight down there, is that affirmative?

Chicken Hawk: OK, listen, OK you're going to have to hold up on that, ahh, our people are getting a little bit ahead of me.

Spooky 41: Spooky 41, tell them we are descending to 7,000 over the target area.

Spooky 41: OK, Chicken Hawk, calm down, get your information down there and just pass that up to me and we'll help you out my friend.

Chicken Hawk: *(Unintelligible)* . . . hold your fire, hold your fire.

Spooky 41: Spad, Spook Spooky 41, go.

Spad 02: Roger, they're moving from the firebase, ahh, to the November about 800 meters and, ahh, you can just watch Hawk here for about a few minutes and see where those lume [illumination] mortars are coming from and they're not friendly.

Spooky 41: OK, understand those lume mortars are not friendly, right?

Spad: That's affirmative, they're from the bad guys.

Spooky 41: OK, now, who's moving the 200 meters to the November, the good guys?

Spad: The good guys are to the November, that's affirmative.

Spooky 41: Thank you much.

Spooky 41 Internal: OK, Lloyd . . . keep them behind us. Tell them I'm going let down in front of them, keep me in sight, I'm going down to 1,500 . . .

Pilot: *(Unintelligible)* . . . behind you, right?

Spooky 41 Internal: Got 2 airplanes behind me . . . too God damn many planes . . . for us to . . .

Transcriber note: [Multiple stations transmitting at same time; too numerous to decipher individual stations accurately. Spooky 41 is trying to get control to clear out some of the stations.]

Unknown Station: *(Unintelligible)* . . . we and a couple of other aircraft out here . . . *(unintelligible)* and the other is Zero Two. We're going to start dropping down to 5,500 here, appreciate it if you'd keep an eye on us so we can both get down there.

Unknown Station: Thank you much.

Control: Five Zero Two this is control over.

Spooky 41: OK, pilot, they're going to clear out for us.

Pilot: OK.

Spooky 41: Chicken Hawk, Spooky 41, go ahead, my friend.

Chicken Hawk:	*(Unintelligible)* . . . one of our people popped a trip flare . . .
Spooky 41:	Chicken Hawk, you'll have to talk a little slower, take it easy, work with me up here. Now what's your situation, go ahead.
Chicken Hawk:	OK, buddy, one of our people . . .
Spooky 41 Internal:	Roger, roger, have a flare at my nine o'clock position at this time.
Chicken Hawk:	OK, a ground flare, ground flare to our November our November, over.
Spooky 41:	Roger, flare to your November, we're looking now . . .
Spooky 41:	. . . ground flare there, Chicken Hawk?
Chicken Hawk:	OK, buddy, why don't we put it to the, ahh, November to the tree line, in the tree line . . . move this strobe, over.
Spooky 41:	OK, I understand you want us to start working to the November, with that flare up into the tree line, is that right?
Chicken Hawk:	Roger, roger, right to the front, right to the November the tree line, right there in the valley.
Spooky 41:	OK and, ahh, Four One Zero to drop its own flares.
Chicken Hawk:	OK, OK . . . ahead of me, my people . . . got ahead of me.
Spad 02:	Spooky 41, this is Spad, target . . .
Chicken Hawk:	Spooky, Spooky this is the Hawk.

Spooky 41:	Roger, Hawk, Spooky 41.
Chicken Hawk:	OK, my people got ahead of me a little bit, they're moving out.
Spooky 41:	OK, real fine, ahh, is Spooky 41 cleared to drop light Chicken Hawk?
Spad 02:	Negative Spooky 41, this is Zero Two, hold the light. Hold the light.
Spooky 41:	Roger Zero Two, Spooky 41 to hold.
Spooky 41:	Hey, ahh, Hawk, understand you're moving out now, is that affirmative?
Spooky 41 Internal:	Pilot do you have that ground flare identified?
Pilot:	Yep.
Spooky 41 Internal:	OK, can you take it 100 or 200 meters north of the tree line?
Chicken Hawk:	That's affirmative, buddy, that's affirmative.
Spooky 41:	OK, good deal, how about moving on down . . .
Chicken Hawk:	. . . affirmative, affirmative, that's what we're doing.
Unknown Station:	Spooky, hold on here a minute.
Spooky 41:	Roger, roger, we're ready whenever you are.
Spooky 41 Internal:	OK, let's let these guys start moving, we don't want . . .
Chicken Hawk:	. . . moving out . . .
Spooky 41:	All right, we're up here ready when you get your men in position out of the way we're going to roll in and give you a hand.

Chicken Hawk:	OK buddy, ahh, we'll keep our heads down, but don't fire to the November, the November, OK?
Spooky 41:	Roger, we understand, ahh, we won't be firing to the November. You want us to stay to the east in that valley down there in the draw down there, right?
Chicken Hawk:	*(Whispering.)* Roger.
Chicken Hawk:	Hey, ahh, we're down at the bottom now and our people are moving out real fine, no trouble so far, WHOA . . . operator, no sweat.
Spooky 41:	Take it easy down there Hawk.
Chicken Hawk:	No trouble so far, no trouble so far. *(Whispering.)* OK, ahh, I'll keep you posted.
Spooky 41:	OK, Hawk.
Spooky 41:	. . . moving north . . . November . . . moving north . . .
Unknown Station:	Roger, roger, understand, we'll stay to the Sierra, we'll be working the . . .
Spooky 41 Internal:	I'd like to get that light out as soon as possible . . . radio . . . drop our flares.
Chicken Hawk:	*(Whispering, breathing hard.)* Hello, Hawk to control, we're moving pretty good.
Kangaroo Control:	Roger that, let me know when you come across that first bald hill and starting down this way, over.
Chicken Hawk:	. . . ahh, correction, OK, buddy, we're by Ambush Hill, Ambush Hill, we're going up on the left side, the left side.
Kangaroo Control:	Roger that, when you come across that hill and start

down into this next wood line you'll be coming into me, over.

Chicken Hawk: *(Whispering.)* Roger, roger on that.

Spooky 41: Chicken Hawk, Spooky 41.

Chicken Hawk: Spooky 41, ahh, hey buddy, what's happening?

Spooky 41: Just want to keep in contact with you down here, ahh, I'm seeing if we can drop our flares, my friend.

Spooky 41: Chicken Hawk, Spooky 41, do you read me?

Chicken Hawk: *(Whispering.)* Hey buddy, give me about One Zero minutes.

Spooky 41: Roger, roger, Chicken Hawk.

Kangaroo Control: Spooky 41, this is Kangaroo, ahh, over.

Spooky 41: Roger, Kangaroo Control, Spooky 41, read you Five By.

Kangaroo: Roger, this is Kangaroo, ahh, appreciate it if no flares are dropped on until you, ahh, get an all clear from me. I got, ahh, four different elements out there . . . en route . . . get these people in and I'm controlling from here, ahh, when they're clear and linked up and on their way to mission, then we'll let it go from there, but let me do it from here and not on the ground, over.

Spooky 41: Roger, roger, I'll coordinate with you, ahh, Kangaroo Control.

Kangaroo: Fine, I'll be finished with this element here about 500 meters to the November Whisky, 500 meters to the November Whisky . . . runs east west . . . and grab any Viking, any Viking is the next call sign you'll pick up with . . . any Viking . . .

Spooky 41:	That's a roger, that's a roger . . . got 500 November Whisky from the element that he's picking up now . . .
Kangaroo:	That's affirmative, that's affirmative . . . on your push.
Spooky 41:	Roger . . . on this push . . .
Chicken Hawk:	Lima Salines, Lima Salines, ahh, this is Chicken Hawk, Chicken Hawk, over.
Lima Salines:	This is Lima Salines, over.
Chicken Hawk:	*(Whispering.)* We got . . . on top of the hill and we'll be coming down the hill into your location.
Shadow 48:	Spooky 41, Shadow 48.
Spooky 41:	Roger, Shadow 48, go.
Shadow 48:	We're going to be coming in over the . . . we're at 8 point 5 . . .
Spooky 41:	Roger, roger, Spooky 41 is at Five Five now.
Lima Salines:	Chicken Hawk, this is Lima, roger that. My people have been notified of this type movement . . . over.
Chicken Hawk:	*(Whispering.)* OK, buddy, right now pushing to top of the hill by the blown out wooded area.
Lima Salines:	. . . I am NOT, I repeat, I am NOT at the location that was given to me, over.
Spooky 41:	Zero Two, Spooky 41.
Spad 02:	Spooky 41, Zero Two.
Spooky 41:	Zero Two . . . contact with Carbon Outlaw, they want to know the name of the ground commander

that was controlling the air strike, do you know who it was?

Spad: No, I don't think, should be able to get that, ahh . . . It was Chicken Hawk that was . . . the air strike.

Spooky 41: Roger, roger, understand. It was Chicken Hawk.

MULTIPLE TRANSMISSIONS.

Chicken Hawk: . . . firebase . . . OK?

Spooky 41: OK, Chicken Hawk, we're going to have to drop light before we can . . . Break, Break, Kangaroo Control, Spooky 41.

Chicken Hawk: OK.

MULTIPLE TRANSMISSIONS.

Spooky 41: Chicken Hawk, hold on, hold on, stand by one, let me contact Kangaroo Control down here.

Spooky 41: Kangaroo Control, Spooky 41.

Kangaroo: Spooky 41, this is Kangaroo Control . . . negative at this time I'll give you the word from here when we want you to . . .

Spooky 41: Roger, roger, Kangaroo Control. Break, break, Chicken Hawk, hold on my friend, ahh, got to get the complete clearance from Kangaroo Control and then we'll hit it.

Spooky 41: Chicken Hawk, Spooky 41, you copy?

Chicken Hawk: . . . *(Loud breathing)* . . .

Kangaroo: Roger, Spooky 41, could you call, ahh, Lima Salines and see if the linkup is complete and also have him relay to me . . . his location . . . over.

Spooky 41: . . . OK . . . location again?

Kangaroo: Roger . . . his element . . . location . . . and . . . with Chicken Hawk, over.

Spooky 41: Roger, roger. Break, Lima Salines, Lima Salines from Spooky 41.

Lima: Spooky 41, this is Lima Salines. Be advised, we still haven't linked up here, we'll give you a call when we do, over.

Spooky 41: Roger, roger. We'd like to know ASAP as soon as you link up so we can get started up here.

Lima: Roger that buddy, I'll let you know as soon as possible.

Spooky 41: Roger, roger. Break Kangaroo, Spooky 41, did you copy?

Kangaroo: This is Kangaroo . . .

Chicken Hawk: . . . Lima, this is Chicken Hawk, this is Chicken Hawk.

Lima Salines: Over.

Chicken Hawk: OK, buddy, we're coming into you now. Look, I'm getting them into a single file, it's a long one, but you're only gonna have one entrance into your perimeter, only one entrance into your perimeter, only one people coming in one line, I'm trying to . . . hope it don't get screwed up by the time it gets down to you, you roger?

Lima Salines:	Roger that, come on in. I'll let my people know.
Chicken Hawk:	Roger, roger. OK, we're moving in now . . . they might be hitting your perimeter now, it'll be a big long line, but don't worry buddy *(whispering)* we only got one line coming in.
Spooky 41:	Kangaroo Control, you copy Lima Salines?
Kangaroo:	Negative, I can't read them . . .
Spooky 41:	Roger, roger, Lima Salines, you have to link up on rebounding tone and, ahh, Chicken Hawk they're just about ready to let us know as soon as they got the linkup.
Lima Salines:	Roger, I'll be standing by.
Spooky 41:	Roger, roger, I'll let you know.
Lima Salines:	It's not complete yet, over.
Spooky 41:	Roger, roger, keep us posted, my friend.
Lima Salines:	Roger, will do.
Unknown Station:	. . . can you hear Chicken Hawk . . .
Spooky 41:	Haven't heard from him in a little while, I've been monitoring.
Spooky 41:	Break, Chicken Hawk, Spooky 41.
Chicken Hawk:	. . . OK.
Spooky 41:	Chicken Hawk, Chicken Hawk, Spooky 41, over.
Chicken Hawk:	. . . Spooky 41, this the Hawk here, ahh, I'd like to contact Lima Salines, over.
Spooky 41:	Lima Salines, this is Spooky 41, Chicken Hawk is trying to contact you.

Lima Salines: Roger, roger, Chicken Hawk, this is Lima Salines, over.

Chicken Hawk: OK, buddy, listen, here's what we're gonna do, we got in the wrong path here a little bit, ahh, wrong path a little bit, so, ahh . . . pulling back up to the wood line, back up to the wood line, instead of this jungle, I am going to be at the November end, November end, and when I get up there and get my people there, could you send us a small party of two or three people out to the wood line and walk to the November and you can link up with us and lead us back to your perimeter, over.

Spooky 41: Roger, roger, is this Chicken Hawk, calling Spooky 41.

Chicken Hawk: Roger, roger, Chicken Hawk calling Spooky 41, Chicken Hawk calling Spooky 41.

Spooky 41: Roger, Chicken Hawk, calm down, my friend, Spooky 41, go ahead.

Chicken Hawk: OK, buddy, somebody's firing on us up there.

Spooky 41 Internal: OK, ask him if he's firing at us and we're clear to fire back at them.

Spooky 41: OK, Chicken Hawk, is this man firing at us or at you, my friend?

Chicken Hawk: OK, buddy, he's firing at me, he's firing at me, what other aircraft is up there?

Spooky 41: OK, all aircraft, attention all aircraft, cease fire, cease fire, you're firing on Chicken Hawk's position.

Shadow 48: Shadow 48, we are not firing.

Spooky 41: Spooky 41 is not firing, Chicken Hawk, are you sure you took any fire from above?

Chicken Hawk: OK, buddy . . . down in this hole and it looked like it was firing on my people from above. I'm gonna get a real close look and I'll let you know, OK?

Spooky 41: OK, Chicken Hawk, just take it easy, my friend, now.

Lima Salines: . . . Hawk to his November . . .

Spooky 41: Roger, roger, Break, Hawk, Spooky 41, Lima Salines is calling and wants you to move to your November, move to your November.

Spooky 41: Chicken Hawk, Chicken Hawk, Spooky 41, did you copy?

Spooky 41: Contact with Lima Salines.

Kangaroo Control: Roger, OK, push . . . down here . . . relay and . . . hear Lima Salines, over.

Spooky 41: Roger, roger, I'll relay anything you need.

Lima Salines: Hawk, this is Lima Salines, over.

Spad 02: . . . handle this thing. We'd like to RTB now . . . Shadow . . . so that we can get back out here early in the morning.

Spooky 41: Roger, roger, Spooky 41, as soon as they can give us clearance to pop flares and stuff we can keep it under control.

Spad 02: . . . we're just kind of spinning our wheels right now staying out of the way and if we can go back right now we can get an early start in the morning.

Spooky 41: Roger, roger, Zero Two, thanks much for your assistance, go ahead and get some good sleep.

MULTIPLE TRANSMISSIONS.

Kangaroo: Zero Two, Zero Two, this is Kangaroo, over.

Spad 02: Roger . . .

Spooky 41: Kangaroo Control, Spooky 41.

Kangaroo: Spooky 41, Kangaroo Control, over.

Spooky 41: OK, Control . . . bit quieter now, how 'bout giving me a rundown and see if we can pinpoint the exact area where you're gonna want us to go in and fire if we can so we can get started as soon after we drop light as possible.

Kangaroo: Wait one.

Chicken Hawk: This is Chicken Hawk, this is Chicken Hawk, any body want me?

Spooky 41: Ahh, Chicken Hawk, this is Spooky 41, I'm talking to Kangaroo Control, how's things going with you, my friend?

Chicken Hawk: Ohh, ahh, a little bit rugged, my friend. This . . . I'll tell you right now is hell. (*Breathing hard.*) I'll tell you. But, ahh . . .

30 November 1969, at Bu Prang

Spooky 41: Got you Lima Charlie now.

Spooky 41: The boys over at Spooky got a little something they want to send to you there and, ahh, we're working it up right now and probably try to get it to you in a few days.

Chicken Hawk: Ahh, jeez, can't imagine what that would be. Ahh, I'll tell you, I've really tried . . . I've really wanted to get up there so damn bad and see all you guys . . . but, ahh, I don't know, things got pretty hot here all of a sudden the past few days.

Spooky 41: Roger, I know what you mean. We been not only hearing it on the radio, ahh, when we're over here, but we been reading about it in the paper. We keep up on you all pretty close.

Chicken Hawk: I can imagine, this kinda like your second home for you guys, isn't it?

Spooky 41: Roger that. I don't think I want to live there, but it still like a second home.

MULTIPLE TRANSMISSIONS.

Chicken Hawk: . . . you know, tell the boys back there that, ahh, we're having some . . . here . . . we're having so damn much trouble here, everybody's trying to get in the act, it's supposed to be a big victory for you know who and you know who's actually doing it too.

Spooky 41: Roger that, I know what you're talking about, over.

Chicken Hawk: Consequently they get into it and they . . .

MULTIPLE TRANSMISSIONS.

Unknown Station: Spooky 41 . . . forty-three decimal seven.

MULTIPLE TRANSMISSIONS.

Chicken Hawk: . . . For instance the other night one of soldiers wanted to know . . . (*static*) and we were in . . . (*static*)

	it was one of the biggest damn hassles . . . I think it was a Shadow and if I was him I woulda just turned around and went home.
Unknown Station:	Spooky 41, Roger.
Chicken Hawk:	Three or four people trying to talk and war game at the same time.
Spooky 41:	Yeah, I know, that's not the thing that bugs us so much, what bugs us is the highers we got up here wanting to know that they get all these coordinates and all these, ahh, clearance numbers and all this other stuff and, ahh, we know that you guys are wanting us to fire soon and we're having to sit up here and wait for them to give us clearance.
Chicken Hawk:	Hey, yeah, I didn't know that . . .
Spooky 41:	Yeah, we have to call back to Carbon Outlaw and he goes back to the big boss to ask and everything and they check it out and plot it out and drink a cup of coffee and finally get his clearance sometimes.
Chicken Hawk:	Oh, that's how it works. How come you . . .
Spooky 41 Internal:	*(Unintelligible.)* . . . Roger. Carbon Outlaw . . . 41, OK.
Spooky 41:	Hey Hawk, you're gonna have to stand by a minute.
Main Tripod:	Spooky 41, Main Tripod.
Spooky 41:	Roger, old buddy, we're going to have to di-di out of the area here in about 6 minutes. I just wanted to give you a call and see how things were going.
Main Tripod:	OK, roger, you planning on coming back tonight?

Spooky 41: Don't know yet, we're gonna go back and regenerate. We may come back.

Tripod: OK, roger. Right now everything seems to be cooled down.

Spooky 41: OK, mighty fine. And, ahh, look, if we don't get back, ahh, as I told Chicken Hawk a while ago, I want to tell all you boys that all the Spookies have enjoyed working with you all, and hope this thing quiets down for you over here. Sorry we can't come over and see you after tonight, but that's the way things go and make sure you tell old Chicken Hawk and 43 and Reeling 28 and all the other boys that we work with, ahh, that we'll be thinking about you fellahs.

Main Tripod: OK, roger, thanks a lot, most of them are right here, the Hawk and 43 are sitting right on this post and listening . . . from you.

Spooky 41: OK, mighty good, like I say, old Spook sure hates to leave you fellows but that's the way it happens sometimes.

Main Tripod: Sure hate to see you go, man.

Spooky 41: OK, we're going to stay over here about 5 minutes, so if you need me, give me a call and then we're going to di-di out of the area.

Main Tripod: OK, roger, we'll see you later.

Spooky 41: Roger that.

Main Tripod: This is Main Tripod, Hawk say again.

Main Tripod: Hear you real good, but you can't seem to hear him . . . He says its been pleasure working with you and hope's to see you prior to going back to the States.

Spooky 41: Roger that. Tell him if he gets over around channel 75 in the next 20 days, he'll probably get to see me.

Main Tripod: OK, roger, I think he heard that. Break, did you get that, Hawk?

Spooky 41: OK . . . this is 41.

Main Tripod: . . . if stuff breaks around here, he'll be up to see you.

Spooky 41: OK, that's good and, ahh, tell him to look around for Alabama Spooky and he'll find me somewhere.

Main Tripod: Roger that. Did you monitor that, Hawk?

Main Tripod: OK, Spooky told me to tell you they'll up there your way so take it easy and good luck. And he wanted to make sure you knew he'd kinda like to see you . . .

Spooky 41: OK, mighty fine, you tell him, ahh, my initials are Mike Alpha Delta Junior.

Main Tripod: OK.

Spooky 41: Roger, buddy, we're fixing to di-di out of the area. You all take it easy and, ahh, tell everybody to keep their head down, tell Hawk to tell old Beak that he makes sure he keeps his nose down.

Main Tripod: Tripod, roger, will do, from all the officers here, so long.

Spooky 41: Roger, roger, old buddy, you all take it easy.

Pilot: Let's go home, sir.

Spooky 41 Internal: Roger.

ACKNOWLEDGMENTS

We are forever indebted to Ken Moffett, who laid the foundation for this book in his capacity as the Veterans Affairs representative in the office of Congressman Bobby Schilling of Illinois. Himself a Vietnam veteran, Ken recognized the heroism of the brave men who fought at Firebase Kate, and was determined that the American people know the truth about this battle.

Ken selflessly gave of his time and effort to locate and recover government documents, newspaper stories, after-action reports, maps, and photographs. He diligently sought out the defenders of Kate as well as those who flew in the skies above. Most wanted to tell their story, but a few chose to not relive the nightmare. Once these contacts were made, he became the central point of contact as well as the repository of all research and information. Without Ken Moffett, there would have been no book and the story would have been lost to history.

We would not have had cause and means to create this book were it not for Reginald Brockwell, who alone kept this story alive over the decades since 1969. Reg also reviewed our final draft, offering numerous suggestions and correcting a number of errors.

We are also indebted to each of the men and women quoted in this work, with whom we have spoken, or who wrote to us, or who shared written accounts of their recollections. In this respect, we are particularly indebted to Major Al Dykes, USAF (Ret.), who saved and shared hours of tape recordings of radio traffic over and around Firebase Kate. These became the basis for the Appendix in this book, and were also useful in helping us to create a timeline for the narrative.

A special thanks to my compadre Ron Staes, who saw this story as a book before anyone else and lit the fuse in me.

Lieutenant Colonel Hugh Pries, USA Special Forces (Ret.), spent countless hours transcribing the taped conversations between myself and the Spooky/Shadow gunships.

Steve Sherman was enormously helpful in my first effort to put memories and fact on paper, aside from maintaining, at his own expense and energy, the world's finest and most complete unofficial archive of Special Forces personnel and activities in Vietnam.

Rita Cann of the National Personnel Records Center provided numerous unit morning reports and many other useful records.

Pat Rolfe transcribed dozens of recordings, creating text from digital files both rapidly and accurately as she learned to love the language of war.

Nelson and Maryellen Koon welcomed Wolf into their home, gave him a wonderful meal, and provided a comfortable bed for an overnight stay.

Likewise, Rocco and Diana DeNote offered Wolf the hospitality of their home, as well as sharing several hard-to-find documents relating to events on Firebase Kate.

Ben and Janet Gay welcomed Wolf into their home, fed him, and later helped guide him back to more-populated parts of Virginia.

Al and Pat Dykes hosted Wolf's stay in their off-the-beaten-path hometown.

Mike and Elizabeth Smith welcomed Wolf with a fabulous meal and warm hospitality.

A special thanks to Dean Fait of the Art Place in Rock Island, Illinois, who created computer-readable disks containing volumes of research and interview transcriptions. Dean enormously facilitated the distribution of research material, which greatly accelerated the flow of information to shorten the time required to complete the project.

While this book was still in its conceptual stage, our literary agent, Doug Grad, shared his industry-tested guidance about its nature, voice, scope, and authorship. He was also relentless in finding the right home for it, and fearlessly negotiated our contract with New American Library.

Our editor at New American Library, Brent Howard, offered sage counsel and marketing savvy, as well as innumerable other helpful acts as he turned a manuscript into a book.

We are indebted as well to the women in our lives: Mary Albracht offered encouragement, proofreading, and support and comfort while her husband relived the perilous events experienced on and around Kate, and the space to participate fully in the project. Tomi Wolf provided her father the vital support that freed him to work on this project, and encouragement when the complexities of completing a book seemed overwhelming. Sage advice and emotional encouragement were provided in unlimited doses by the Munchkin Queen.

While this book is therefore the product of the efforts of many people, we alone are responsible for any errors, mistakes, or misstatements.

Captain William Albracht, USAR (Ret.),
Moline, Illinois

Captain Marvin J. Wolf, USAR (Ret.),
Los Angeles, California

Index

A-1 Skyraider, 164
Abbott, CW2 James L., 204, 205, 276
Abrams, General Creighton, 192, 220
AC-47 Spooky gunship, xv, 96, 163–70, 226, 232, 233, 237–38, 249, 254
  transcript of recordings, 297–343
AC-119G Shadow, 120, 158, 166–68, 202, 224, 226, 232, 249, 254
AC-130H Spectre gunship, 207
Adam, Captain Klaus, 37–42, 74, 79, 156, 267–68, 282
Adam, Ursula Viera-Vazquez, 38–39
Aerial reconnaissance, 16–18
Afghanistan, 34
Agent Orange, 291
AH-1 Cobra, 103
A1H Skyraiders, 223–24, 227, 231
Ahearn, WO John, 174, 176–79, 249, 268–69
Alamo, the, 219
Albracht, Bob, 15, 46–48, 51, 57, 59–60, 62–63
Albracht, Captain William, xiv–xvi, 273
  basic training and, 51–53
  birth of, 45
  brother Bob and, 47–48
  at Bu Prang, 62–63
  Bu Prang attack and, 253–54
  childhood of, 46
  commissioned second lieutenant, 57
  education of, 46–47, 59
  enlistment of, 49
  escape and evasion from Kate and, 231–40, 243–48
  family of, 294
  joins Mike Force, 263–64, 292
  on Kate, 81, 85–92, 95–97, 99–105, 107–12, 119, 120, 135, 136, 138, 141–42, 144, 146–50, 155–58, 161, 167–70, 173–82, 185–96, 209–15, 219, 222–27, 229, 250–51
  medals awarded to, 254, 256, 293, 295–96
  media interview of, 254–55
  at Officer Candidate School, 54–58
  parachute training and, 57–58

Albracht, Captain William, (*cont.*)
parents of, 46, 56
planning escape from Kate, 214–15, 220, 223–27, 229–30
with Secret Service, 293–94
solo reconnaissance by, 243–44
training Royal Thai Army and, 15, 60
transcript of recordings by, 297–43
weapons carried by, 85–86, 147
Albracht, Don, 46
Albracht, Germaine, 46
Albracht, Leander, 46, 56
Albracht, Mary Beth, 46
Albracht, Nancy, 46
Alvarez, SP4 Rafael, Jr., 276
Ambush Hill, 30, 86, 87, 95–96, 100–2, 136, 214, 224, 230–33, 235–38
AN/GRC-46 radios, 65–66
An Khe, 50, 124
An Lac, 29, 112, 269
AN/PRC 25 radios, 96
Anderson, Colonel, 31, 36
Antiwar protests, 3
Arbizo, Staff Sergeant Santiago, 29, 69, 79, 89
Arc Light Mission Golf 476, 177, 178
Army of the Republic of [South] Vietnam (ARVN), 2–6, 14, 80, 123–26
First Airborne Division, 19, 126
23rd Infantry Division, xv, 19, 20, 126, 158, 190–92, 200
Special Forces, 28
Artillery, history of, 23–25
Artillery forward observers (FOs), 62
"Artilleryman's Vision, The" (Whitman), 84
ARVN (*see* Army of the Republic of [South] Vietnam)
Australian Special Air Service, 14
Ayres, B. Drummond, Jr., 259

B-52 bomber, 175, 177, 178, 237
B-40 rocket, 117
Bahnar people, 15
Balaklava, 22
Ballistics, discipline of, 25, 68
Baltzly, Ed, 55, 58, 60
Ban Don (Trang Phuoc), 28, 29, 69, 79
Báo Dai, 12, 124
Barham, Captain Lucian "Luke," 29–30, 41, 69–70, 78, 80, 86, 89, 90, 120, 269–70
Barnes, SP4 Francis "Butch," 156, 270
Barthman, SP4 Peter, 275
Battle for LZ Kate, The (Brockwell), 273–74
Battlefield communications, 24
Beckwith, Colonel Charles, 124
Beehive rounds, 119, 143, 157
Beers, Ethelinda, 208
Ben Het, 26, 29, 116–17, 261
Berlin blockade, 163
Binh Dinh province, 16
Binh Thuan province, 16
Black, Carol Marks, 134, 135, 270–72
Black, CWO Nolan, 133–35, 142–44, 146–50, 249, 270–72
Black, Laura Kristina, 134, 135, 271–72
Blake, SP4 Robert E., 276
Bledshaw, SP4 Johnny D., 276
Bomb damage assessments, 109, 179, 267
Bore sighting, 113
Bowers, Colonel Francis, 34, 191–92, 210
Bowie, Jim, 219
Brockwell, First Lieutenant Reginald, 32, 34–37, 153–54, 188–89, 191, 192, 272–74, 289–90, 294
Brydon, Major William J. "Bill," 196, 214, 233, 274
Bu Prang Special Forces Camp, xiii, 9, 15–16, 19, 20, 28, 32–37, 62–63, 79, 81, 89–91, 96, 101, 112, 114, 125, 126, 143, 145, 146, 158, 173, 176, 178, 189–91, 196, 201, 202, 233, 248–49, 253, 259, 261, 285, 286
Bu Prang town, 10, 12, 18
Buddha's Child (Wolf), 3*n*
Bundros, SP5 Gregory, 276
Buon Ma Thuot (BMT), 10, 18–20, 34, 62, 80, 115, 125, 126, 145, 158, 174, 178, 201, 220

C rations, 68, 69
C-4 explosives, 89
C-47 "Gooney Bird," 162–64

C-119 Flying Boxcars, 163–64
Ca Mau Peninsula, 177, 178
Caldwell, Sergeant Mike, 187, 193, 275
Cam Ranh Bay, 108, 284
Cambodia, xiii, xiv, 2, 9, 10, 14, 17–19, 36, 68, 79, 86, 89, 90, 101, 178, 188–89, 200
Camp La Rolland, Cambodia, 188–89
Canada, Sergeant Clyde, 143, 150, 249
Cannon, development of, 24
Cardigan, Earl of, 22
Central Highlands, 1, 10, 12, 62, 66, 132, 200
Central Intelligence Agency (CIA), 12, 13, 18, 60
CH-47 Chinook, 26, 113–14, 186
CH-54 Sikorsky Flying Crane, 26
Cham people, 10, 12, 14
Childers, Captain Charles, 196
Childs, Rudy, 99, 110
Civilian Irregular Defense Group (CIDG), xiv, 12–14, 20, 28, 35, 70, 71, 78
Claymore mines, 88–89, 144
Close, SP4 Edward J., 276
Cobra gunship, 103, 110, 186
Cole, CW2 James C., 201, 205, 275
"College Colonel, The" (Melville), 228
Collins, CW2 Robert, 275
Collins, Lieutenant Colonel, 192
Colt Automatic Rifle (CAR-15), 85, 147
CONEX containers, 31–32, 99
Conscientious objectors, 48
Coonce, WO1 John "Jack," 135, 136, 276
Corcoran, Lieutenant General Charles A., 16, 220–22, 255–56, 260
Cosmos, WO1 Charles "Pete," 204, 276
Craig, SP4 Jesse, 276
Crane, Lex, 55, 58, 60
Crites, Lieutenant, 169
Crockett, Davy, 219

Dak Lak Province, 10, 174, 268
Dak To, 19
Davison, WO John "Les," 135–37, 186, 201, 203–5, 240, 249, 275–76
DC-3, 162
De Sio, WO1 David J., 276
Degar Highlands Liberation Front, 13
Degar tribes, 10, 12, 15
Delaune, Lieutenant Colonel Elton J., 34, 154, 155, 174, 210, 288–90
Demilitarized Zone, 15
DeNote, Staff Sergeant Rocco, 81, 186, 189–90, 192, 220, 222, 277, 298, 299
Diem, Ngo Dinh, 12, 13
Dien Bien Phu, xiv, 37, 86
Donovan, CW2 Kenneth, 199–202, 204, 206–7, 249, 259–60, 275, 277–78
Draft, US, 3, 27, 47, 48, 134, 135
Draft dodgers, Vietnamese, 5
Drang River Valley, 18
Duc Lap Special Forces Camp, 9, 18–20, 32–34, 35, 36, 69, 112, 133, 136, 154, 191, 200, 201, 259
Dykes, Captain Al, 162–70, 173, 207, 230, 237, 249, 278, 297, 298

EC-47s, 16–17, 163, 207
Eisenhower, General Dwight D., 162–63
ELINT (electronic intelligence), 16
Enuol, Y Bham, 14

F-4 Phantom, xiii, 108, 109
F-100 Super Sabre, xv, 108, 109, 142, 174
FADAC (Field Artillery Digital Automatic Computer), 66, 225
Falcon gunship, 135–38, 176, 186, 203, 206
Farlow, SP4 Richard, 276
FDC (*see* Fire direction center)
Fenlon, WO1 Dennis, 206, 275
Field guns, development of, 24
Fire direction center (FDC), 32, 34, 77–78, 100, 118, 155–57, 188
Fire direction specialists, 25
Firebase Annie, 31, 32, 36, 65, 67, 156, 174, 268
Firebase concept, 34
Firebase Dorrie, 36, 282

Firebase Helen, 36, 191
Firebase Kate
air support for, 96, 100, 103, 107–8, 111–12, 141, 142–50, 158, 161, 166–70, 176–80, 188–89, 195, 223–24, 249
ammunition shortage on, xv, 144, 146, 150, 186–87, 195, 213, 257
ARVN and, xiii, 190–92
attack on, 95–105, 107–20, 123, 137, 141–44, 146–50, 155–58, 167–70, 174–82, 186–96, 209, 211, 212, 250
bomb damage assessment of, 267
building, xiii–xiv, 29–32
communications on, 65–66, 166–67, 225
cross-border strike and, 189
escape from, xv–xvi, 231–40, 243–48
food on, 68–69
geography of, 30, 86, 87, 89
operational chain of command on, 34–35
perimeter breached, 175–76
perimeter defenses of, 87–89
planning escape from, 214–15, 220, 223–27, 229–30
recon expeditions from, 69–71
recreation on, 71, 89, 90
registering of guns on, 67–68
reinforcements for, 112, 116, 120, 141
replaced howitzer, 114, 119
rescue plan for, 192–94, 196, 211–13
sanitation and hygiene on, 70, 72, 90
size of, 65
supplying, xiv–xv, 80–81, 144, 146, 150, 186–87, 202–3, 206–7, 275–76
troop rotation on, 81
underground FDC built on, 77–78
water on, 185–87, 213
weapons on, xiv, 26, 31, 34, 67–68, 86, 188
weather and, 66, 71–72
wounded on, 98–100, 102, 104, 105, 109–10, 135–38, 147–49, 179, 187, 194, 195
Firebase Martha, 36, 191
Firebase Mike Smith, 284, 288, 290
Firebase Susan, 31, 32, 36, 65, 67, 68, 156, 174, 268
Firebase Swinger, 29
Flight school, 130–31
Forward air controllers (FACs), 62, 143, 147, 150
Foster, First Lieutenant Walter, 276
Franco-Prussian War of 1870, 23
French, in Vietnam, xiv, 12, 37, 86
Friendly fire, 4, 176
Frye, Mary Elizabeth, 140

Galloway, Joseph L., xiii–xvi
Gay, CWO Harold Benjamin, 115, 130–33, 135, 142–44, 146–50, 249, 279
Geneva Accords of 1954, 12, 135
Geromin, SP4 Warren, 72–73, 78, 112–13, 115, 148–49, 194, 233, 247, 248, 279
Ghost soldiers, 5
Gia Nghia, 104, 107, 112, 126, 146, 174
Giáp, General Vo Nguyên
Gillikin, SP4 Larry, 275
Gooch, Sergeant First Class Jimmy, 76, 284
Graft, in ARVN, 4, 5
Gulf of Tonkin, 15
"Gunga Din" (Kipling), 184
Gunpowder, invention of, 23
Guthrie, Wilbur, 144–47, 149, 150

H-34 helicopter, 129
Hall, Colonel Charles, 35–37
Hare, Phil, 295
Harrell, WO2 Denny, 136–38
HC-47, 163
Healey, Colonel "Iron Mike," 254, 257
Hearne, WO2 Maury, 143, 148–50, 249
Helmich, Major Gerald R., 224, 227, 279–80
Henry V (Shakespeare), 266
"High Flight" (Magee), 198
Hill 875/Dak To, Battle of, xiv
Hitch, First Lieutenant James A., 206
Hmong people, 15
Ho Chi Minh Trail, 17, 19, 163, 188
Hon Tre Island, 62
Honest John rockets, 74–75

Hopkins, Kenn, 25, 30, 31, 71, 73, 91, 97–98, 108, 113–19, 141, 142, 154–55, 157, 192–94, 211, 248, 280–81, 284
Houghtaling, Sergeant, 28, 113, 168–69, 173, 177
Houston, Sam, 219
Howitzers, 24, 31, 34, 67–68, 73, 76–77, 86, 97–98, 101, 107, 113–14, 119, 225
Hue, 20
Huey gunship (*see* UH-1 gunship)

Ia Drang, Battle of, 18–19
Ia Drang Valley, xiv
Indian Wars, 34
Indirect fire, concept of, 21
Ingram, WO1 Larry D., 276

Jarai people, 15
Jesuits, 11
Johnson, Lyndon B., 3, 14
Johnson, Marlin, 174, 269
Johnson, Peewee, 225
Johnson, SP4 Bob, 32, 66–67, 69, 77–78, 99, 118, 155–56, 214, 220, 224, 236–37, 239, 247, 281

Kadel, SP4 David E., 275
Kampuchean people, 14
Kate (*see* Firebase Kate)
Kennedy, John F., 292
Kerr, Lieutenant John, 25, 65, 67, 68, 77, 78, 80, 87, 91, 99, 108–11, 119, 120, 141, 146, 147, 155–57, 173, 177, 248, 282–83, 290
Kerry, John, 189
Khe Sanh, siege of, xiv
Khmer Krom people, 15
Khmer people, 10, 12
Khmer Republic, 270
Kinh people, 10–12
Kinnard, Major General Harry, 124–25
Kipling, Rudyard, 64, 128, 160, 184, 242
Klein, First Lieutenant Tom, 154, 289
Kontum province, 16, 20
Koon, SP4 Nelson, 73–75, 77–79, 96, 98, 113, 115, 118, 120, 137, 138, 154, 155, 157–58, 187, 192, 194, 210–11, 225, 226, 230, 235, 237, 246–48, 283–85
Korean War, xvi, 31, 33, 222
Ky, General Nguyen Cao, 3, 5, 14

Lam Dong province, 16
Laos, 2, 10, 14, 17, 18, 101
Larson, Lieutenant General Stanley "Swede," 125
Lartéguy, Jean (Jean Pierre Lucien Osty), xiv
Lattin, Major George, 107, 109, 111, 188, 249, 273, 285–86
Law of the Jungle, The (Kipling), 64
Leaves of Grass (Whitman), 84
Lillie, Gordon W., 222
Long Binh, 61
Longfellow, Henry Wadsworth, 106
"Lost Legion, The" (Kipling), 242
Lott, SP5 Douglas Hugh, Jr., 143, 150, 249
Love, SP4 Thomas W., 275
Lu Lan, General, 222
LZ Albany, 18
LZ X-Ray, 18

M16 rifle, 85, 147, 192
M60 machine gun, 120, 145, 192, 194
M79 grenade launcher, 114, 192
M1918 Browning Automatic Rifle, 85
MACV (Military Assistance Command, Vietnam), 13, 190
MACV RECONDO Combat Operations Course (COC), 62
Maddox, Bob, 136, 137
Magee, John Gillespie, Jr., 198
Malvestuto, Terry, 286
Matlock, Jim "Herbie," 144–50, 249, 286–87
Matson, SP4 Richard D., 276
McFarland, Sergeant, 98, 113, 154, 225
McKim, Randolph Harrison, xxvi
McNamara, Robert, 109
Melville, Herman, 218, 228

Mike Force (Mobile Strike Force), xv, xvi, 14, 15, 18, 41, 62, 112, 192–94, 196, 211–13, 224, 231–33, 237–39, 244–47, 263
Military Occupational Specialty 13B, 75
Ming, General Duong Van, 13–14
Moffett, Ken, 290, 294, 295
Monsoon season, 17
Montagnard soldiers, v, xiii–xv, 6, 10–14, 26, 28–30, 69–71, 78, 87–91, 95–96, 123, 124, 148, 175, 190, 192, 213–14, 220, 223, 226, 234, 235
Moore, Major, 176
Moore, PFC Thomas M., 275
Mortars, development of, 24
Mosher, SP5 Craig W., 275
Murphy, Joe, 47–50
My Lai massacre, 53

Nachtigall, Dave, 136
Nadine, PFC Dennis, 120
Napalm, 4, 147, 176
National Security Agency (NSA), 16
Native Americans, 11–12
Newsweek magazine, 189
Nha Trang, 16, 37, 61, 125, 254, 293
Nha Trang Bay, 62
Nixon, Richard M., xiii, 3, 126, 189–91
North Vietnamese forces (*see* People's Army of [North] Vietnam)
Norton, PFC Michael R., 114, 249–50, 274, 280
Nung troops, xv, 15
NVA (*see* People's Army of [North] Vietnam)

O-1 Bird Dog, 17, 104, 107, 111, 112, 114, 129
Officer Candidate School, 49–58, 67
Officer promotions, 40–41
OH-6 Cayuse (LOACH), 103–4
Olsen, SP4 Pete, 145, 146
Operation Switchback, 13
OV-1 Mohawk, 17
Owen, Major Dean M., 201–4, 249, 260, 276

Palmer, Captain William, 62, 63
Parachute training, 57–58
Parker, Steven, 272
Patton, George S., Jr., 94, 152
PAVN (*see* People's Army of [North] Vietnam)
People's Army of [North] Vietnam (PAVN), 1, 2, 6, 14, 15, 36–37, 70, 79, 80, 86, 89, 90, 96, 97, 101–4, 107, 112, 115–16, 119, 124–26, 141–44, 147–50, 156–58, 167–69, 174–79, 186, 188–91, 194, 202, 206, 207, 209, 211, 212, 224, 226, 230–31, 235–38, 245–47, 250, 253–54
  24th Infantry Regiment, 19
  28th Infantry Regiment, 18, 212
  32nd Infantry Regiment, 19
  40th Artillery Regiment, 18
  66th Regiment, xiv, 18–19, 81, 207, 212
  174th Infantry Regiment, 19
  K-393 Artillery Battalion, 18
Pepke, Major General Donn R., 125–26
Phan Rang, 34, 170, 174
Phuc, Phan Thi Kim, 4
Phyllis Ann project, 162, 163
"Picket-Guard, The" (Beers), 208
Pierelli, Sergeant Dan, 79–80, 86, 87, 89, 90, 95, 99, 101, 102, 161–62, 166, 168, 169, 174, 187, 191, 195, 211, 225, 226, 232–36, 243, 245, 246, 248, 263–64, 273, 287
Platt, Air Force FAC William E., 112, 179, 287
Plei Me Special Forces Camp, 124–26
Pleiku City, 15, 16, 62, 124, 125, 145
Pluhar, Larry, 268
Plummer, SP4 Ernest C., 276
Post-traumatic stress disorder (PTSD), 33, 195
Pries, Colonel Hugh, 297
Project Friday Gap, 269–70
Pugh, Dick, 278

Quang Duc province, 16
Quang Tri province, 19

"Reaper and the Flowers, The" (Longfellow), 106
Recoilless rifles, 97
Relief columns, 123–24
Republic of Korea troops, 16
Resquist, Lieutenant, 169
Rickenbacker, Captain Eddie, 223
Riovo, Major, 77
Rock Island, Illinois, 45
Rogers, Gerald "Tex," 69, 73, 77, 98, 229, 230, 232, 245, 248–49, 288
Roosevelt, Theodore, 19
Ross, First Lieutenant Ronald A., 153–56, 173, 174, 180–82, 195, 215, 274, 288–90
Ross, John, 290
Ross, Trisha, 290
ROTC (Reserve Officer Training Corps), 49, 53, 62
Royal Thai Army, 15, 60
Ryder, First Lieutenant Ken, 142

Saigon Cowboys, 5
Schilling, Bobby, 290, 294–95
Schmidt, Elvira, 291
Schulz, Charles, 223
Scott, Forrest, 29, 30, 80–81
11 Corps, 16, 34, 261
Serain, SP4 Calvin, 136, 275
Shadow (*see* AC-119G Shadow)
Shakespeare, William, 266
"Sheridan at Cedar Creek" (Melville), 218
Shriver, WO1 Kenneth, 276
Sidle, General Winant, 36
Simmons, Lieutenant Colonel Frank, 9, 10, 192
Simmons, Sergeant First Class Don, 248
Simpson, First Lieutenant Norman, 275
Smith, Elizabeth Clark, 27, 291
Smith, First Lieutenant Mike, 26–31, 67, 68, 70, 71, 77, 78, 80, 87, 91, 97, 99–100, 110–11, 116, 154, 209–11, 214, 226, 230, 235, 237, 243, 245, 246, 248, 256, 288, 290–91
Smith, Justin, 291
South Vietnam Air Force (VNAF), 3, 4, 14
South Vietnamese forces (*see* Army of the Republic of [South] Vietnam), 2–3
Special Forces (*see* United States forces)
Spectre (*see* AC-130H Spectre gunship)
Spooky (*see* AC-47 Spooky gunship)
Stevens, Sergeant First Class, 246–48
Strange Captain John, 104, 105, 114, 249
Sullivan brothers, 60

Tennyson, Alfred, Lord, 8
Tet Offensive, 2–3, 145
TH-55 Osage, 131
Thanh Hoa, 18
37 mm anti-aircraft gun, 142
Tidmore, Sergeant, 76
Tierney, Lieutenant George, 63
Tiranti, PFC Bernie, 98, 113, 118, 154, 157, 187, 248, 284, 291
Trace ammunition, 147
Trang Phuoc (Ban Don), 28, 29, 69, 79
Travis, William, 219
12.7 mm machine gun, 235–36
Typhoon, The, magazine, 191–92

U-2 spy plane, 16–17
UH-1 gunship, 110, 114–16, 131, 132, 142, 144, 176
Uhring, WO1 Frank G., 276
United Front for the Liberation of Oppressed Races Front (Front Unifié de Lutte des Races Opprimées, FULRO), 14
United States forces
First Air Cavalry Division, 18–19, 124
First Aviation Brigade 48th AHC, 114, 132, 133, 134, 142, 249
First Aviation Brigade 155th AHC, 131, 133–35, 144–46, 199, 201, 203, 240, 249, 259
First Aviation Brigade 189th AHC, 144, 145, 249
1st Cavalry Division, xiv, 19
I Field Force Vietnam (IFFV), 36, 41, 42, 16, 17, 19, 32–34, 125, 191, 220, 260
First Infantry Division, 221

United States forces (*cont.*)
4th Infantry Division, xv, 19, 125, 126, 132, 190
Fifth Special Forces Group, 13–15, 35, 59–62, 190, 257
6th Special Operations Squadron, 223
17th Cavalry, 103
22nd Artillery, 34, 153, 154, 210, 289
27th Artillery, 28
35th Tactical Fighter Wing, 108
46th Special Forces Company, 60
52nd Artillery Group, 41
71st Evacuation Hospital, 177
92nd Artillery, 25–26, 28
101st Airborne Division, 38, 51, 133, 134
155th Assault Helicopter Company, 18
173rd Airborne Division, 19
185th Recon Company, 80, 104
486th Bomb Squadron, 177
559th Tactical Fighter Squadron, 108
after-action reports, 70, 125, 148
Air Force, 129–30
Army Air Corps, 129, 162
Army Security Agency, 16
Army Signal Corps, 53
Army Special Warfare Center, 58
Military Intelligence, 18
Special Forces Officers' Course, 58–59
Special Forces Team A-233, 28, 29, 69, 79–81
Special Forces Team A-234, 29, 112, 269
Special Forces Team A-236, 9, 10, 12, 15, 81, 253
Special Forces Team A-239, 19
Special Forces Team B-23, 9, 81, 112, 150, 158, 192, 220
Strategic Air Command, 175
Task Force Alpha, 125
Task Force Fighter, 125–26
USS *Juneau*, 60
Ut, Nick, 4
Utapao Royal Air Base, Thailand, 173–75, 177

Viet Cong, 2, 3, 12, 13, 15, 80, 123–25, 177, 221
Viet Minh, 12, 37, 86
Vietnam Memorial, Washington Mall, 2
Vietnamization, xiii, 3, 5, 6, 126, 190, 259–61
Vinh Loc, Major General, 124, 125
VNAF (*see* South Vietnam Air Force)

War Between the States, 23
Ware, Major General Keith, 221, 222
Watson, WO1 Jerry, 275
Weapons, history of artillery, 23–25
Weather conditions, 66, 71–72, 132
Weaver, SP4 Billy, 220
Wells, CPT, 298
Whiteside, Captain Richard, 150, 257
Whitman, Walt, 84
Wilcox, SP5 Mike, 202–4, 207, 275
Wiles, SP4 Ronnie, 276
Wolf, Captain Marvin, xvi, 50
World War II, 31, 33, 54, 60, 74, 129
Wright, Colonel B. R., 204, 276

"Young British Soldier, The" (Kipling), 128

Zollner, First Lieutenant Maurice "Moe," 174, 176–78, 195, 211, 214, 237, 243, 245, 246, 248, 268, 292, 299

AUTHOR PHOTO COURTESY OF THE AUTHOR

WILLIAM ALBRACHT is a highly decorated Vietnam veteran and retired Secret Service agent whose twenty-five-year White House career included the protection details of four American presidents and numerous foreign dignitaries. Upon retirement, Albracht managed executive security operations at the Ford Motor Company before returning to his hometown to open a security consulting business.

MARVIN J. WOLF is a decorated Vietnam veteran and the author or coauthor of many nonfiction books, including *Where White Men Fear to Tread* and *Buddha's Child*. Visit him online at marvwolf.com.